WOODTURNING METHODS

MIKE DARLOW

Fox
Chapel Publishing Co. Inc.

1970 Broad Street • East Petersburg, PA 17520 • www.foxchapelpublishing.com

Printed by H & Y Printing Limited, Hong Kong.

The other books in this series are: The Fundamentals of Woodturning, Woodturning Techniques, and Woodturning Design (late 2002). Distributed in North America by Fox Chapel Publishing Company Inc., 1970 Broad Street , East Petersburg, PA 17520. Tel: (717) 560 4703   Fax: (717) 560 4702   www.carvingworld.com

Darlow, Mike, 1943- .
    Woodturning methods.

Includes index.
    ISBN 1-56523-125-2

1. Turning. 2. Woodwork. I. Title.

684.083

CONTENTS

ACKNOWLEDGMENTS

I have used many of turning's specialist methods during my twenty years of professional turning. But to cover all the methods in this book thoroughly I had to seek help from others. That help included advice, supplying transparencies and photographs, allowing me to photograph, and enabling me to trial and use equipment. I thank the people, companies, and organizations listed below.

Australia
Rhonda Howell of John Heine & Son, Bob Harris of Hunter Woodturning, Ross O'Brien of Illawarra Woodturning Supplies, Michael Richter of MIK International, Garry Pye of Garry Pye Woodturning, David Laundry of Record Hand & Power Tools Australia, Vic Verrrecchio of Vicmark, Mike Jeffreys of The Wood Works Book & Tool, Len and Jean Smith of The Woodsmith, and John Ewart of The Woodturning Centre.

Frank Bollins, Bob Chapman, Don Dickson, Michael Doyle, Don Greenhalgh, John B. Hawkins, Peter Herbert, Michelle Kane, Jonas Kirk, Bruce Leadbeatter, John Morgan, Dennis Moulang, Bernard Oke, Courtney Williams, and John Wooller.

Producing a book demands long periods of uninterrupted concentration. Doing it at home imposes particular stresses because you are easily accessible, but don't want to be. I thank my wife Alice for her proofreading and help in so many other ways, and my sons Joshua and Samuel for not bugging me too much.

France
Gerard Bidou, and Daniel Guilloux.

Switzerland
Sigi Angerer.

Germany
Ulrike Meyerdierks of Verlag Th. Schafer.
Gottfried Bockelmann, and Johannes Volmer.

New Zealand
Peter Battensby, Fred Irvine, and Andy Whyman.

United Kingdom
Peter Hindle of Ashem Crafts, Roy Child of Peter Child, Christopher Proudfoot at Christie's South Kensington, Crown Hand Tools, Terry Porter and Rosemary Mundy of GMC Publications, Multitool, Mark Baker of Robert Sorby, and Peter Flewitt of Turbo RCD.
John F. Edwards, E.W. (Bill) Newton, and David Springett.

United States of America
Robert F. Morse of Cushman Industries.
Christian Burchard, Paul Ferraglio, Jerry Glaser, Hugh Foster, Michael F. Kehs, and Mark Sfirri.

INTRODUCTION

Woodturning Methods is my third book, and the first of two on special methods for turning particular forms. Some of the methods in this book you may use frequently, some occasionally, some you may never use. The immediate relevance of a method will vary from turner to turner, but knowing of these methods and where to find them detailed expands and interconnects your woodturning vocabulary. The second book on methods titled *Woodturning Techniques* was published in 2000.

Woodturning Methods is also the second book of a series which will build to a complete woodturning library. The first and base book of the series is *The Fundamentals of Woodturning*, an essential text which introduces turning. It covers lathes, turning tools, and tool sharpening; and describes the fundamental techniques of hand turning in detail. The advantage of an integrated series of books is that I need to detail information only once. Thus when information is relevant in another book of the series, I can refer the reader to the primary source instead of having to repeat the information.

Woodturning Methods concentrates on methods which are essentially in-lathe, or are directly associated with turning. Many of these methods and their associated equipment were developed long ago—not surprising in a 3000-year-old craft which utilizes a common natural material. With modern technical sophistication we can perhaps push the old methods a little further, but the potential for radical developments is limited. Therefore this book is not filled with new methods, still less with methods which I can claim to have originated; instead it seeks to make turning's specialist methods more accessible, to make their relationships clearer, and to explain them better. As the acknowledgments demonstrate, I have sought input from many contemporary turners, manufacturers, and suppliers. I have also borrowed from woodturning writings both old and new. I have however acknowledged my sources, both material and inspirational. And where another writer has explored a relevant area well and that writing is readily accessible, I refer you to that writing rather than rehash it.

I have presented the methods with little subjective comment. Judgements on a method's aesthetic and other merits, the value of the associated equipment, the income-producing potential, etc., I leave you to decide.

You may find some of this book heavy going—for example parts of chapter 7 on turning ellipses. You may wish to turn ellipses without understanding their geometry and the intricate workings of the various mechanisms; and by reading chapter 7 selectively you can achieve that aim. Other readers may wish to delve more deeply, and they can because the

detail is there. While I cannot tailor this book precisely for you, by providing the information in an approachable form I hope to please most readers, and tempt them to inquire more deeply than they have before.

Endnotes are rarely included in woodturning books, perhaps because publishers believe that these features of academe make a book too highfalutin and thus scare away potential buyers. Readers of my books are made of stronger stuff, and I hope many will find these notes of interest and worth pursuing.

The bibliographies list most of the turning and ornamental-turning books published in English: they also detail most of the relevant magazines and journals, and some books in languages other than English. I have therefore only given brief details when referring in the text and endnotes to books and magazines which are fully specified in the bibliographies.

The drawings and photographs are mostly by me, those not are usually acknowledged. I used Agfa CT precisa 100 film. The lathe shown in almost all the photographs is my Vicmarc VL200 which has the electronically-variable-speed option.

I laid this book out using Adobe Illustrator, Photoshop, and Pagemaker on a Macintosh G3 computer. These products may be marvellous, but I wish that they were more stable. As one who is forced by advancing decrepitude to wear spectacles to read, I have departed from the usual practice of putting captions, endnotes, and the index in smaller type.

In *The Fundamentals of Woodturning* I give both English and metric units. Here again I usually give both despite metric being better suited to turning, except where this would give an undesirable mass.

This is a book to use in the workshop, and to read at leisure. You can dip into it; you do not have to work through it from front to back. However you use it, I hope that it will help you to enjoy your turning more.

Mike Darlow, August, 1999.

KEYS

Center lines and axes

Hidden detail

Pointing and dimensioning arrows

Diameter

Vertical distance from bottom of object

Wood in elevation

Wood in section

Cast iron, mild steel, in elevation

Cast iron, mild steel, in section

Tool and special steels

Tool cuts

Note, extra colors are used and there may some departures from the colors specified.

Chapter One

CHUCKING

In woodturning, a chuck is a device for holding a workpiece or a drill rigidly in alignment in a lathe.

The *Oxford English Dictionary* suggests that the term "chuck" comes from the Old Northern French *chuque*, *choque* or *chouque* meaning a lumpy piece of wood, especially one to be burnt In his *The History of the Worthies of England* of 1662, Thomas Fuller used *chocketh* for stopping something moving by chocking it with a piece of waste wood. In 1678 Joseph Moxon published *Mechanick Exercises or the Doctrine of Handy-Works*, the first English text on woodturning. In it *chock* is used to refer to a work-holding device similar to a cupchuck which is mounted on a lathe mandrel. (Moxon was also the author of *Mathematicks Made Easie* published in 1679, the forerunner of many similar but sometimes misleading titles). By 1807 Olinthus Gregory in *A Treatise of Mechanics* was using the modern spelling *chuck*.[1] "Chucking" was in use by 1869.

I have divided the development of woodturning chucking into three phases:

1. An early phase to about 1800.
2. The industrial metal-turning phase from 1800 to about 1960.
3. The hobby-dominated phase starting from about 1960.

1.1 CHUCKING TO ABOUT 1800

In pole lathes (figure 1.1) and early Great-Wheel-driven lathes (figure 1.2), a cord was wrapped around and rotated the workpiece which was mounted between two iron-spike centers called pikes (figure 1.3). For other types of workpiece the cord could be wrapped around what Joseph Moxon in *Mechanick Exercises* called driving mandrels (figure 1.4). These driving mandrels could be considered as the first lathe chucks.

Moxon's book was the first to detail trade methods. It enabled those who wanted to gain trade skills to teach themselves; bypass the rigid, overlong, and archaic training practices dictated by the guilds; and take advantage of the shortage of craftsmen at the end of the 17th century. But the hand-turning equipment Moxon pictured was technically obsolete, remaining in widespread use only because of the Luddite-like opposition from the turners' guilds to the most important advance since turning was invented. This advance, the two-bearing headstock, ushered in the modern era of turning in both wood and metal. The first firm evidence of the two-bearing headstock is a drawing by Leonardo da Vinci

of about A.D. 1500 (figure 1.5). Whether this seemingly obvious advance was already used in lathes before 1500, and if not why it was so late coming, are unknown. Significantly, spindles housed in or between two bearings were in use earlier, for example in tower clocks and windlasses.

Figure 1.1 **Turning on a pole lathe.** The driving cord runs from the top of the springy pole, is wrapped around the workpiece, and tied to the treadle. Pushing down on the treadle rotates the workpiece against the tool's cutting edge. Lifting the foot allows the pole to straighten which rotates the workpiece in the reverse direction so that the tool does not cut. Jonas Kirk of Sydney, Australia, is the turner here and in figures 1.3 and 1.4.

The potential advantages of the two-bearing headstock over the "headstock" with a fixed pike were that:

1. The driving belt could be moved well away from the workpiece allowing greater tool access and easier speed variation with a stepped pulley.
2. Workpieces other than spindles could be held in alignment more rigidly while being rotated.
3. One face or end of a workpiece could be freely accessed by turning tools.

These potential advantages could not be realized by merely retaining a pointed or even a pronged pike on the projecting right-hand end (nose) of the rotatable headstock spindle. The spindle nose needed to be designed so that a range of devices could be rigidly mounted onto or into it, these devices being designed to grip or hold workpieces of different shapes and sizes during different turning operations. These devices are of course chucks if we extend our modern use of the term to include faceplates and drive centers. Supporting this extension, Frank Pain throughout his 1956 book *The Practical Wood Turner* calls a drive center a "driving chuck".

The practice of threading the headstock spindle's right-hand nose to receive chucks started almost immediately after the adoption of the new two-bearing headstock design. It is unlikely that noses were internally tapered like cupchucks on the evidence of Moxon. In 1678 he describes a spindle nose on a two-bearing-headstock oval-turning lathe as having "a wide Hole about an Inch and a quarter Diameter, and an Inch deep: And in this wide Hole is Turned a Female Screw with a course Thread, to receive a Male Screw made behind [on a spigot that projects from the left-hand end of] the Mandrel that the Work is fixed upon."[2] This internally-threaded nose design would have particularly suited wooden chucks as male-threaded chuck bosses were easier to make than female, and would have been less likely to split. Externally-threaded spindle noses were probably introduced at about the same time as internally-threaded, and are almost universal today. Figure 1.6 shows headstock spindles with internally- and externally-threaded noses. Figure 1.7 shows a tap of the type which was supplied with the lathe. Both figures are from Charles Plumier's *L'Art de Tourner* of 1701, the first major text on turning. Plumier was written not for artisan hand turners, but for ornamental-turners[3] who were aristocrats or were employed by them. Ornamental turners sought and could afford the most sophisticated workholding devices, and Plumier therefore shows: chucks for turning ellipses, a cage chuck for holding irregular workpieces (figure 1.8), a cupchuck, and a jam chuck and sphere chuck for turning spheres (figures 4.24 and 4.72).

The second major turning text was *Manuel du Tourneur* by Louis-Eloy Bergeron, first published in 1792.[4] In 1816 a revised and expanded edition by Pierre Hamelin-Bergeron, son-in-law of Louis-Eloy, was published.[5] It shows a range of basic chucks including a faceplate, a screwchuck, a

cupchuck,[6] a spring chuck (figure 1.9), and screw-bell chucks (figure 1.10). It also anticipates the next chucking phase, and shows two four-jaw independent chucks and a self-centering chuck, types which are discussed in the next section.

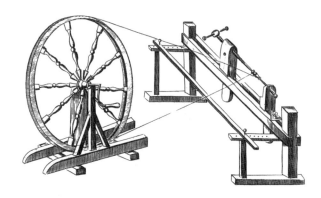

Figure 1.2 A Great Wheel lathe pictured by Joseph Moxon in 1678.[7] A helper turned the Great Wheel which through an endless cord, in this case wrapped around the workpiece, rotated the workpiece continuously forwards. This arrangement was especially used for larger workpieces. It gave a relatively constant depth of cut unlike the continually-reversing rotation of the pole lathe which gives a series of separated cuts, each one varying in its depth. Twisting the endless cord into a figure "8" as shown increases the length of cord in contact with the workpiece and thereby reduces the possibility of slippage.

Figure 1.3 The driving cord is wrapped around the spindle several times so that it [the cord] does not slip as it rotates the workpiece.

Figure 1.4 **Using a flat mandrel** to hold and drive a bowl workpiece on a pole lathe. Moxon called this a flat mandrel because the end of the mandrel which is forced against the workpiece is flat. The flat end has driving spurs or spikes projecting from it to grip the workpiece. Moxon also described a pin mandrel for driving drilled workpieces, and a hollow mandrel for cupchuck turning which had to be used with a boring collar (figure 8.34).[8]

Figure 1.6 **Two headstock spindles** pictured in 1701 in Plumier's *L'Art de Tourner*,[9] The top spindle has a hollow nose which is almost certainly internally threaded. The bottom spindle has an externally-threaded nose.

Figure 1.7 **A chuck tap and cupchuck** pictured in plate 7 of Plumier.

Turners commonly made their simpler chucks, especially cupchucks, from wood or brass. A turner bored and threaded each chuck to screw directly onto his or her headstock spindle's externally-threaded nose. Each lathe manufacturer had his own unique nose threads, and therefore supplied a tap with each lathe. This practice started to retreat after Joseph Whitworth first proposed thread standardization in 1841,[10] but there is still an unnecessarily large number of woodturning nose threads manufactured.

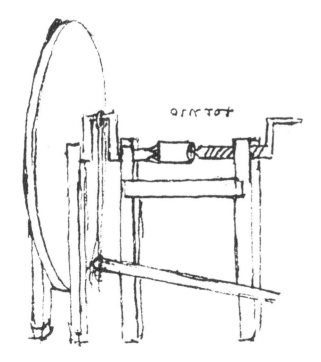

Figure 1.5 **Not a two- but a three-bearing headstock** lathe driven by a treadle, crank, and flywheel. The flywheel converts the reversing rotation characteristic of the treadle alone into a unidirectional rotation. A sketch by Leonardo da Vinci c.1500 in the *Codex Atlanticus*.

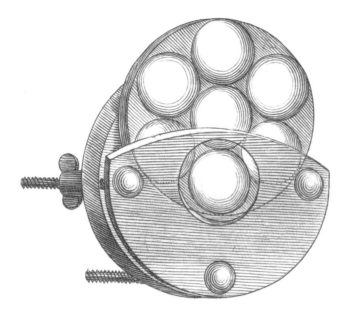

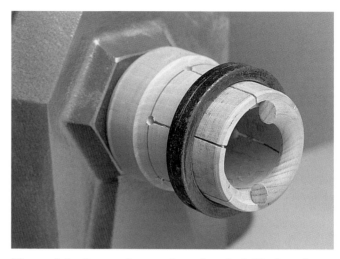

Figure 1.9 **A wooden spring chuck drilled and threaded to screw directly onto a headstock-spindle nose.**[11] One of the earliest and commonest chuck types; and still used today as section 1.5 shows. Here the chuck's fingers are forced to grip the wooden-ring workpiece by pushing a steel ring to the left. A plywood ring could be substituted for the steel ring.

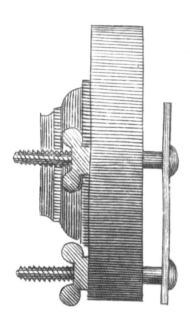

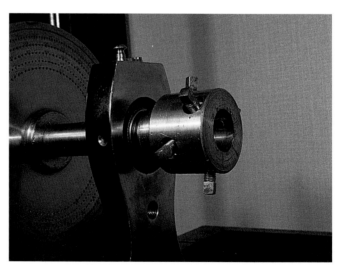

Figure 1.10 **A six-screw bell chuck** by Holzapffel & Co. The number and arrangement of the screws varies from chuck to chuck. The chuck cavity can be round, square, or triangular in cross section. Bell chucks were among the forerunners of both independent and self-centering chucks.

The workpiece has to be hard because it is held between the tips of the screws. These chucks were therefore used to hold the ivory and hard-wood workpieces preferred by ornamental-turners rather than the softer woods typically used in hand woodturning.

The drilled circular plate on the left is a dividing plate. It is used to index, to rotate the workpiece by set amounts between operations.

Photograph by John Edwards.

Figure 1.8 **A cage chuck** pictured in plate 46 of Plumier. In the front elevation, *top*, the chuck has been used to turn seven recesses in a circular workpiece. Cage chucks are much used today to reverse-chuck bowls to finish-turn their bottoms.

1.2 CHUCKING FROM 1800 TO 1960

Ornamental-turning had been largely abandoned by the European courts by 1800, but was growing in popularity among wealthy dilettantes. In Britain the ornamental lathe (figure 1.11) became more popular than the rose engine (page 152). Compound slides, rapidly-rotating cutters driven by overhead gear, and ever-more-complicated chucks were introduced during the late 18th and 19th centuries, and made possible ornamental-turnings of increasing complexity (figure 1.12). And it was a family at the forefront of these advances, the Holtzapffels, who published the next major source of chucking information.[12]

John Jacob Holtzapffel had emigrated to London in 1784. His son Charles published the first two volumes of *Turning and Mechanical Manipulation* in 1846 and 1847. Charles' son, John Jacob, completed and published volume III in 1850, and wrote and published volume IV on hand turning in 1881 and volume V on ornamental-turning in 1884.

The efforts of the Holtzapffels and others promoted ornamental-turning as a fascinating hobby for the wealthy and as a service trade to jewellers and security-printing plate engravers. Josiah Wedgewood had even used the techniques to decorate leather-hard pottery before the end of the 18th century.[13] But the technical advances pioneered by ornamental-turners were overwhelmed by those of the Industrial Revolution which gathered pace in Britain, and then spread through Europe and North America. Hand woodturning was also affected, becoming predominantly an urban-, even a factory-based trade which progressed technically through poaching advances first developed for industrial metal turning. Major examples of this poaching included:

1. Cast-iron lathe beds displaced wooden lathe beds.
2. Turner-power was replaced by steam which was then replaced by electricity. These two later power sources were in the form of large, central power units which drove many machines through a forest of line shafting. Stopping and starting a lathe (pages 39 and 40) was not as convenient as it is now, and the taper chuck (figure 1.13) allowed spindle turners to work without having to stop their lathes. Individual electric motors started to fitted to lathes from about 1920. V-belts started to replace leather belts from around 1930.
3. Plain steel bearings gave way to cast, split, soft-metal and bronze bearings. These in turn were superseded by ball bearings from the 1920s.

There were also advances in headstock spindle design which included:

1. A through hole which allows rod or dowel to pass through the spindle. The through hole also facilitates vacuum chucking.
2. Morse-tapered swallows at the right-hand ends of spindles with through holes. These swallows are mainly used to grip taper-shank drills and chucks permanently mounted on tapered arbors. The through hole allows you to easily eject items with tapered arbors from the swallow with a knock-out bar.
3. A projecting nose on the left-hand end of the headstock spindle which allows outboard turning.
4. Locking facilities which prevent threaded chucks and faceplates unscrewing if you brake the spindle.
5. Division plates (figure 1.10) and similar for indexing which were adopted from ornamental-turning lathes.

In chucking, collet chucks were invented, but because hand-woodturning versions were not manufactured much before 1980, they are not discussed until the next section 1.3.

The self-centering chuck was also developed during this period. Its earliest predecessors were probably those shown in Bergeron: the screw-bell chuck (figure 1.10), the screw-faceplate chuck (figure 1.14), and the independent-jaw chuck (figures 1.15 and 1.16). Henry Maudsley (1771-1831) developed a two-jaw self-centering chuck (figure 1.17) in London early in the 19th century. Screw-operated independent and self-centering chucks continued to be developed (figures 1.17 to 1.19), but now only screw-operated independent-jaw chucks continue to be manufactured because scroll-operated self-centering chucks took over from about 1880.

The scroll principle had been foreseen by Leonardo in about 1500 in a pipe-boring mill.[14] The self-centering chuck of Holtzapffel & Deyerlein first manufactured in 1811 (figure 1.20) and a similar chuck shown in Hamelin-Bergeron (figure 1.21) both had nascent scrolls (figure 1.23), and were amongst the earliest. While ingenious, they generated too much friction. The breakthrough came in 1842 when the Scot James Dundas patented the self-centering scroll chuck (figure 1.22).[15]

Scroll chucks quickly became hugely important in engineering and were further refined (figure 1.24)—their construction is further detailed in the next section in figures 1.38 and 1.39. Small-diameter scroll chucks were listed in woodturning-lathe catalogues as optional accessories for most of the 20th century, but did not start to become popular until special jaws suited to woodturning were introduced in the mid-1980s.

Another important area for development in this period was drill chucking. The Jacobs chuck (figure 1.25) was patented by A.I. Jacobs in 1902 when he had moved to Hartford, Connecticut.[16] Jacobs chucks can also be used to hold small wooden workpieces.[17]

Exciting as the new developments were, the simple basic chucks continued to be the most used by hand woodturners. For example, in the late 19th century woodturning lathes were supplied with up to a dozen cupchucks of different sizes.[18]

Figure 1.12 19th-century ornamental-turnings in lignum vitae. *John Hawkins Antiques*.

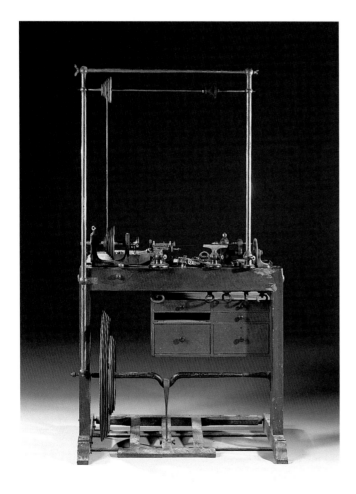

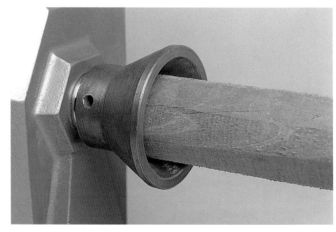

Figure 1.11 An ornamental-turning lathe of 1822, No. 1232 by Holtzapffel & Deyerlein, London. Immediately to the right of the headstock is the slide rest. A boring collar is at the right-hand end of the mahogany bed. The treadle drives the headstock spindle through an endless belt (missing). The headstock spindle drives the overhead gear, which in turn using the right-hand stepped pulley can be used to drive rotating cutters held in cutting frames mounted on the slide rest. The overhead gear is also used to drive drills. *Christie's South Kensington*.

Figure 1.13 A taper chuck. Taper chucks allow rapid mounting and demounting of square or circular cross-section spindle workpieces. The tapered inside of the chuck can be smooth or facetted, and has a diametrical taper of about 2 in 1. Taper chucks are usually used with a taper tail center which has a similar but left-facing recess. Taper chucks are used in some automatic lathes because of their self-centering ability, but pronged drive centers and cone or ring tail centers are better for hand turning.

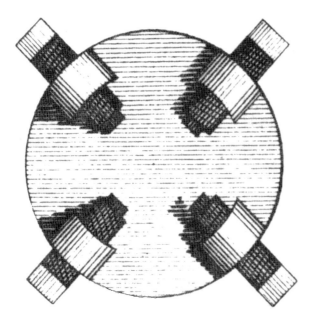

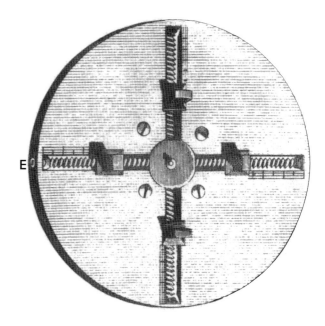

Figure 1.14 A screw-faceplate chuck pictured in Hamelin-Bergeron, a shallow version of the screw-bell chuck. It is an independent-jaw chuck because each jaw is moved separately. It has three disadvantages:

1. The tip of each screw is small and rotates as it tightens on the workpiece: it therefore tends to drill into and alter the alignment of the workpiece.
2. The tip of each screw is small in area which restricts the gripping strength of the chuck.
3. Workpieces which already have square or circular cross sections cannot be gripped concentrically without going through a special procedure.

The first two disadvantages were overcome by adding a separate free-to-rotate jaw onto the tip of each screw, or, as in the next figure, restraining each screw longitudinally and mounting an internally-threaded jaw onto it. The third disadvantage lead to the development of the self-centering chuck in which the jaws move radially in unison.

Figure 1.15 A four-jaw independent chuck, also pictured in Hamelin-Bergeron. Each jaw is moved independently by rotating its screw. Each screw has a square outer end **E** accessible at the periphery of the chuck body for a key with a square socket.

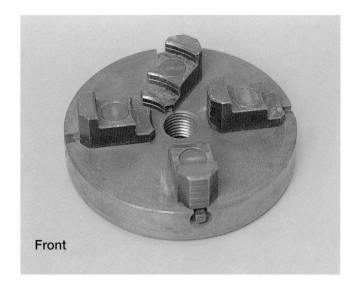

Front

Rear

Figure 1.16 A light-duty, modern, independent-jaw chuck. Its front shows few changes from the chuck in the preceding figure. Again each jaw is moved independently and radially by rotating the square end of its radial screw with a key. Each jaw top half can be rotated for inside and outside gripping and for gripping irregularly-shaped workpieces.

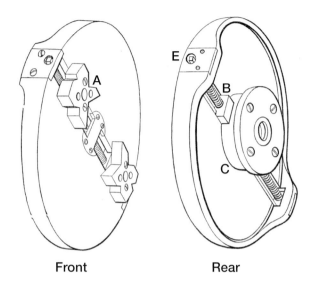

Front   Rear

Figure 1.17 A two-jaw, self-centering chuck invented by Henry Maudsley (1771-1831).[19] The two jaws' top halves **A** can be fixed in any of four orientations on their bottom halves **B** according to the size and shape of the workpiece and whether it is being gripped internally or externally. The screw is continuous through the center boss **C** which is internally threaded to screw onto the lathe nose. One half of the screw has a right-hand thread, the other half a left-hand thread. By engaging a key with one of the screw's square ends **D**, and rotating the screw, the jaws can be moved towards and away from the lathe axis in unison.

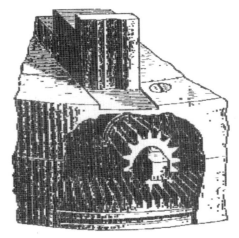

Rack down

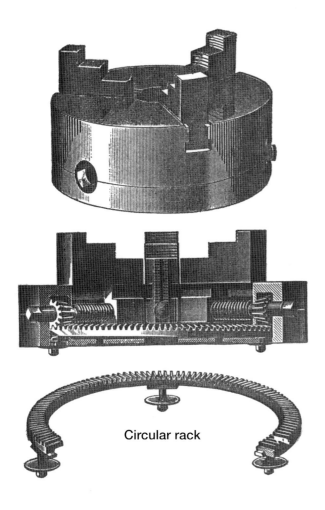

Circular rack

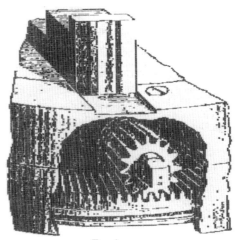

Rack up

Figure 1.18 A three-jaw, self-centering and independent chuck.[20] This late-19th-century chuck incorporates a circular rack. When the rack is screwed up (using the three screws below) to mesh with the three pinions, the chuck's action is self-centering because rotating one radial square-ended screw with a key revolves the rack. The rack then rotates the other two pinions so that all the jaws move radially in unison. When the rack is screwed down and does not mesh with the pinions, each jaw can be moved independently using its own square-ended screw. The principle of a circular rack being used to give self-centering jaw movement was invented by American A.F. Cushman, and is described in the next figure.

Figure 1.19 The working of Cushman's combination chuck of about 1875. A.F. Cushman worked in Hartford, Connecticut. Building on the 1840 invention of Simon Fairman of Stafford, Connecticut, Cushman developed a chuck with jaws which could be self-centering or be moved independently. Each jaw could be moved independently and radially by a screw passing through a threaded hole in the lower part of the jaw. In addition each screw had a pinion fixed onto it. A circular rack with a threaded periphery could be revolved within the chuck body and thus be brought to engage with all the pinions. Rotating one screw using a key on its exposed square end then operated all jaws simultaneously. This chuck was manufactured with three and four jaws in diameters from 9 to 36 in. (225 to 915 mm).[21]

This type of chuck represented the summit of screw-operated chuck development. Meanwhile in the Old World the scroll chuck had been under development since the end of the 18th century.

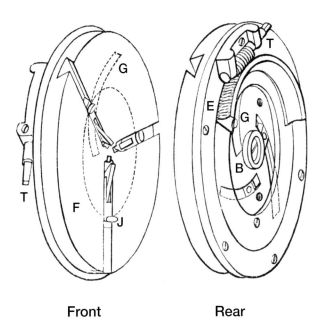

Front   Rear

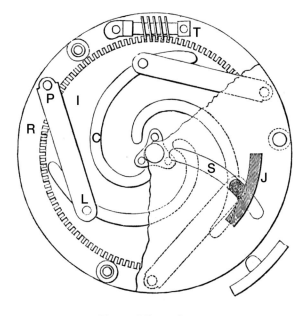

Front Elevation

Figure 1.20 A self-centering three-jaw chuck first manufactured in 1811 by Holtzapffel & Deyerlein, London.[22] The front plate **F**, has three straight radial grooves in which the three jaws **J** slide. A tangent screw **T** is fixed to the rear of front plate **F**. Also fixed to the back of the front plate is a central internally-threaded boss **B** which is used to screw the chuck onto the headstock-spindle nose.

The chuck has two further plates which are screwed together. The intermediate plate contains three curved grooves **G**. The rear plate is externally-toothed, **E**. By turning the tangent screw **T**, the rear and intermediate plates are rotated relative to the front plate. This causes the crossovers between the front plate's radial grooves and the intermediate plate's curved grooves to move inwards or outwards in unison.

The jaws have two parts pinned together which are able to swivel relative to each other. The rear parts are curved and slide in the intermediate plate's curved grooves. The front parts are basically rectangular and slide in the front plate's radial grooves. Projecting from each front part is a stud which can grip workpieces internally or externally. The jaw front part also contains a supplementary jaw which is pinned and housed within the front jaw. This supplementary jaw can be pulled out to project from the front plate to hold small workpieces externally.

Figure 1.21 A self-centering chuck pictured in Hamelin-Bergeron,[23] similar in principle to the chuck in the previous figure. A tangent screw **T** is fixed to the rear plate **R**. By rotating the tangent screw the intermediate plate **I** with the toothed rim and longer curved slots **C** is rotated. The three straight arms each have one end **P** pinned to the rear plate, with the other end **L** located in one of the slots in the intermediate plate. Each jaw **J** slides in a radial, almost-straight slot **S** in the front of the chuck (which is fixed to the rear plate). Each jaw is also pinned to the located end **L** of one of the arms. Rotating the tangent screw thus causes the jaws to move radially inwards or outwards in unison.

Ingenious as the curved-slot-based mechanisms in this and the preceding figure were, they were but a harbinger of a more efficient and elegant device for moving jaws radially in unison, the scroll.

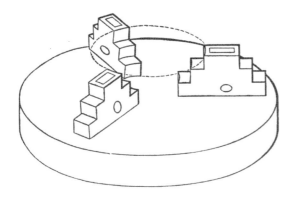

Figure 1.22 The first scroll chuck, invented by James Dundas in 1842.[24] Like earlier self-centering chucks, this chuck has a front plate (shown) and a rear plate (hidden). The jaws cover and are held in and guided by stopped radial slots in the front plate. The rear plate has a scroll machined into it. The scroll-chuck principle is explained in the next figure.

In the Holtzapffel & Deyerlein chuck (figure 1.20), the rear plate was revolved relative to the front plate with a tangent screw: in the Dundas chuck the rear plate incorporating the scroll was revolved by hand or by levering. This second method is still used in light-duty chucks and in the modern Nova chuck shown in figure 1.36. None of these methods for operating the chuck was suited to one-handed operation and strong gripping. Cushman's rack and pinions supplied the solution.

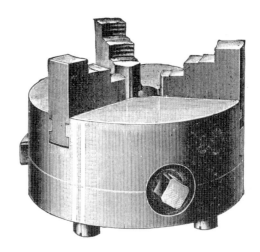

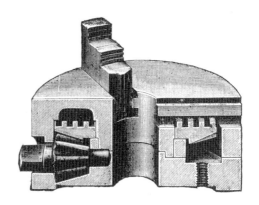

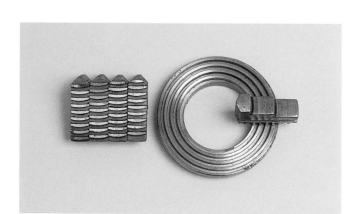

Figure 1.23 A chuck scroll. Although related to the curved slots shown in the previous two figures, it is different because there is only one groove. Rotating the scroll causes the jaws to move radially in unison. However the teeth of each jaw need to be machined at the offset corresponding to that jaw's position in the chuck's front plate. Therefore the teeth in a set of jaws cannot align, *left*, and must be fed into the chuck in the correct order.

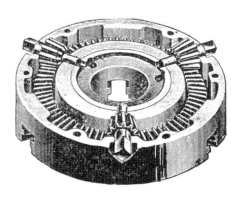

Figure 1.24 Scroll chuck of late 19th century fitted with outside-gripping jaws.

This chuck design is still current. It shows the final major development in the hand-operated scroll chuck in which Cushman's pinions and annular rack are applied to revolve Dundas's scroll. This resulted in a thicker and heavier chuck, but greater ease and speed of operation and gripping strength.[25]

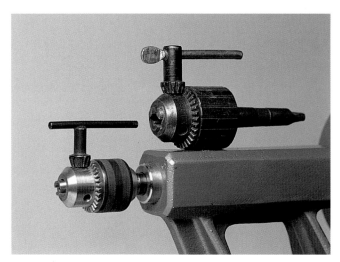

Figure 1.25 Jacobs chucks mounted on Morse-taper arbors. The chuck on the right was made by the Jacobs Manufacturing Company, the chuck on the left is a generic version supplied by Peter Child, England. The dimensions of Morse tapers are detailed on page 177.

1.3 MODERN WOODTURNING CHUCKING

The potential rewards from commercially-exploitable hardware since the explosion in hobby woodturning which started in Britain during the 1960s have apparently spurred many innovations in woodturning chucking. (I say *apparently* because the important chuck types have barely changed in decades or even centuries, and because some "new" chucks could more accurately be called rediscoveries). The innovations have been of twelve types:

1. The introduction of simple multipurpose chucks which use rigid components which fit or screw together (figure 1.26).
2. The application of the collet principle (figure 1.27) to chucks for woodturners, and the development of collet-based multipurpose chucks (figures 1.28 to 1.34).
3. The introduction of various jaw and front-half-jaw types, many based on the dovetail. These are used with collet and scroll chucks.
4. Small chucks for the many hobbyists who have small lathes or turn small items (figure 1.34).
5. From about 1985, the development of scroll-based chucks specially for woodturning (figures 1.35 to 1.41).

6. Advances in screwchucks: these have included: improved screw geometry (figure 1.42), removable screws, left-hand screws for outboard turning, and multiple body diameters.
7. The introduction and rediscovery of new and neglected chuck types including pin chucks (figures 1.43 to 1.45), loose rings which mate with dovetail jaws (figure 1.46), and chucks which have sharp circular blades (figure 1.47).
8. The increased use of chucks which the workpiece screws onto or into, including chucks based on taps and dies (figure 1.48).
9. More methods for mounting chucks, see section 1.4.
10. The adaption of ornamental-turning chucks.
11. The utilization of modern technology in chucks which turners make for themselves, for example: homemade wooden chucks not drilled and tapped to screw directly onto the headstock-spindle nose, but fitted onto metal chucks; and the use of steel components and fastenings in spring and cage chucks. (Homemade chucks are detailed in pages 29 to 32).
12. The development of vacuum and lowered-pressure chucking, described in pages 33 to 37.

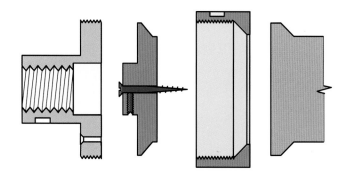

Figure 1.26 The features of the Myford three-in-one chuck. This chuck provided a faceplate, *left*, and a screwchuck. The screwchuck was assembled by screwing the collar to the left along the threaded rim of the faceplate to grip the intermediate plate containing the screw between the collar and the faceplate. A flanged workpiece, *right*, could be gripped between the faceplate and the collar. Among the earliest of the multiple-use chucks produced for the hobbyist, this type was overtaken late in the 1970s by the collet-based chucks.

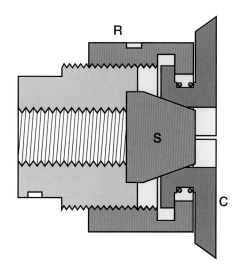

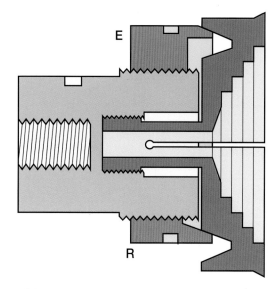

Expanding collet. Screwing the ring or collar R to the left forces the collet C to expand as it is pulled "up" the tapered spigot S. The collet is usually in four separate pieces, often held together by a rubber band.

An outside-gripping step collet. Screwing the expanding collar E (*top*) to the right forces the outer dovetail jaws to expand into and grip in a recess in a workpiece. Screwing the other closer R (*bottom*) to the right closes the steps. Inside-gripping step collets are sometimes used in engineering.

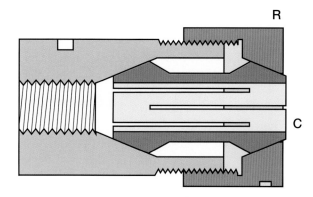

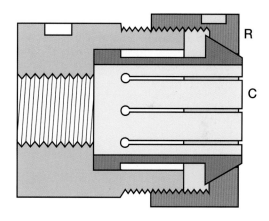

Double-taper collet. Screwing the collar or closer R to the left contracts the collet C at both ends equally.

Dead-length collet. Screwing the closer R to the left squashes only the right-hand end of the collet C.

Figure 1.27 Collet chuck types shown in longitudinal section.[26]

The engineering term collet is derived from the word's earlier meanings related to neckband. Collet (or split) chucks are developments of the earlier wooden spring chuck (figure 1.9), but contain an extra component, the collet, typically a split tube incorporating jaws.

The first collets were of the draw-in type. They were first mated with through holes through spindles by Joseph Whitworth in England, and in 1871 in the United States by Edward G. Parkhurst. Round bar could be passed through the lathe spindle to be gripped and machined as it emerged from the headstock-spindle's right-hand end. I have not shown the draw-in collet here because it is not used in hand woodturning. However it is still much used in engineering, and in some automatic woodturning lathes.[27]

Collets have limited adjustment. The more their gripping diameter is varied from the nominal, the less circular the gripping surface of the collet.

Figure 1.28 The 6-in-1. This 1970's chuck added an expanding collet of four dovetail jaws held together by a rubber band to the Myford three-in-one, and thereby increased the number of gripping options to six.

Figure 1.29 The Craft Supplies Handy Collet Chuck. It was produced during the 1970s, and utilized the double-taper collet principle. The internal diameter of the collet can therefore remain constant along its length. Three diameters of collet were supplied.

Figure 1.30 The Craft Supplies Precision Collet Chuck utilizes the dead-length collet in which the internal diameter of the collet is reduced as the external collar is screwed to the left. The chuck has many accessories and offers many chucking options.

Figure 1.31 Contracting and expanding collet chucks. *Left,* the Record Power RP3000 X1 chuck in screwchuck mode; *right,* the Craft Supplies Maxi-Grip 2000. Other similar brands include the Masterchuck designed by Roy Child, not shown, and Multitool shown in figure 1.34.

Collet chucks borrowed from scroll chucks and started to incorporate the two-piece jaws and add-on turnable segments described in figures 1.35 and 1.36. But the most recent innovation has been the facility to expand *and* contract the jaws' diameter without having to disassemble the chuck and swap major parts.

Figure 1.32 The Raffan multi collet chuck made by Woodfast Manufacturing in South Australia between 1988 and 1993.

This step-collet chuck was supplied with two collars, one to expand the collet, the other to contract it. The appropriate collar must be screwed onto the body before the step collet is screwed in. The rim of the expansion collar shown fits within the rim of the collet. Screwing the expansion collar to the right expands the dovetailed outer rim of the collet to grip into a shallow 3 inch (75 mm) diameter recess in the workpiece.

Figure 1.34 A small collet chuck, the Multistar Micro, to the left of its bigger brother the Multistar Duplex. Both chucks grip in expansion and contraction, and have a wide range of accessory jaws. The Micro chuck can grip by expansion into circular recesses from 15 to 35 mm in diameter; and by compression onto spigots from 6 to 25 mm in diameter, and onto squares 4 to 22 mm thick.

Collet-based chucks remain popular because they are compact and are without dangerous projections. However the scroll chuck is now the preferred multi-use type because of its greater ease and range of adjustment.

Figure 1.33 The Raffan chuck with the contracting collar screwed onto the body. After screwing the collet fully into the chuck body, screwing the contraction collar to the right contracts the jaws. The taper inside the rim of the collar compresses the tapered shoulder on the back of the collet.

An externally-stepped collet was also available for this chuck. Stepped accessory jaws are available for most brands of woodturners multi-jaw collet and scroll chucks.

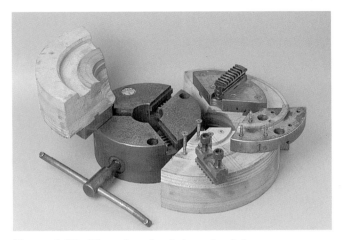

Figure 1.35 The chuck-plate principle.

Although there had not been any major changes in the design of scroll chucks since the mating of Dundas's scroll with Cushman's circular rack and pinions, there had been one advance which was to have special relevance to woodturners. This was the splitting of chuck jaws into two half-jaws. A set each of inside- and outside-gripping jaws are always supplied with engineers chucks, but sets of two-piece jaws are also available for some brands. These jaws have back and front halves which screw together. The rear or back half-jaws engage with the scroll and the radial slots in the front plate of the chuck. Various front half-jaws could be screwed to the rear-half jaws to quickly adapt a chuck to a particular gripping role.

In 1985 Mike Darlow published an article showing how front accessory jaws could be fitted to a scroll chuck's back half-jaws to give a variety of woodturning chucking options.[28] For chucking bowls by their rims Mike patented the arrangement shown where segments of wood or similar turnable materials could be fixed to chuck plates which were in turn fixed to the back half-jaws.

You first turn a recess or groove in the segments equal in outside diameter to the outside of your bowl's rim. Then when you hold your bowl's rim inside the recess or groove and tighten the chuck, the rim is gripped with an even pressure all around. Therefore you can grip the rim tightly without risk of fracturing it. The principle can be used to grip other workpieces besides bowls.

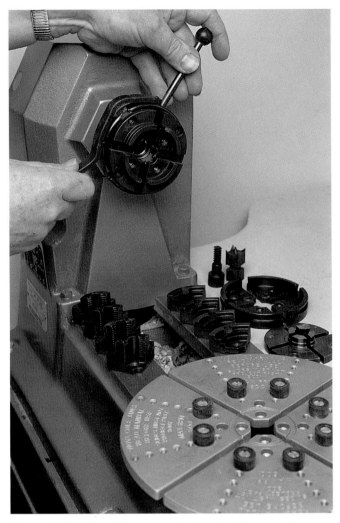

Figure 1.36 The Nova scroll chuck introduced in 1988 by Latalex of New Zealand.

The weight, cost, and concerns about the risk of injury from their projecting jaws meant that for decades engineers' scroll chucks had been little used by woodturners. In the 1980s inexpensive engineers' scroll chucks started to be exported from Asia and central Europe. But these cheaper chucks only had one-piece jaws, and in the more useful larger diameters were still too heavy for most woodturning lathes. There were also concerns that they had poorly-cast cast-iron bodies which might shatter at the high speeds used in woodturning. In response Latalex in New Zealand was the first company to develop a lightweight, steel, lever-operated chuck with a range of front half-jaws. Over the next few years other manufacturers introduced similar chucks, and more accessory jaws were introduced.

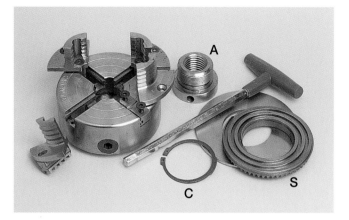

Figure 1.38   Top of a Vicmarc VM120 scroll chuck.

The four jaws slide radially in unison. Each jaw is two-piece: the top halves here are for cupchuck turning and are called "shark jaws" by Vicmarc. Each top half is screwed to a bottom half. Each bottom half is grooved to slide smoothly in its radial slot in the top face of the chuck body, and toothed to engage with the scroll. The scroll **S**, like a gramophone record, has only one groove. It is held in contact with the teeth of the bottom half-jaws by the circlip **C**. The chuck has a rear cover plate, and an adapter **A** with an external thread which screws into the internally-threaded boss in the rear of the chuck body. When you buy the chuck, you buy an adapter **A** which has the same internal thread as your headstock-spindle's right-hand nose. By changing adaptors you can use the one chuck on the left- and right-hand ends of different lathe headstock spindles.

Figure 1.37   A key-operated Vicmarc VM120 scroll chuck.

You need two hands to operate a lever-operated scroll chuck, and a third hand to hold the workpiece against or into the chuck until the jaws are tightened. For those lacking a fifth limb, the return to the key operation used by engineers' chucks was a boon. This chuck also has a steel body, and a range of accessory jaws for woodturning: its construction is shown in the next two figures.

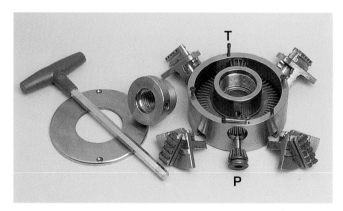

Figure 1.39   Back of a Vicmarc VM120 scroll chuck.

The special threaded pins **T** locate the pinions **P**. To rotate the scroll you rotate one of the pinions using the key.

Figure 1.40 The Supernova four-jaw scroll chuck by Latalex, New Zealand, introduced in 1997. Its features are explained in the next figure.

Figure 1.42 Screwchuck screws. *Left*, the modern Glaser-inspired screw of a Vicmarc screwchuck; *right*, the conical screw of a screwchuck made by Wadkin of Leicester, England up to about 1980.

The conical screw was manufactured for about two centuries up to the 1970s, perhaps because it was supposed to hold better in a short pilot hole or because turners used to drill their pilot holes with drills with long tapered tips. In 1980 Jerry Glaser of Los Angeles introduced his Glaser Screwchuck. Its square thread pattern, constant diameter shank, and high-tensile steel have been increasingly copied.

Turners made and still make screwchucks by adding wooden backing plates with wood screws to faceplates.[29] This was mimicked in the early multipurpose chucks, and almost all current chucks incorporate screwchuck facilities.

Most screwchuck screws are designed for inboard turning. Multi-purpose-chuck and screwchuck screws with left-hand threads are available for outboard turning. They are a worthwhile purchase if you have, as you should, a lathe on which you can turn outboard.

Figure 1.41 The rear of a Supernova four-jaw scroll chuck. A typical engineers' scroll chuck has a rear cover plate and two or three pinions which engage with the annular rack on the back of the scroll. By incorporating the pinions into the key, and eliminating the back cover plate, this chuck has been lightened and is cheaper to manufacture, but it will need internal cleaning a little more often.

Figure 1.43 The earliest form of manufactured pin chuck. This one is an accessory to a Craft Supplies Precision Combination Chuck.

A hole equal in diameter to the pin chuck spigot is drilled in the workpiece. The workpiece is then pushed onto the spigot. When the lathe is started the chuck starts to rotate before the workpiece. As the chuck rotates forwards, the loose pin remains stationary, jams between the wall of the hole in the workpiece and the rear of the groove in the chuck spigot, and thus enables the chuck to grip and drive the workpiece. As workpieces can slide off this type of pin chuck, it is sensible to use the tailstock to hold the workpiece in place.

Figure 1.45 1-inch pin chuck accessory jaws screwed to a Craft Supplies 2000 collet chuck. The ridges on the outsides of the jaws help prevent a workpiece sliding off. Small-diameter workpieces can be chucked within the jaws.

Figure 1.44 A pawl-operated pin chuck for holding predrilled pepper mill bodies. As the lathe starts, the pawl jams against the wall of the drilled hole in the workpiece. The chuck is marketed by Jack Crawford of Sydney, Australia.

Figure 1.46 Dovetailed loose rings are screwed directly to the workpiece and are then gripped by their parent chuck's dovetailed jaws. Similar loose rings are available for most brands of multipurpose chuck.

Figure 1.47 **A sharp-ring chuck** by Alex. Geiger.[30] These chucks are used in continental Europe and Asia, but rarely in English-speaking countries. The workpiece is hammered onto and gripped by the sharp edges of the rings.

Figure 1.48 **Chucks based on engineers taps and dies** designed by Bruce Leadbeatter of Sydney and made by Woodfast Manufacturing in South Australia. *Left,* the screw spigot chuck; *right,* the screw cup chuck. Both chucks cut a thread on the workpiece.

Threaded chucks, for example Dennis Stewart's NUT chuck, have long been available, but usually squash the wood into a thread rather than cut it.

1.4 MOUNTING CHUCKS

Figure 1.9 shows a wooden chuck drilled and tapped to screw directly onto a headstock-spindle nose. Ornamental-turners have made such chucks from the 16th century. Until the middle of the 19th century, each lathe manufacturer manufactured the metal chucks which would be used on its lathes, and supplied them pre-threaded to suit. Chuck manufacture was then increasingly taken over by specialist companies, and a backing plate had to be machined to enable a particular chuck to be mounted on a particular lathe. As threads and lathe noses standardized, pre-threaded chucks and backing plates for the common lathe-nose threads became available. At the other end of the lathe, the widespread adoption of the tapers developed in the United States by Steven Morse was a boon to the manufacturers of drills, and to the manufacturers of small chucks such as the Jacobs which could be mounted on arbors.

Hand woodturners normally lack the ability to thread chucks and make metal backing plates. Woodturning-chuck manufactures have therefore long supplied chucks or backing plates pre-threaded for the most common spindle noses. The most recent introduction has been to thread chucks to accept a range of inserts with different internal threads. Figure 1.49 illustrates the three common mounting methods. Now instead of threading the wooden bodies of homemade chucks, woodturners hold them in manufactured metal chucks as shown in the next section 1.5.

Figure 1.49 **Chuck-mounting alternatives.** *Left,* a Vicmarc VM 120 chuck threaded to take inserts; *center,* an engineer's scroll chuck with a backing plate marketed by Axminster, England; *right,* a Multitool chuck threaded 30 x 3.5 mm RH (sometimes called a dedicated thread) which can only be mounted on a spindle nose with that particular thread.

1.5 HOMEMADE CHUCKS

Although there is a wide range of proprietary chucks, you can save time and money on some jobs by making your own chucks. The wood-disk chuck in figure 1.50 is perhaps the crudest: the jam or press-fit chuck (figures 1.51 and 1.52) the most common. Other types are shown in figures 1.53 to 1.62. Chuck types shown elsewhere in this book include the sphere chuck (figures 4.70 to 4.72) and the screwed mandrel (figure 8.50).

Homemade chucks are usually made from wood, plywood, or other wood-based board, and often incorporate steel fasteners. Strengthening the chuck can be worthwhile, particularly with steel rings to resist circumferential tension (figure 1.56). Homemade chucks usually replicate types developed long ago, but recent technological developments, for example the hose clip in figure 1.55, can be utilized to advantage.

Figure 1.50 A wood-disk chuck. Flat-backed or flat-bottomed workpieces can be held on or against the trued flat face of a wooden disk screwed to a faceplate by: hot-melt glue, sealing wax, a paper joint (strong paper glued between the two flat wood faces), or tailstock pressure.

To center the workpiece you can:

1. Have a small spike projecting from the center of the wood disk. The spike could be fixed, or be sprung as described in figures 1.67 and 1.68.
2. Turn a spigot on the wood-disk chuck and drill a matching recess in the workpiece, or vice versa.
3. With a compass or during an earlier turning operation, pencil a circle on the back of the workpiece a little larger in diameter than the wood disk of the chuck. You then adjust the workpiece's position until the margin between the wood-disk chuck and the pencilled circle is even. The converse can also be useful.

Figure 1.51 The jam or press-fit chuck is the most used homemade chuck. Its front can be wood with axial or radial grain, plywood, or a suitable composition board. The chuck front is now usually mounted on a faceplate or in a steel chuck rather than being drilled and threaded by you to screw directly onto your lathe's headstock-spindle nose.

You should always provide and skim a true radial bearing surface. You then seat a face, rim, shoulder, or similar workpiece feature against this bearing surface to ensure that the workpiece axis is coaxial with the lathe axis.

Jam chucks are also used to provide the accurate workpiece centering and alignment for several other chuck types such as cage chucks (figure 1.8) and vacuum chucks (figure 1.63).

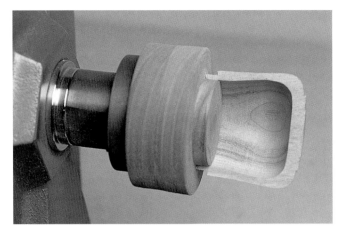

Figure 1.52 A jam-spigot chuck can only used for light turning: the workpiece is likely to slip or split if you take heavy cuts because the workpiece is in circumferential tension. It is always better to grip a workpiece by putting it into circumferential compression as the previous and most other chucks do.

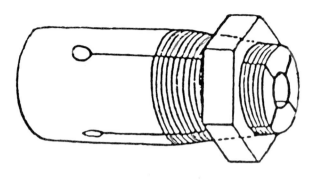

Figure 1.54 A nut-operated spring chuck[31] requires a tapered external thread on the chuck body. Ideally the thread inside the nut should have the same taper.

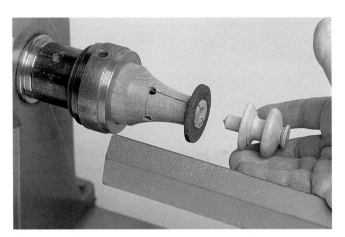

Figure 1.53 A ring-operated spring chuck being used to hold a knob to finish-turn the waste from the knob's front. Turn a plywood ring if you cannot find a metal one of suitable diameter.

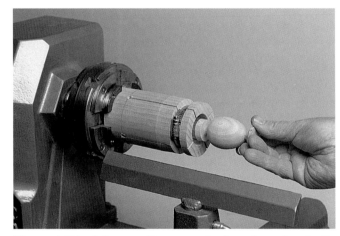

Figure 1.55 A hose-clip-operated spring chuck. To lessen the risk of injury, recess the hose clip and have its loose tail trailing when the lathe rotates forwards.

Figure 1.58 **An wooden expanding-mandrel** operated by the tailstock ram. Expanding mandrels ideally grip both ends of a workpiece through hole, unlike tapered mandrels.

Figure 1.56 **A square-hole chuck.** The hole is tapered, reducing in cross section from right to left. Small versions, useful for driving lace-bobbin blanks, are still manufactured as inserts for multipurpose chucks or with Morse-taper shanks. You can easily make your own square-hole chucks from hard wood or metal. They can be held in a chuck or on a faceplate, or be turned with a Morse-taper shank which fits into your lathe's headstock-spindle swallow.

Figure 1.59 **A drawbar-operated wooden expanding-mandrel.** The mandrel is expanded by pulling the knob on the left of the headstock to the left. The knob is attached to a drawbar (a length of 10 mm diameter threaded rod) which passes through the hollow headstock spindle. The right-hand end of the drawbar is shown in the next figure.

Figure 1.57 **A tapered mandrel.** A mandrel made of a compressible material like wood should have a very slow taper. Too steep a taper and the workpiece will not be held securely. If the mandrel is steel it need not be tapered provided that you can drill a suitably-sized hole in the workpiece.

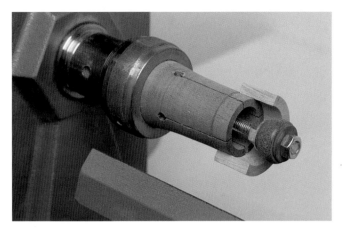

Figure 1.60 The expanding mandrel and the right-hand end of the drawbar of the chuck in the preceding figure. Both the wooden collar on the drawbar and the swallow of the mandrel decrease in diameter to the left.

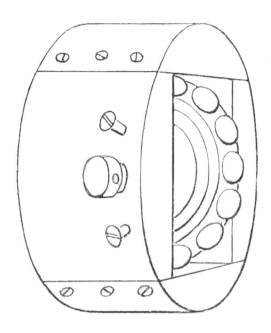

Figure 1.62 A chuck for turning half pearls, another of the many chucks you can make shown in J.J. Holtzapffel's *Hand or Simple Turning*.[32] Other excellent sources for special-purpose chucks are *Der Drechsler* by von C.A. Martin and *Das Drechslerwerk* by Fritz Spannagel.

Figure 1.61 The mandrel of the chuck shown in the preceding two figures expanded to grip the workpiece by pulling the knob to the left.

1.6 VACUUM CHUCKING

Mounting and demounting the workpiece takes a couple of seconds with this 20th-century chucking method in which the workpiece is sucked onto or into a suitable chuck. Sucking is perhaps a confusing term because it could be thought to imply that the workpiece is pulled against the chuck by negative pressure. Alas negative pressure is impossible, and the workpiece is pushed against or into the chuck by atmospheric pressure. There is an lesser and opposing pressure, and the holding power of the chuck is proportional to the difference between these two pressures (figure 1.63).

The first vacuum chucks did not use vacuum pumps to lower the pressure on the headstock side of the workpiece (figure 1.64). However a vacuum pump (figure 1.65) is far superior because the chuck will still hold if there is minor leakage of ambient air into the evacuated cavity.

With a vacuum pump the air is extracted through a hose. To run the lathe without coiling and destroying the hose there needs to be a rotatable seal or union connecting the hose to the headstock spindle. For a headstock spindle with a through hole, the union and the vacuum chuck are mounted on opposite ends (figure 1.66).

You need to be able to center and align the workpiece on a vacuum chuck. For this you can use a circular or annular recess in the chuck, a spigot, the tail center, or a sprung center pin. All but the last also give extra chucking security, lessening the chance of sudden leakage and preventing the workpiece from becoming airborne if a leak does suddenly occur.

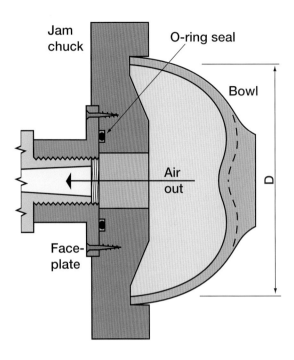

Figure 1.63 The principle of vacuum chucking.
At sea level the weight of air above exerts an atmospheric pressure p_a of 14.7 psi (1.0 atmosphere or 101 kPa). Atmospheric pressure acts not just downwards but in all directions.

In vacuum chucking the vacuum pump removes air from the cavity of diameter **D** to the left of an inboard workpiece, and lowers the pressure within the cavity to p_c. The force then pushing the workpiece into the chuck is the net pressure pushing on the workpiece to the left multiplied by the area of the cavity

$$= 0.25 \ (p_a - p_c) \ \pi \ \mathbf{D}^2$$

The forces generated can be considerable. The force pushing a 12 in. (300 mm) diameter bowl into a vacuum chuck can be as high as 1660 lb (750 kg).

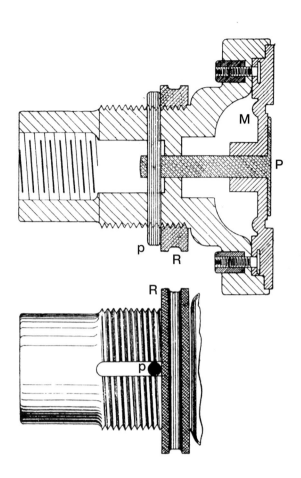

Figure 1.64 A German vacuum chuck of 1905.[33]

Screwing ring **R** to the left pulled pin **p** and piston **P** to the left. Thus **M**, a rubber membrane, was pulled into the hollowed body of the chuck, and the volume of the cavity between the workpiece and the membrane was increased. The decrease in pressure within the cavity was proportional to the increase in volume of the cavity. And as the pressure within the cavity decreased, so did the holding power of the chuck.

Although the pressure within the cavity could theoretically be reduced to almost zero, any leakage of air into the cavity though gaps between the membrane and the workpiece or through the pores of the workpiece would have caused the chuck to let go. The development of suitable vacuum pumps (next figure) and rotary seals called unions allows continuous evacuation. This enables the pressure within the cavity between the workpiece and the chuck to be kept very low and the hold maintained even when there are minor leakages.

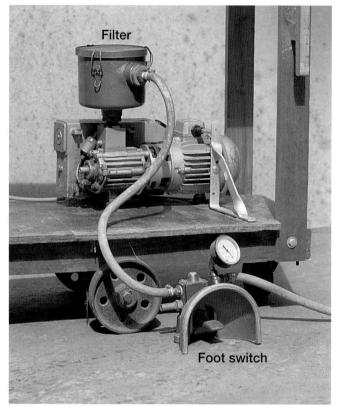

Figure 1.65 A 1/2 hp rotary vacuum pump. Vacuum pumps can readily reduce the pressure in the cavity between the workpiece and the chuck to almost zero. These pumps have minute clearances between their moving parts. The air which is extracted through the pump must therefore be properly filtered.

Depressing the foot switch allows air to enter the system for workpiece mounting and demounting.

Even with a vacuum pump, vacuum chucking is only secure as long as there is no or minimal leakage. To help prevent leakage:

1. All screwed joints should be sealed with plumbers' plastic tape.
2. Where surfaces are pressed together there should be O-rings. O-rings are available in a huge range of diameters from engineers and bearing suppliers.
3. Seal the surfaces of all wood, plywood, and MDF chuck components with PVA glue or similar because they are likely to be porous.

Figure 1.66 The headstock arrangement for vacuum chucking.

With a headstock spindle with a through-hole and threaded noses at each end, the vacuum chuck can be mounted inboard, as here, or outboard. Two vacuum chucks for holding flat-backed workpieces are shown. Have the effective diameter of the chuck as large as possible to increase the hold and to lessen the possibility of levering the workpiece out of alignment and causing a leak.

The hose from the vacuum pump cannot be fixed directly to the other spindle nose or the hose would be twisted to destruction when you switched the lathe on. The hose has to be connected to a vacuum-union, a rotatable seal, which is screwed onto the headstock-spindle nose if the threads are compatible. If the threads are not compatible, use a suitably threaded adaptor between the union and the spindle nose as here.

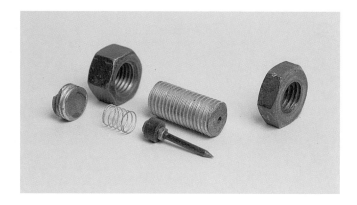

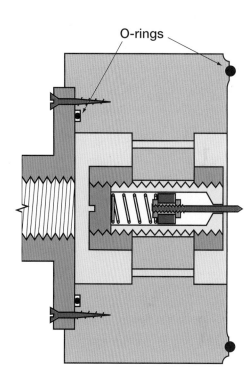

O-rings

Figure 1.68 The construction of the vacuum chuck with the sprung center pin shown in the preceding figure. A short, fixed, projecting pin or screw such as those shown in figure 1.66 are useful centering aids for flat-backed workpieces with punched center holes, but the sprung center pin makes chucking faster still. The construction is very simple requiring only hacksawing and drilling in the lathe. In the top photograph the cylinder which houses the center pin is 2 in. long, is cut from a 1 in. BSW screw, and is bored with 9/16 in. and 3/16 in. holes. The sizes and threads can of course be varied.

Figure 1.67 A vacuum chuck with a sprung center pin. The construction is detailed in the next figure.

1.7 PARTIAL-VACUUM CHUCKING

The systems described in the preceding section cause the workpiece to be forced onto or into the chuck so hard that the workpiece can be turned without any mechanical fixing if the effective diameter of the chuck is more than 4 in. (100 mm). From the early 1990s, related systems were introduced which used domestic vacuum cleaners and even expelling blades to create a partial vacuum in the chuck cavity. Unless augmented by mechanical fixings, these systems permit the workpiece to be sanded but not turned. Whether such systems are worthwhile is debatable, particularly when compared to the far greater security offered by mechanical cage chucks and similar.

When a domestic vacuum cleaner is used to lower the pressure in the cavity there is negligible air flow through the cleaner, so ensure that you do not use a cleaner which needs some air flow to cool the cleaner's motor. However vacuum cleaners only reduce the pressure within the chuck cavity by about 30% of an atmosphere—you wouldn't be able to move the cleaner's head across the carpet if the pressure reduction were high. An efficient union is not warranted therefore, and that in figure 1.69 you can make yourself to use with the chuck types shown in the preceding section. Partial-vacuum faceplates with resilient-material facings and incorporated unions have also been commercially introduced (1.70).

A novel partial-vacuum chuck was the Turbo RCD. Introduced in 1997 by Peter Flewitt of Nottingham, England, it combined a jam chuck with expelling blades. The outside of the bowl rim was axially located in an step jam chuck. You had to briefly support the workpiece when starting (and stopping) the lathe if the workpiece rim was not a tight fit in the jam chuck. As the chuck rotated, its blades expelled air from the cavity. The faster the chuck's rotation, the lower the pressure within the chuck cavity and the better the hold.

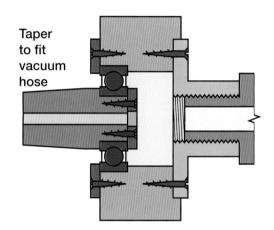

Taper to fit vacuum hose

Figure 1.69 A homemade union based on a sealed bearing. In the photograph the bearing is crudely but effectively held into its wooden housing with four screws. The drawing shows a neater arrangement. The central spigot needs to be tapered so that the end of the vacuum-cleaner hose fits snugly.

Figure 1.70 A vacuum chuck by Vicmarc. It has a closed-cell, foam-covered front face, and incorporates a union for use with a vacuum cleaner. The most efficient way to center a workpiece on this and similar flat chucks is to use the tailstock. Leave the tailstock in place for as long as possible.

1.8 SUMMARY

This chapter has described chucks comprehensively but not exhaustively. Chucking applications are shown in the remaining chapters of this book; in *The Fundamentals of Woodturning*, in particular in chapter 7; and in *Woodturning Techniques*.

1.9 ENDNOTES

1 A thorough dissertation on the word is given by Frank Berry in "Chuck-The Last Word," *The Society of Ornamental Turners Bulletin*, No. 90, pp. 191–192.

2 Joseph Moxon, *Mechanick Exercises or the Doctrine of Handy-Works*, p. 228 of the Praeger facsimile edition.

3 I have used a hyphen between *ornamental* and *turners* so that present-day practitioners will not be thought to be just physically and sartorially endowed. I also use a hyphen between *ornamental* and *turning* to give the combination the status of a compound noun, and thus raise it above the mere turning of ornaments.

4 The true author was Louis-Georges-Isaac Salivet who asked his friend Louis-Eloy Bergeron to be identified as the author. Reference: S.G. Abell, J.Leggat, and W.G. Ogden, Jr, *A Bibliography of the Art of Turning and Lathe and Machine Tool History*, third edition, 1987, p. 9.

5 Abell, Leggat, and Ogden, *A Bibliography of the Art of Turning and Lathe and Machine Tool History*, p. 10.

6 Modern versions of the three preceding chuck types are shown in: Mike Darlow, *The Fundamentals of Woodturning*, figs 3.9, 7.1, 7.4, and 7.11.

7 Moxon, *Mechanical Exercises*, plate 14 of the turning section.

8 Moxon, *Mechanick Exercises*, plate 13 of the turning section.

9 The upper spindle is pictured in plate 7 of the 1701 1st edition, the lower spindle in plate 12. The plate numbers may be different in different editions of Plumier.

10 L.T.C. Rolt, *Tools for the Job* (London: B.T. Batsford Ltd, 1965), p. 118.

11 This chuck is based on that in: J.J. Holtzapffel, *Hand or Simple Turning*, p. 222, fig. 269.

12 A family tree and brief history is given in *The Society of Ornamental Turners Bulletin*, No. 60, pp. 66–67.

13 John B. Hawkins, "Staffordshire Engine Turned Pottery 1760–1780," *The Society of Ornamental Turners Bulletin*, No. 100, pp. 213–220.

14 L.T.C. Rolt, *Tools for the Job*, p. 29.

15 J.J. Holtzapffel, *Hand or Simple Turning*, p. 231.

16 Mike Darlow, "Jacobs the Man," *Woodturning*, No. 68 (October 1998): pp. 59–60.

17 Mike Darlow, *The Fundamentals of Woodturning*, p. 130, fig. 7.3.

18 J.J. Holtzapffel, *Hand or Simple Turning*, pp. 101–102. See also Mike Darlow, *The Fundamentals of Woodturning*, p. 130, fig. 7.1.

19 The two drawings are adapted from: J.J. Holtzapffel, *Hand or Simple Turning*, p. 232, figs 286 and 287.

20 Elliott L. Brookes, *20th Century Machine Shop Practice* (Chicago: Frederick J. Drake & Co. 1906), pp. 233–234.

21 Details from *American Machinist*, Vol. 1, No. 1 (November, 1877): p. 1.

22 J.J. Holtzapffel, *Hand or Simple Turning*, p. 229, figs 282 and 283.

23 Also pictured in: J.J. Holtzapffel, *Hand or Simple Turning*, p. 230, fig. 285.

24 J.J. Holtzapffel, *Hand or Simple Turning*, p. 231, and p. 229 fig. 284.

25 von C.A. Martin, *Der Drechsler*, p. 36, figs 46, 47, 48.

26 These drawing were adapted from figures in: Tubal Cain, *Workholding in the Lathe* (Hemel Hempstead: Argus Books, 1987), ch. 7. Tubal Cain is a pseudonym of T.D. Walshaw. Tubal-Cain is described in Genesis 4:22 as a forger of "all kinds of tools out of bronze and iron."

27 L.T.C. Rolt, *Tools for the Job*, pp. 120 and 166.

28 Mike Darlow, "The Gripping Story," *Woodworker* (January 1986): pp. 61–62.

29 Mike Darlow, *The Practice of Woodturning*, p. 60, fig. 4.5.

30 This illustration is in part scanned from a catalog of Alex. Geiger Maschinenfabrik KG, Germany. Sharp-ring chucks are also pictured in: Fritz Spannagel, *Das Drechslerwerk*, fig. 64; Rolf Steinert, *Drechseln in Holtz*, fig. 4.7; and Gottfried Bockelmann, *Handbuch Drechseln*, p. 54.

31 J.J. Holtzapffel, *Hand or Simple Turning*, p. 222, fig. 271.

32 J.J. Holtzapffel, *Hand or Simple Turning*, p. 559, fig. 755.

33 von C.A. Martin, *Der Drechsler*, p. 277, fig. 571.

Chapter Two

SPINDLE TURNING

This chapter describes methods used in eight areas of spindle turning:

1. Mounting and demounting workpieces without stopping the lathe.
2. Cutting different pommel details.
3. Sizing.
4. Turning captive rings.
5. Turning loose rings.
6. Inletting split rings.
7. Turning trees.
8. Swash turning and pumping.

2.1 MOUNTING AND DEMOUNTING WITH THE LATHE RUNNING

Professional turners save time and electricity by mounting smaller spindle blanks and demounting the finished turnings with the lathe running. This practice would have been universal among woodturners who used lathes driven from line shafts by leather belts because it saved time, and saved wear to the journal bearings (figures 2.1 to 2.3).

Figure 2.1 A forest of leather belting in the machine shop of John Heine Ltd, Leichhardt, Sydney, Australia in 1918. Line shafts, countershafts, shifter rods and belt poles are suspended from the ceiling.
Through the 19th century and into the 20th, a single power source, a steam engine or later a large electric motor, drove all a factory's fixed machines. Power was transmitted through the factory by line shafting which rotated throughout the working day at a constant speed. The hanging belt poles allowed the power to a machine to be readily engaged and disengaged as described in the next two figures.

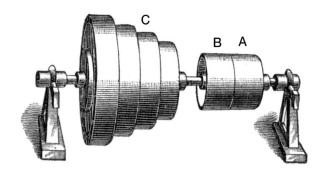

Figure 2.2 **A countershaft** was typically mounted above each machine, and driven from a line shaft by an endless leather belt.[1] This belt could drive *fast* or *tight* pulley **A** which was fixed to the countershaft. Alternatively when the operator wanted to stop his machine, he shifted the belt across to drive the *free* or *loose* pulley **B** which was free to rotate on the countershaft. The stepped pulley **C** was fixed on the countershaft, and formed a pair with a stepped pulley fixed on the lathe-headstock spindle, the two stepped pulleys being connected by their own endless leather belt.

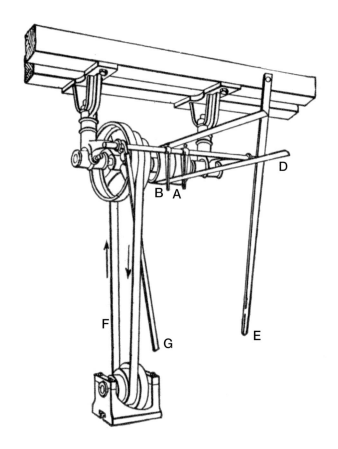

Figure 2.3 **A countershaft driving a lathe headstock.**[2] The fast pulley **A** and the loose pulley **B** acted as a crude but effective clutch. To disconnect the drive to his lathe a turner had to flick or shift the leather belt **D** from the fast to the loose pulley, To restore power to his lathe the turner flicked or shifted belt **D** back again. This was accomplished by moving the handle of the belt pole **E** to the left or right. This took a few seconds, which would not have been desirable to woodturners on piecework or to their foremen. Hence the practice of mounting smaller spindle blanks and demounting the finished turnings with the lathe running.

Turners also changed their lathe's speeds with the lathe running. Endless belt **F** was first thrown by hand to the next-smallest pulley to that for the new required speed on the lathe spindle's stepped pulley. Belt **F** was then shifted to the appropriate pulley on the countershaft stepped pulley, here by using a second belt pole **G**. Finally belt **F** was shifted by hand onto the correct pulley on the headstock spindle.

2.1.1 MOUNTING

Mounting a workpiece in a lathe which is running is not necessary or even wise for amateurs. You should not attempt it unless you are an experienced and competent turner, and never with larger workpieces.

The practice is aided by having a suitable drive center (figure 2.4). Try first with small cylindrical workpieces and a lowered lathe speed. You can use the technique which is described in figures 2.5 to 2.10 whether the turning is to be demounted whole, or parted off.

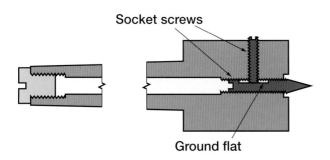

Socket screws

Ground flat

Longitudinal Section

Figure 2.4 A drive center with an adjustable center pin. You can readily modify a suitable manufactured drive center if you can drill and tap, and have a chuck which can grip the larger-diameter end of the drive center. For center pins I use $1/4$ in. (6 mm) socket screws.

Both mounting and demounting involve keeping the left-hand end of the workpiece clear of the revolving prongs while it is supported on the center pin. A suitable drive center's center pin therefore needs to project from $1/8$ to $5/16$ in. (3 to 7 mm) past the ends of the prongs. The softer the wood and the larger the blank's size, the greater the ideal projection of the center pin. An adjustable center pin allows you to cope with a wider range of workpieces, and to maintain suitable projections as the prongs are shortened through resharpening.

Keep the drive center in good condition. Damaged or burred prongs can hamper demounting. Prongs of unequal length drive poorly.

Mounting and demounting is far easier if you have prepunched the centers of the workpiece ends. Take care with the depth and included angle of these cone-shaped holes. When the blank is first located on the drive center's center pin, the driving prongs should be 1 to 3 mm clear of the blank's left-hand face.

Figure 2.5 Starting to mount a workpiece with the lathe running. The banjo, toolrest, and tailstock are locked in positions which should not need to be altered once the batch is under way.

Position your head so that you can clearly see the blank's left-hand end and your drive center. Gently push the blank to the left with your right hand, and use your left hand to guide the punched hole in the workpiece's left-hand end over your driving center's center pin. If the center pin's projection and the punched hole are suitably sized, the workpiece will rest safely on the rotating center pin with the prongs clear of the end of the blank. Continue to push the workpiece gently to the left.

Figure 2.6 Changing hands. Shuffle to the right, and bring your left hand to also grip the blank's right-hand end. Your left hand's fingers should pass beneath the toolrest, your thumb above. Maintain the gentle push on the blank to the left.

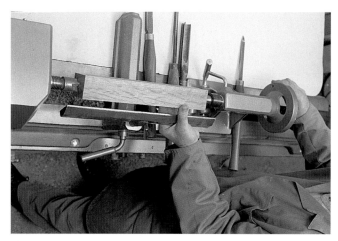

Figure 2.7 **Starting to operate the tailstock.** While your left hand supports the blank's right-hand end and takes over the push to the left, transfer your right hand to the tailstock handwheel. Slowly wind the ram to the left, and watch the point of the tail center into the punched hole in the blank's right-hand end.

Figure 2.9 **Move your left thumb back onto the nearside of the toolrest** so that it cannot become trapped between the blank and the toolrest. Your fingertips should still be preventing the blank from rotating.

Figure 2.8 **The prongs start to engage.** As you continue winding the handwheel you will hear and feel the drive center's prongs start to scrape the blank's left-hand end.

Figure 2.10 Releasing the blank. As you wind the tailstock ram to the left, the engagement of the drive center prongs increases. Continue winding slowly. As the rotation of the blank becomes hard to resist, release the blank by lowering the fingers of your left hand. Continue to wind the tail center into the wood until the blank is securely held. Finally lock the tailstock ram so that it cannot creep to the right, and you are ready to start turning.

2.1.2 DEMOUNTING

You gain little by mounting a blank with the lathe running unless you can also demount the finished turning with the lathe running. There are two demounting situations: demounting the whole finish-turned workpiece (figure 2.11), and parting off leaving a waste stub (figure 2.12). You should always leave the waste stub at the headstock end of the workpiece.

Figure 2.11 Demounting a finished turning with the lathe running. Unlock the tailstock ram. Position your left hand to close onto the left-hand end of the turning—if the turning has a long pommel at its left-hand end, you can safely grip the pommel once the workpiece has ceased rotating. If the pommel at the left-hand end is short, you can position your hand just to the right of the pommel. Have your palm and fingers passing beneath the toolrest. Position your left thumb on the nearside of the toolrest, well clear of the rotating turning. Slowly wind the tail center to the right with your right hand. The left-hand end of the turning should slowly spring off the drive center's prongs while its right-hand end continues to be located by the tail center.

Once the turning's left-hand end is free of the prongs but still supported on the center pin, support and then grip the workpiece with your left hand. Continue retracting the tail center until there is enough distance between the turning and the drive center for you to safely remove the turning.

It is safest to stop the lathe if the turning does not spring free. The problem may be that your drive center's prongs are burred, or that the included angle of its center point is too small.

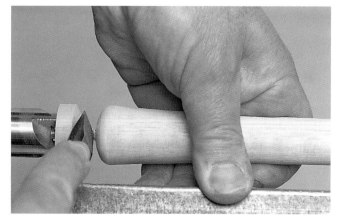

Figure 2.12 **Parting off.** First V-cut down. Once the waste pin is small, slacken the tailstock so that the turning will come free and not be jammed in after parting.[3]

The waste stub normally falls off unaided. If not, carefully lever it off with a tool tip, taking care not damage the tool tip by bringing it into contact with the drive center.

2.2 POMMELS

The standard pommel is square in side elevation, but there are other commonly-used designs (figures 2.13 and 2.14). Figure 2.15 explains how to cut pommel details.

Figure 2.14 **A show-wood pommel below upholstery.** In better-quality work, the hidden wood above the show wood is carved away so the upholstery lies fairly flush with the show wood.

The outer corner of each stool leg is rounded. It is necessary therefore to cut the lower end of the pommel square—cutting it convex as in **B** of the previous figure would leave a strange, non-horizontal edge.

Figure 2.13 **Pommel variations.** *Left to right*: **A**, square; **B**, slightly convex; **C**, ogee-cornered; and **D**, ogee-cornered with a cylindrical section.

In all four legs the bead is separated from the pommel by a cylindrical section. This cylindrical section is commonly included because it allows you to roll the right-hand (here lower) half of the adjacent bead with the same wide skew that you would use to turn the rest of the workpiece.

Figure 2.15 Cutting a pommel detail. Pommel corner features such as those shown in figure 2.13 are straightforward to cut. Imagine that, as here, the square is integral within a cylinder, and that the pale waste miraculously disappears when you have finished. You therefore use the tools and tool presentations that you would for a workpiece of circular cross section. To achieve a smoother surface:

1. Have the lathe speed high—this shortens the durations that you are cutting air between cutting wood.
2. Manipulate your tools more slowly and keep their presentations at minimum clearance.

2.3 SIZING

Figures 2.16 and 2.17 show tools called sizers which are used to cut pins which will be glued into sockets. You can also set other diameters with a sizer, but because you have to rough the section close to its finished diameter before sizing, it is quicker to caliper with a parting tool or gouge. Figure 2.18 shows a sizer in use.[4]

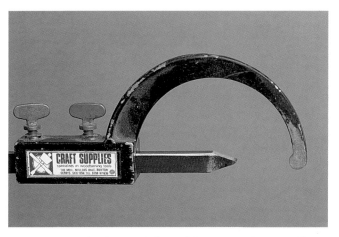

Figure 2.17 A sizer of the add-on crook type. The crook is manufactured for Craft Supplies Ltd of Derbyshire, England. You should arris the two lower edges of the tool blade to help it slide easily on and not damage your toolrest.

You set the diameter you want to size between the cutting edge and the facing inside projection of the crook. The tip of the crook should be narrower than the width of the sizer's cutting edge. When you first present a sizer the rake angle is positive; it also tends to be larger for smaller pin diameters. Therefore although a sizer finally scrapes, you need to sharpen its lower bevel at a smaller angle to the blade's axis than a scraper's 70°. Having a top bevel increases the sharpening angle, and gives the cutting edge more durability.

Turners do not usually set diameters on what will become a finished and visible surface with a sizer because the cutter's scraping action tears the wood badly.

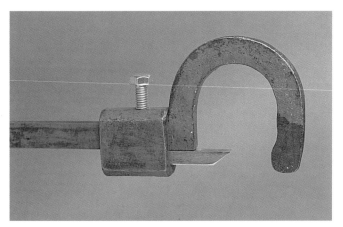

Figure 2.16 A sizer of the add-on tool bit type.

Figure 2.18 Sizing a pin, here on a chair stretcher. You do not use calipers with a sizer, and can therefore grip the sizer with one or with both hands. I often prefer two-handed gripping because of a sizer's greater tendency to grab. If you use a sizer one-handed, grip it as you would a parting tool with your right hand holding the tool well forwards and the handle beneath your forearm.

Sizing is straightforward. You lever the sizer downwards to cut the pin, and lever the sizer back up to free the tool. During both actions you must also pull on the sizer to avoid cutting the diameter undersize.

The cutting edge of a sizer is pulled forwards during a cut by the tip of the crook. If you leave a pin's diameter too big before sizing, typically more than 10% oversize, the sizer's cutting edge will attempt to scrape away an excessively-thick shaving and you are likely to lose control.

There is no need to rock a sizer as you might a parting tool because you should only be removing a small thickness of wood.[4]

2.4 CAPTIVE RINGS

A ring which is turned "into" a spindle and then remains trapped but loose on that spindle is termed a captive ring. These rings are usually circular rings, that is they are circular in cross section. They are mostly used for quirky ornament (figure 2.19).[5]

Captive rings can also be functional (figure 2.20). Captive rings can be turned with skew chisels or with ring-cutting or ring-scraping tools (figures 2.21 to 2.26).

I am against using bead-forming scrapers to produce beads or flush beads which are not the outer surfaces of captive rings. These scrapers leave an inferior bead surface with most woods as figure 2.31 shows. Those turners who use bead scrapers to avoid bead rolling with a skew restrict their vocabulary of bead shapes and sizes, and prevent themselves from realizing their turning potential. The use of bead-forming scrapers to cut the outsides of captive rings in cooperative woods has some validity.

Figure 2.19 A goblet with ten captive rings[6] turned with the captive ring hook shown in figure 2.25.

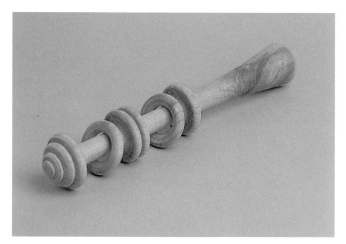

Figure 2.20 A baby's rattle similar to the mid-19th-century rattle in the Pinto Collection in the Birmingham Museum and Art Gallery, England.[7] As there is a danger of a baby breaking the rings and swallowing some of the pieces, this may be an unwise item to sell in these increasingly litigious times.

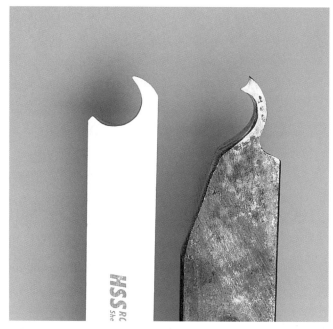

Figure 2.22 An Improved captive-ring scraper, *right*, which has its long jaw widening towards its scraping tip. This feature lessens the likelihood of damaging the inside surface of a captive ring if you have not previously cleared the waste. Also, the cutting edge is concave, the two side points giving a cleaner cut.

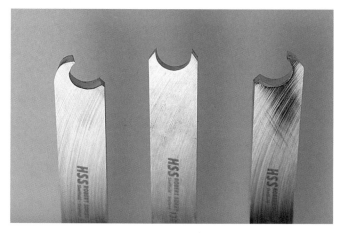

Figure 2.21 Captive-ring-turning tools. *Left*, left-hand captive-ring scraper; *center*, bead-forming scraper; *right*, right-hand captive-ring scraper. Manufactured in HSS, these tools are typically available for 1/2, 5/16, and 3/8 in. (13, 11.5, and 10 mm) ring diameters. These tools are by Robert Sorby. Similar tools are available from some other manufacturers.

The longer jaws of these captive-ring scrapers narrow toward their scraping tips. Therefore as you cut a ring's inside surface, if you have not previously cleared away the waste, that waste will press against the outside of the long jaw. The inside of the long jaw will thus be forced against and crush or cut into the ring's inside surface—this damage can be lessened by tuning (figure 2.23).

These scraping tools are sharpened by flat-honing their top faces.

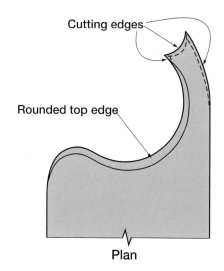

Cutting edges

Rounded top edge

Plan

Figure 2.23 Tuning captive-ring scrapers. You should round the sharp top edge around the inside of each captive ring scraper so that it will not damage the already-cut ring surface when you use that surface as a circular fence. Use a slipstone or circular diamond file, and start from just behind the scraping tip of the longer jaw.[8] Also arris the blade's bottom edges so that the tool slides freely on your toolrest.

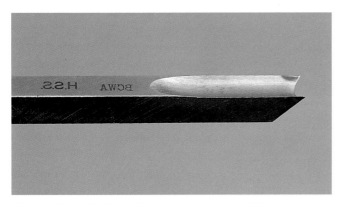

Figure 2.24 A Bob Chapman bead-cutting tool. It is used flute-down in a *semi-cutting* presentation.

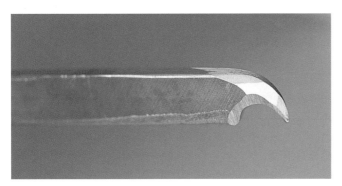

Figure 2.25 A captive-ring hook similar to that shown by David Regester in *Turning Boxes and Spindles Step-by-Step.*[9] The tool can cut in from both the left and the right.

Figure 2.26 A captive-ring gouge by the author. This tool leaves an improved finished surface on the insides of captive rings.

2.4.1 TURNING CAPTIVE RINGS

You produce a captive ring in five stages:

1. Turn the ring's outer half as if it were a flush bead.
2. Turn most of the ring's inner half, then sand its exposed surface.
3. Cut the ring free.
4. Finish-turn the cove which contains the captive ring(s).
5. Sand the inner surface of the ring where it was parted free.

TURNING CAPTIVE RINGS' OUTER HALVES

You have a choice of methods for most stages. For example, you can turn a captive ring's outer surface with any of several tools (figures 2.27 to 2.30). Figure 2.31 demonstrates the benefits of using a *cutting* tool like a skew.

Figure 2.27 Turning a captive ring's outer half with a skew. The first operation is to clear the waste, here by canted V-cutting, just as if you are leaving a pommel. I have taken the final V-cut on the left well down past the inside of the ring.

Figure 2.28 Rolling the outer half. For the flush bead to be truly semicircular in cross section, your skew's facing bevel when at the end of rolling cut should finish square to the lathe axis in plan and in a vertical plane.

Figure 2.29 Turning a flush bead with a Bob Chapman tool. The cutting action of this tool is between that of a skew and a bead-forming scraper. You present the Bob Chapman tool at minimum clearance with the handle low and the flute facing the workpiece.

Figure 2.30 Turning a flush bead with a bead-forming scraper. You push the scraper into the wood in a scraping presentation with the blade square to the lathe axis in plan. Using a slightly-negative rake angle (having the top face pointing slightly below the lathe axis) lessens tear-out. Fanning the tool slightly from side to side speeds the process.

Figure 2.31 Flush beads cut in different woods: *top*, in fast-grown radiata pine; *bottom*, in a dense hardwood. *Left*, cut with a Bob Chapman tool; *center*, with a bead-forming scraper; and *right*, cut with a skew. While it is quicker to scrape the flush bead, the quality of the scraped surface can be between very poor and good depending on the wood. When the scraped off-the-tool surface is poor, extra sanding will be needed and the outside surface of the finished ring will be flattened.

TURNING CAPTIVE RINGS' INNER HALVES

You have to remove waste from alongside each side of the inner half of a captive ring before you can finish-turn it. You can use a skew, gouge, or parting tool, either singly or in some combination, to remove this waste. The optimum choice of tool depends on the tool(s) used before and after. The amount of waste is influenced by the tool to be used to finish-turn, with the skew requiring the most, and captive-ring scrapers the least. Figure 2.32 shows waste removal with a parting-off tool, prior to the finish-turning with ring scrapers (figures 2.33 and 2.34).

To achieve a circular cross section is most difficult with a skew and easiest with a captive-ring scraper. The captive-ring hook lies between the two.

You have to remove waste on both sides of the ring to make room for the tool you will use to cut the ring's inside surface, and to prevent that tool being deflected against and damaging and misshaping the ring's inside surface. You might use a skew, a parting tool, a parting-off tool or a detail gouge to remove this waste.

The turning of the captive rings with *cutting* tools is described in figures 2.35 to 2.37. Figures 2.38 to 2.40 show sanding, and how to finish-turn the containing cove.

Figure 2.33 **Scraping the right-hand inside of a captive ring.** You need to remove waste which would press against the outside of the scraper's long jaw and thus press the inside of the jaw into the inside surface of the ring.

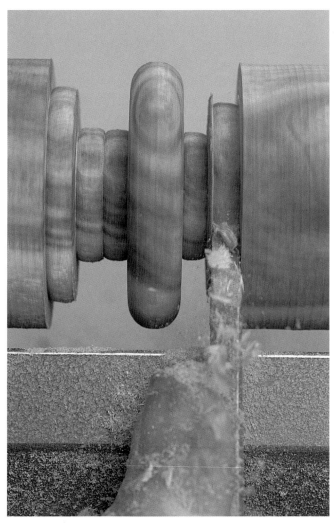

Figure 2.32 **Parting away the waste** to allow access for the captive-ring scrapers.

Figure 2.34 **Scraping the left-hand inside.**

Figure 2.35 *Cutting* the inside of a captive ring with a captive-ring gouge. This tool can be used from both the left and the right.

Figure 2.36 *Cutting* the inside of a captive ring with a skew's long point after cutting the waste away with a skew's short point.[10]

Figure 2.37 *Cutting* the inside of a captive ring with a captive-ring hook. The workpiece is the rattle shown in figure 2.20.[11]

Figure 2.38 Sanding the accessible captive-ring inside surface just before separating the ring.

Figure 2.39 Finish-turning the cove with a detail gouge. Normally you can let the rings rattle around, moving them out of the way with your finger or a harmless part of the tool. You may need to tape them to one side with masking tape. If turning, say, a very thin stemmed goblet, you may need to suspend the captive rings with string so that they are not in contact with the stem.

2.5   LOOSE RINGS

You could use the method used to turn captive rings to produce batches of loose rings from axially-grained, cylindrical workpieces. However because the minimum distance between adjacent rings is relatively large and the wood wastage therefore high, the modified procedure outlined in figure 2.41 is preferred. The extra tool needed is shown in figure 2.42. The procedure for a workpiece mounted between centers is shown in figures 2.43 to 2.47. Alternatively, you can cantilever the workpiece from a chuck and bore out the internal waste if you have a drill of the required size (figures 2.48 to 2.50).[12]

You can cut also turn loose rings from radially-grained workpieces, and this is described in *Woodturning Techniques*.

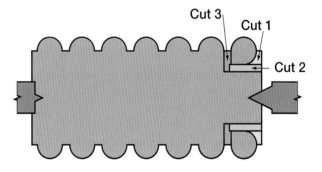

Longitudinal Section

Figure 2.40 Sanding the inside of a captive ring. Abrasive paper or cloth is wound around the bottom of the cove clockwise (looking from the tailstock), and taped to the surface of the cove. The unsanded area of the ring can then be readily sanded by holding and revolving it against the revolving abrasive.

Figure 2.41 Cutting loose rings from the surface of a cylindrical spindle. The rings are separated by waste of width equal to your parting-off tool. The sequence of cuts described in figures 2.43 to 2.47 is:

1. Part down half the rings' diameter between all the rings with a parting-off tool.
2. Finish-turn the rings' outer halves with a skew or bead scraper.
3. For each ring in turn: cut the right-hand inner surface with a right-hand captive-ring scraper **1**; cut in from the tailstock **2**; sand as much of the ring as is accessible; and free with a parting-off tool **3**.
4. After freeing all the rings, hold each ring in a spring or jam chuck to trim and sand the unfinished area.

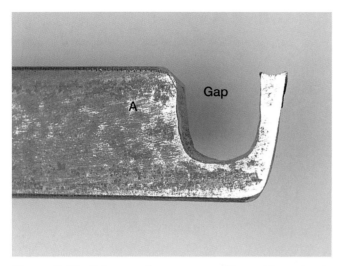

Figure 2.42 **A loose-ring scraper.** The cutting edge is a touch wider than the rest of the jaw so that the inside of the jaw is less likely to be pressed against the already-cut surface of the ring. The cutting edge is also ground concave to give two cutting points which will leave an improved surface on the ring. The width of the gap is wider than the diameter of the ring, and fairly parallel so that when the toolrest is close to the workpiece, shoulder **A** is still supported by the toolrest.

Figure 2.43 **Starting a cut type 1 (see figure 2.41) the with a right-hand captive-ring scraper.** Here all the outsides have been formed with an outside ring scraper. The cylindrical workpiece could, of course, be longer.

Figure 2.44 **Continuing to cut with the captive-ring scraper.** Cease cutting once the tip has cut just past the center. Try to take this cut too far and you can loose control.

Figure 2.45 **Parting to the left** (cut type **2**) with a loose-ring scraper. Sand the accessible surface before parting the ring free.

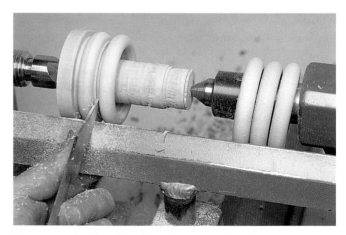

Figure 2.46 **Parting free** (cut type **3**) with a narrow parting-off tool.

Figure 2.47 **Finish-turning a ring where it was parted free.** The chuck is a spring chuck.

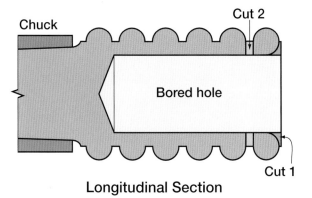

Longitudinal Section

Figure 2.48 **Turning loose rings after boring away the rings' inside waste.** You may have to limit the depth of the hole and the turning of the rings' outside halves to retain stiffness. The right-hand inside of the rings can be shaped with an inside ring scraper or similar, or a detail gouge.

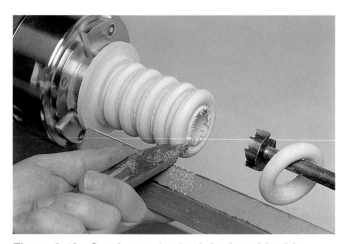

Figure 2.49 **Cutting a ring's right-hand inside** after boring the cylindrical workpiece to the inside diameter of the rings.

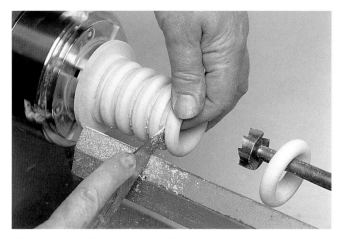

Figure 2.50 **Parting off with a parting-off tool.** The ring is then finished as shown in figure 2.47.

2.6   SPLIT RINGS

Figure 2.51 shows how you can gain diameter economically and/or inlet a contrasting wood using a split loose ring with a D-shaped cross section.

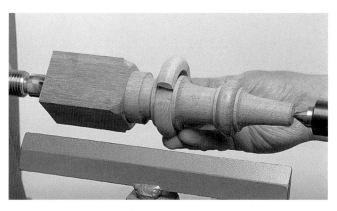

Figure 2.51 **A split ring** used to produce a larger-diameter bead on a leg than is possible from the leg's square cross-section blank.

The loose ring can be axially or radially grained. After turning it, I rived it along a diameter. The halves are about to be rejoined and glued into the groove in the leg.

2.7 TURNING TREES

Perhaps not the most significant of techniques,[13] but, as figure 2.52 shows, useful as a party piece and for toy and model makers. The ideal tool for turning wood into trees is shown figure 2.53, and its use in figures 2.54 and 2.55.

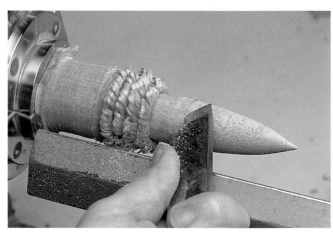

Figure 2.54 Starting a curling cut on the short point with the straight cutting edge at about 45° to the lathe axis.

The workpiece was first turned to a carrot-like form. Its diameter in the region of the lower foliage should be about 5/8 in. (16 mm) less than the overall desired diameter of the finished tree. The cutting path of the short point should then be horizontal or slightly down so that the shaving thickens slightly through the cut. The chisel can be traversed along the toolrest to the left at a constant side rake. Pivoting the chisel to increase the side rake during the cut curls the shaving less towards the end of the cut, and tends to lessen any damage to the curl.

Figure 2.52 A Cretaceous scene. The trees are about 5 in. (130 mm) high. The *Triceratops hamburgi* and *Brontosaurus mcdonaldi* glow in the dark, and are from the Samuel Darlow collection of takeaway ephemera.

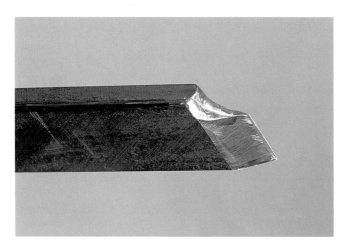

Figure 2.53 A tree-turning chisel, a skew modified by having a segment of about 1/4 in. (5 mm) radius ground away at its original short point. The larger the diameter of the workpiece, the larger the radius of the ground-away segment needs to be. You can also use an unmodified skew, although it seems to curl the shaving less well.

Figure 2.55 Completing the curling cut started in the preceding figure. The technique is especially effective with unseasoned wood.

2.8   SWASH TURNING AND PUMPING

The headstock spindles of some lathes can rotate *and* move longitudinally. This facility of a headstock spindle to pump to-and-fro along its axis is used in three ways, particularly in ornamental-turning, to produce:

1.   Threads by using a traversing mandrel (figure 2.56).
2.   Swash turnings (figure 2.57).
3.   Especially-ornate effects by using crowns (figure 2.62).

Swash was used by Moxon in the late 17th century to mean "with mouldings oblique to the axis," and is a contraction of the earlier word aswash, the derivation of which is unknown. The construction of lathes used to produce swash turnings is shown in figures 2.58 to 2.60. But more complicated longitudinal motions are possible, for example the urn in figure 2.62 and the wave patterns on the side of the gold box shown in figure 7.12. The device used to control this more complicated pumping is a crown (figure 2.61). Figure 2.63 shows a modern lathe with the crown and rosette combined into a crown-rosette.

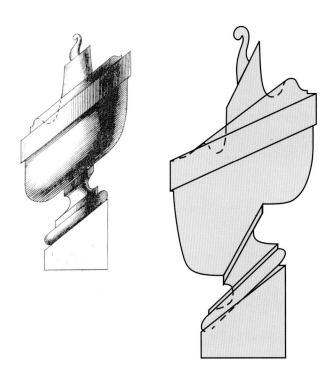

Figure 2.57   Two urns. *Left,* a far-from-accurate engraving of swash-turned urn pictured in plate XLI of Hamelin-Bergeron. *Right,* a more-accurate representation. Each point on a swash-turned workpiece pumps longitudinally to-and-fro the same distance irrespective of that point's distance from the lathe axis. Therefore small-diameter sections are more oblique than large unless, say on the lathe below, the distance of wheel **W** from the lathe axis is lengthened when smaller diameter surfaces are being cut.

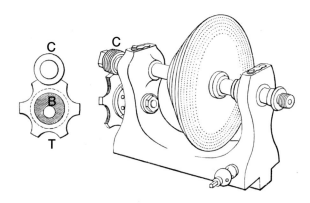

Figure 2.56   A headstock with a traversing or screw-cutting mandrel.[14] The headstock mandrel or spindle can slide longitudinally through its bearings. To cut a particular thread, a collar **C** threaded externally with the desired pitch is fixed on the left-hand end of the spindle. A turret **T** with six segments in its periphery is mounted on the left-hand end of the headstock casting. The surface of each segment has a thread of a different pitch. The turret is rotated to bring the appropriately-threaded segment to the top, and that segment is then pushed up to engage with the collar by rotating the eccentric bush **B**. Rotating the headstock spindle will then cause a fixed tool to cut a thread with the same pitch as that on the collar on a workpiece mounted on the right-hand end of the mandrel.

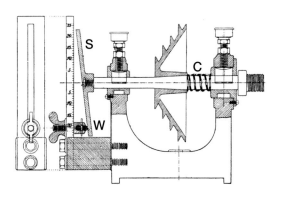

Figure 2.58   A German swash-turning lathe of about 1905.[15] The headstock spindle is pushed to the left by compression spring **C**. Swash plate **S** is attached to the left-hand end of the headstock spindle. A wheel **W** bears against the swash plate, and by varying the vertical distance of the wheel from the lathe axis the stroke of the pumping is varied.

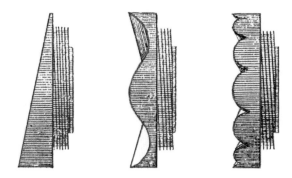

Figure 2.59 **An ornamental lathe fitted with a swash plate** S shown in plate XLI of Hamelin-Bergeron. The swash plate's tilt is adjustable as detailed in the next figure. The wheel to the left and in contact with the swash plate is usually called a rubber.

This lathe also has a traversing mandrel. The levers projecting from the side of the headstock incorporate threaded semicircular cutouts similar to the segments around the turret shown in figure 2.56. Raising a lever engages that lever's threaded segment with a like-threaded section on the headstock spindle. Rotating the headstock spindle then causes a fixed tool to cut a thread on the workpiece with the same pitch as that on the engaged threaded segment and spindle section.

Figure 2.61 **Three crowns**, that on the left is a swash crown. If the swash plate in figure 2.59 is removed and replaced by the center or right-hand crown above, the pumping can be more complex. The next figure shows what is possible. A range of different but related pumpings can be obtained from one crown by replacing the wheel-like rubber in figure 2.59 with rubbers of tighter curvatures which can follow rose undulations more closely.

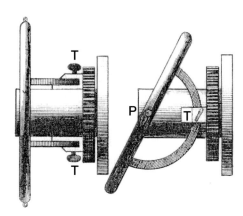

Figure 2.60 **A pivoting swash plate** shown in two elevations at right angles to one another. This illustration is taken from Hamelin-Bergeron plate XLI. The plate pivots about pins **P**, and is locked in position with thumb screws **T**.

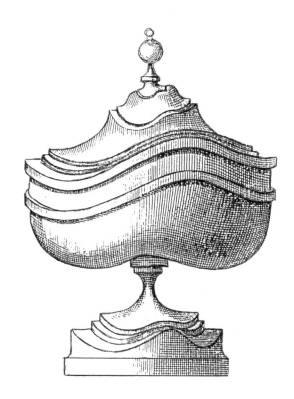

Figure 2.62 **An urn produced by pumping** from plate XL of Hamelin-Bergeron. The lathe used would have been similar to that in figure 2.59. The crown would have been similar to the central one in figure 2.61, and the workpiece would also have been mounted on an elliptical chuck.

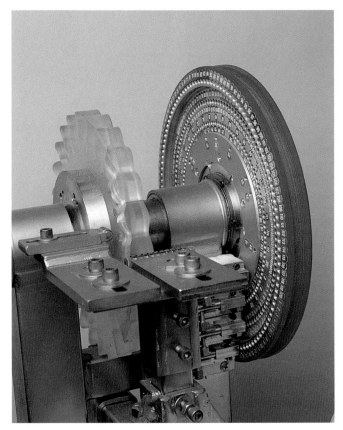

Figure 2.63 A rose engine with a crown-rosette, made by John Morgan of Frankston, Victoria, Australia. The transverse swaying of the headstock and the longitudinal pumping of the headstock spindle result from the crown-rosette's continuous contact with the two fixed roller rubbers in the foreground. Unusually, the dividing plate is to the right of the right-hand headstock bearing.

2.9 ENDNOTES

1 This illustration is taken from *International Correspondence Schools, Ltd. Reference Library* (1903), Section 43, p. 6.

2 This illustration is taken from *International Correspondence Schools, Ltd. Reference Library* (1903), Section 43, p. 16.

3 Parting off a handle is detailed in *The Fundamentals of Woodturning*, p. 113, fig. 6.100, and p.117, fig. 6.112.

4 Sizing with a parting tool is described in *The Fundamentals of Woodturning*, page 116, fig. 6.107.

5 A fine example is the turner's or "thrown" chair which has captive rings on most of its component spindles shown in Wolsey S.W. and Luff R.W.P., *Furniture in England: The Age of the Joiner* (New York: Frederick A. Praeger, 1969), plate 88.

6 Suggested by a goblet pictured in: Rolf Steinert, *Drechseln in Holtz*, p. 185.

7 The original rattle is shown in: Edward H. Pinto, *Treen and Other Wooden Bygones*, plate 218.

8 An article which gave a good introduction to the sharpening and use of these tools is: Mick O'Donnell, "Captive Rings," *Practical Wood Working* (March 1993).

9 Pictured in: David Regester, *Turning Boxes and Spindles Step-By-Step*, p.83, fig. 105.

10 Cutting a cove with a skew is shown in *The Fundamentals of Woodturning*, page 123, fig. 6.127.

11 The turning of a similar rattle is described in: Fred W. Holder, "A Ringed Rattle," *American Woodturner* (Dec 1994), pp. 26–27.

12 Both methods are outlined in: Fritz Spannagel, *Das Drechslerwerk*.

13 The only reference I have seen to this technique is in: Rolf Steinert, *Drechseln in Holz*, pp. 185–186.

14 Adapted from: J.J. Holtzapffel, *Hand or Simple Turning*, p. 107, figs 111 and 112.

15 von C.A. Martin, *Der Drechsler*, p. 230, fig. 493.

Chapter Three

SLENDER SPINDLES

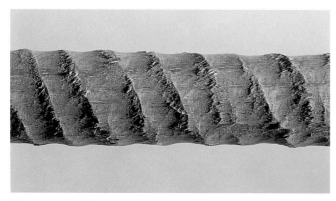

Figure 3.1 **The type of spiralled surface typically left on an unsteadied, slender workpiece.**

You get a surface such as that in figure 3.1 when a spindle is sufficiently slender to be deflected and bounce under your turning tool. The problem is usually worse near the center of a spindle's length. A slender workpiece will also attempt to climb up over your tool tip, especially if you are using a parting tool or detail gouge. And if a workpiece is very slender, it will whip like a skipping rope, and may tear itself out of the lathe if you turn it at the speed you would normally turn a non-slender workpiece of similar diameter.

There is a second and troublesome problem associated with slender turnings which is not directly due to slenderness. When you start to turn off the waste wood from an internally-stressed workpiece, that workpiece will want to start to bow. The magnitude of that bowing increases as you turn, and can in extreme cases lead to the workpiece being scrapped. The cause of bowing and how to overcome it when it is not too extreme are discussed in section 3.10.

You can use overcome the problems of slenderness by:

1. Modifying your tool use.
2. Minimizing the thrust you exert with your tailstock.
3. Ordering your sequence of tool use to preserve workpiece stiffness for as long as possible.
4. Reducing your lathe's speed.
5. Holding the headstock end of the workpiece rigidly in alignment with your lathe's axis in a chuck.
6. Modifying your turning's design to increase its effective stiffness.
7. Using one or more steadies. A steady holds a short part of a workpiece's length in alignment with the lathe axis.

8. Instead of turning a long spindle from one piece of wood, turning it as a number of short component spindles which you then assemble to create the desired long spindle.

These eight resorts are described in sections 3.1 to 3.8. You can use these resorts singly or in combination. Resorts 1 to 4 are simple to employ, and should be tried first. Resorts 5 to 8 are best tried in that order. It is better to hold a spindle's left-hand end in a chuck or modify a spindle's design than use rigid mechanical steadies. And a long, slender spindle turned in one piece is substantially stronger than a similar long spindle assembled from short component spindles.

3.1   MODIFYING TOOL USE

You can lessen the tendency of a workpiece to deflect while being turned by preferring tools which cut more gently, and by presenting each tool in the optimum way. Use a *cutting* tool with a small sharpening angle in preference to one which scrapes. If using a gouge, prefer one with a smaller flute radius; if using a parting tool, use a narrower one—smaller versions of the same tool type take a narrower shaving and therefore exert less force on the workpiece. To reduce the tendency of a workpiece to climb up over your tool's tip, use a skew in preference to a gouge because the skew's long point projects further past the length of cutting edge where cutting is taking place. If you have to use a detail gouge, present it with more side rake so that it cuts further back from the tip. Avoid using a parting tool if you can.

3.2   LESSENING TAILSTOCK THRUST

If you are using a conventional drive center, use sufficient tail center force to properly embed the drive center's prongs into the left-hand end of the spindle blank. Then retract the tail center a touch so that it does not force the workpiece to bow, but still exerts sufficient thrust to securely locate the workpiece's ends.

3.3 OPTIMIZING THE SEQUENCE OF TOOL USE

You optimize your sequence of tool use in two ways:

1. Use the different tools in the optimum order—for turning spindles that optimum order is: roughing gouge, skew, detail gouge. Using this sequence tends to preserve stiffness in the workpiece because the coves are cut last.
2. Work along a workpiece so as to preserve its stiffness. You work from right to left when finish-turning a cupchucked workpiece. You should usually finish-turn a slender spindle by working from the center of its length towards its ends.

The optimum marriage of the two sometimes-conflicting sequences for a particular spindle is not always obvious.

3.4 REDUCING LATHE SPEED

Figure 3.2 shows the recommended maximum lathe speeds for stiff workpieces. Using lower lathe speeds reduces the amplitudes of a workpiece's flexing. You may find it worthwhile to reduce the lathe speed to as little as a sixth of that you would use for a stiff workpiece of similar diameter. If you have a variable-speed lathe, try small changes in lathe speed, either up or down—these can significantly alter the amplitudes of a workpiece's vibration.

As you reduce the lathe speed, shavings sever less readily, subsurface damage increases, and the macro-cut surface becomes more rippled. You can minimize these effects by using *cutting* tools, presenting them with more side rake, traversing them more slowly along the toolrest, and reducing the depth of cut.

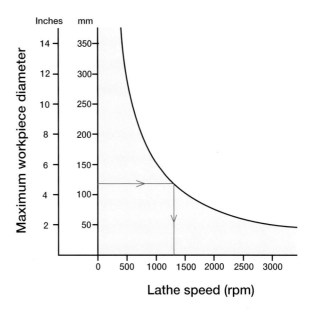

Figure 3.2 Lathe speed. The curved line gives the maximum recommended lathe speeds for stiff workpieces. You should turn slender workpieces at slower, sometimes far-slower, speeds.

3.5 CHUCKING THE LEFT-HAND END

Figure 3.3 illustrates how building-in one end of a loaded beam reduces its deflection. You can similarly reduce the amplitudes of a slender spindle's transverse oscillations by holding the spindle's left-hand end rigidly in axial alignment. For this you can use:

1. A four-jaw scroll chuck fitted with jaws suited for gripping square cross sections (figure 3.4). For small, square cross sections you could use a four-jaw, self-centering mini-chuck.
2. A square-hole chuck.
3. A scroll, collet, Jacobs, mini, or screw-socket chuck after preturning what will be the workpiece's left-hand end to a cylinder.
4. Your headstock-spindle swallow. Preturn what will be the workpiece's left-hand end to the appropriate Morse taper, and then force it into the swallow.[1] (The dimensions of Morse tapers are listed in table 8.2).

You may need to increase a blank's length to enable the workpiece to be chucked without sacrificing length from the finished turning. You then finish-turn working from right to left to retain the chuck-induced stiffness for as long as possible.

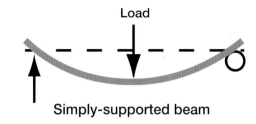

Load

Simply-supported beam

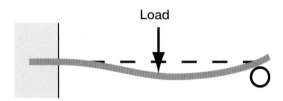

Load

Beam built-in at left-hand end

Figure 3.3 **The deflection of two similar beams loaded at their centers.** The ends of the upper beam are simply supported and are therefore free to rotate in a vertical plane. The deflection of the lower beam is about 55% less because its left-hand end is built in and therefore not free to rotate in a vertical plane.

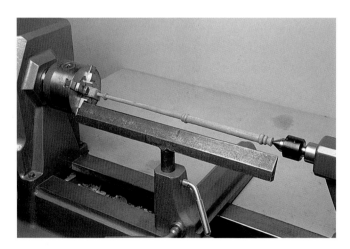

Figure 3.4 **Stiffening a workpiece by chucking its left-hand end.** The corners of the left-hand end of the workpiece have been chamfered off. This allowed the workpiece to pass further into the engineers scroll chuck and be gripped by the full length of the jaws, thus increasing the stiffening effect. The workpiece is a candle-snuffer handle which is being finish-turned from right to left to best preserve workpiece stiffness.

3.6   MODIFYING A SPINDLE'S DESIGN

You can often improve a spindle's stiffness without adversely affecting its appearance and utility, especially by:

1. Increasing the diameter of sections which are small in diameter.
2. Shifting thinner sections towards a spindle's ends.

Figure 3.5 illustrates how these and related steps lessen the need to resort to steadies.

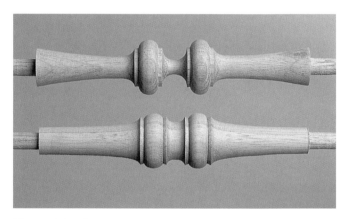

Figure 3.5 **Increasing stiffness.** The lower spindle is a stiffer version of the upper spindle. The changes comprise:

1. Making the beads shallower.
2. Kicking up the fillets instead of turning them horizontal.
3. Narrowing the width of the center cove and making it still shallower by flattening its bottom.
4. Narrowing the two long sections towards the spindle's pins instead of towards the spindle's center.

3.7 STEADIES

A steady prevents a workpiece deflecting at the point of the steady's installation. A steady creates a node on a spindle, thereby reducing the amplitudes of a spindle's transverse oscillations elsewhere. There are three types of steadies:

1. *Friction steadies*. The bearing surfaces of such a steadies are fixed and rub on the surface of the rotating workpiece (figures 3.6 to 3.15).
2. *Planetary steadies* (figures 3.16 and 3.17). At the interfaces between the steady and the workpiece the surfaces of both ideally move with the same velocity. There is therefore negligible friction between the two surfaces and just a little crushing damage to the workpiece surface.
3. *Collar steadies* (figures 3.18 to 3.22). The collar is rigidly fixed around the workpiece. The outside of the collar is then held in a friction or planetary steady. This arrangement should ensure almost no damage to the workpiece surface.

Steadies are also used as boring collars. When a non-rotating drill is fed into the right-hand end of a workpiece, a boring collar locates and allows the workpiece's right-hand end to rotate (see figures 8.34, and 8.41 to 8.45).

Figure 3.7 An open vee type of friction steady.[2] A traditionally based design which is noisy, and soon crushes and a little later chars the surface of a fast-rotating workpiece. To lessen these effects: use a soft wood for the jaws, line the jaw with a slippery heat-resistant plastic, lower the lathe speed, and wax the interface. You will need to leave the workpiece area which rubs against the steady slightly oversize. After removing the steady, you then turn or carve off the partially-crushed and wax-impregnated excess waste wood. The final operation is to sand the area.

This type of steady can only prevent the workpiece springing towards you by being pushed against the workpiece's far side; the more slender and more bowed the workpiece the harder that push has to be. But there is a limit: exceed it and the workpiece will fly out of the lathe.

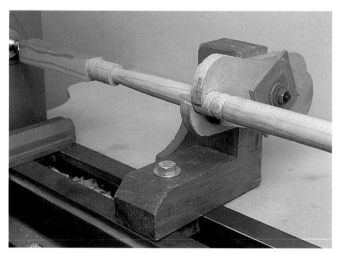

Figure 3.6 An adjustable-jaw, fixed, friction steady. Abrasive paper is glued onto the arm and steady-upright surfaces so that the arms don't creep open once locked. This steady is "closed" as it prevents the workpiece moving towards you.

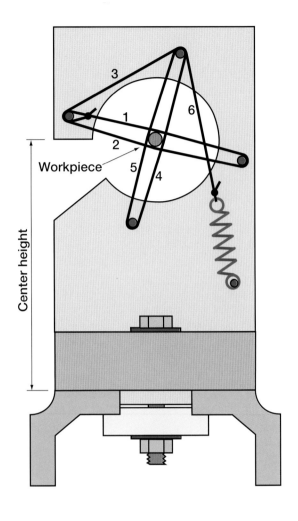

Figure 3.8 A string steady supporting a trembleur—section 3.13 shows how to turn trembleurs. The string is soft and has "give", and therefore does not damage the surface of the workpiece. String steadies are used to provide gentle support to sections after they have been turned, with more supportive steadies being mounted near to the area being turned.

An alternative to a string steady would be one lined with piano felt. It would also barely damage the workpiece surface.

Figure 3.9 The string path for a string steady is shown by the numbers. A bowline knot is used to form the loop which goes round the left-hand screw. The other end of the thick string can be tensioned with a spring, by a hanging weight, or by tying.

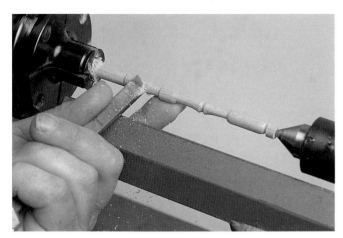

Figure 3.10 **Your forefinger is a handy mobile friction steady** for very small spindles. You need to use the tied-underhand grip, and a toolrest with a top member which is compact and preferably uniform in cross section. The left-hand end of the lace-bobbin blank is held in a Nova chuck fitted with 25 mm jaws.

Figure 3.12 **Steadying with the left hand while planing to the right.** Your left hand makes an ideal mobile steady, and does not damage the workpiece surface although classified as a friction steady. Use your left thumb to position the chisel and brace your left hand. You move the skew, your left thumb, and your left hand along the toolrest as a rigid unit.

The left-hand steadying illustrated in this and the following three figures can be used for a wide variety of cuts, not just planing.

Figure 3.11 **End steadying with thumb and fingers** while parting free the right-hand end of the lace bobbin from the previous figure. You can trim and then sand the end using the same steadying.

Figure 3.13 **Steadying with the left hand while cutting to the left.**

Figure 3.14 Left-hand steadying when planing to the left towards a pommel which prevents the left hand being positioned to the left of the tool as in figure 3.13. The striking part of my left hand is referenced to and runs along the toolrest. I am pressing down with my left wrist to reference the skew.

Figure 3.16 A two-wheel planetary steady. Each skateboard wheel is mounted on a 5/16 in. BSW socket screw. The threaded end of each screw is screwed into a tapped hole in a length of 1 in. diameter steel bar, the bar being locked into an extra banjo. This design is ideal for balusters and other spindles which are moderately slender. This type of steady causes minimal damage to the workpiece surface; and is relatively quiet, due in part to the resilient plastic of the wheels and their wide contact.

Figure 3.15 Left-hand steadying when planing to the right away from a pommel. My left wrist is pressing down onto the tool blade to locate it against the toolrest.

Your left hand becomes less effective as a steady as workpieces get bigger—you then have to resort to mechanical steadies.

Figure 3.17 **A three-wheel planetary steady** takes longer to mount onto the workpiece than the two-wheeled version, but prevents the workpiece from moving towards you. A three-wheeler is therefore better for more slender workpieces and for those which are internally stressed: it can also be used as a boring collar.

Figure 3.18 **A collar steady constructed by mounting a flange-mounted self-aligning bearing on a plywood structure.** The workpiece is being turned from right to left. The corners of the workpiece have been roughed to a slow taper. The steady was then pushed to the left until the workpiece jammed inside the bearing's inner race.

After finish-turning the length to the right of the steady, more of the corners to the left will be roughed off. The steady will then moved a little to the right to allow the corners where the steady was to be reduced. The steady will then be pushed to the left until it again jams on the corners. The process is then repeated as many times as necessary, with, if necessary, the addition of extra steadies to the right.

A disadvantage of collar steadies is that they are normally too bulky to allow a long toolrest to run past them.

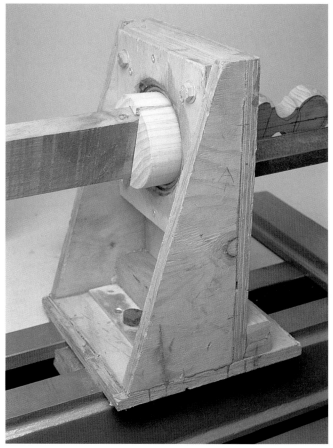

Figure 3.19 A pillow-block collar steady. The block is tilted to enable the toolrest to be mounted closer to the workpiece. The roughed cylindrical workpiece is wedged into the bearing's inner race with a split annular "wedge". The wedge tapers on its outside, has a hole equal in diameter to the workpiece diameter bored through it, and is sawn longitudinally into two halves. So that they cannot vibrate out, the two halves of the wedge should be screwed to the inner race of the bearing, or be tacked or taped to the workpiece.

Figure 3.20 A large collar steady incorporating a large sealed bearing. A fence picket is wedged inside the inner race so that a decorative top can be turned on its right-hand end. The wedges have been tacked (or could have been tied or taped) to the picket so that they cannot vibrate out.

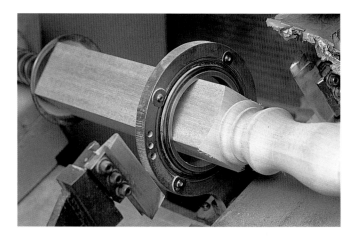

Figure 3.21 A mobile carriage-mounted collar steady on an automatic lathe. The cutter is also mounted on the carriage, adjacent to the steady so that the workpiece cannot vibrate relative to the cutter.

3.8 USING STEADIES

In general, the more support a steady gives and the less it damages the workpiece surface, the longer it takes to mount a workpiece against or through that steady. This may influence your choice of steadying method, as should:

1. The workpiece's slenderness and length.
2. The ease of later turning or carving off surface waste wood damaged by the steady.
3. Whether a particular type of steady is more compatible with the design of the workpiece.
4. Whether the workpiece design requires multiple steadies or moving steadies.
5. Whether you suspect that the wood is internally stressed.

A fixed steady is best located on a section of the workpiece which will be relatively easy to finish-turn after moving or removing the steady. A single steady is most effective if located near the center of a workpiece's length. If the workpiece is internally stressed, it may be better to plane, carve, and sand away the damaged excess wood where the steady was located than attempt to turn that wood off. Therefore locate steadies where the design of the workpiece is without detail. Where planetary or collar steadies have been mounted, you may only have to sand heavily to reveal an undamaged surface.

The greater a workpiece's slenderness and length, the greater the likelihood that you will need to:

1. Move your one steady along the workpiece in steps during the turning, keeping it close to where you are cutting.
2. Use multiple steadies fixed in position—they do not have to be of the same type.
3. Leapfrog steadies, usually from the center of the workpiece's length towards its ends.

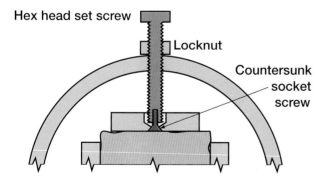

Figure 3.22 **A collar steady for large, square-cross-section workpieces** supported on a friction steady. This type of collar is related to the screw-bell chuck and the cat-head. If greased or waxed, the outer surface of the collar will rotate smoothly at slow speed in a crude wooden friction steady. The bottom drawing shows a cross section through a jaw of the collar steady.

3.9 TURNING A LONG SPINDLE IN COMPONENTS

You can redesign long, one-piece spindles as assemblages of shorter components. Socket-and-spigot joints are commonly used to connect the components (figure 3.23).

Another and often-stronger alternative is to axially bore the component blanks, finish-turn them using the through hole to center them in the lathe (pages 183 and 184), and then thread and perhaps glue them in line over a long wooden dowel or a steel rod. The steel rod can be plain, threaded, or plain with threaded ends. You can use this solution where a one-piece workpiece would be too slender or longer than your lathe's between-centers capacity. It is also applicable when the blank for a slender turning has high internal stresses and would bow too much.

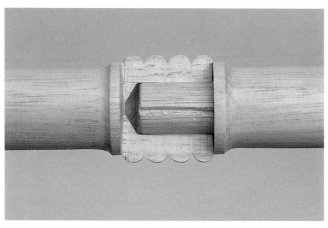

Figure 3.23 A disguised socket-and-spigot joint.
There is a thickening for strength and a discontinuity (here the meeting of a bead with a fillet) which hides the joint. Make the diameter of the spigot about 60% of the finished diameter of the turning to maximize the joint strength. Make the spigot's length at least 50% greater than its diameter. Cut a groove in the spigot to allow the air and any excess glue to escape when you press the two parts together.

3.10 INTERNAL STRESSES IN WOOD

If a spindle bows as you machine or turn it, its wood is internally stressed. (Stress is force per unit area). This bowing makes turning more difficult. It also leads to misalignment between areas you turn early, and abutting or overlapping areas which you turn later (figure 3.24). This section explains internal stressing and how to cope with it.

A living tree is a stressed structure. In a tree which is straight, vertical, tall, symmetrically branched, and not subjected to a prevailing wind from one direction, the load transmitted down to a cross section low through the trunk will be spread evenly over the whole area of the cross section. Planks or square sections cut from the straight, clear trunk of such a tree will be unlikely to bow during machining or turning.

The branch wood in figure 3.25 is not evenly stressed. To support the branch to the right of vertical section **CD**, the fibers running through **CD** must resist the weight of the branch to the right in shear. The fibers are additionally stressed because the weight of the branch to the right of **CD** is centered a considerable distance to the right of **CD**. This distance is often called the lever arm. To resist the product of the weight of the branch to the right of **CD** multiplied by its lever arm, the stresses in the fibers across **CD** must sum to an equal and opposite rotational force or moment. The stresses in the fibers across **CD** must therefore be similar to those shown in figure 3.26. It is these bending-induced stresses rather than the shear stresses which cause the bowing.

The shear and rotational forces which have to be resisted by the fibers crossing vertical section **AB** must be higher those crossing **CD** because of the additional weight and moment due to branch length **ABCD**. Also the moment due to the branch to the right of **CD** is larger at **AB** than at **CD** because that branch weight's lever arm is longer by the length of **ABCD**. But although in the living tree the fibers in branch length **ABCD** are unevenly stressed, they are in equilibrium—if not the right-hand end of the branch would rise or fall until there was equilibrium. These stresses in living wood are considerable as anyone who has shifted much freshly-felled wood would realize. Trees therefore modify their growth to better cope with these high and uneven stresses (figure 3.27).

If you cut the short log **ABCD** out of the tree it would no longer have to support itself or the wood and leaves to its right. The log would therefore shorten along its top where the fibers had been growing in tension. It would also lengthen along the bottom where the fibers had been growing in compression. This shortening and lengthening would take some minutes or hours to cease. At this stage the log would have relaxed into a new equilibrium by bowing (figure 3.28). However in reality the bowing would be barely perceptible because of the relatively large cross-sectional area and short length of **ABCD**.

Wood fibers are bound together by lignin and interconnected by medullary rays. Wood is a material which has considerable stiffness. After log **ABCD** is cut from the living tree, it cannot bow sufficiently to allow the stresses present in the fibers in the living tree to relax to zero. The fibers in the log will therefore still be stressed after the initial relaxation, though at lower levels than in the living tree.

If you rip the log **ABCD** into smaller sections, each section will, like **ABCD**, have its top fibers in tension and its bottom fibers in compression (figure 3.29). The shallower the cross section, the greater its flexibility and therefore its ability to relax by bowing to lessen the internal stressing.

Signs of internal stress in a spindle blank are bowing during and after machining prior to mounting in the lathe. When you first dress wood with internal stresses you start to realize that as you dress away wood you keep creating a fresh situation, which in turn demands a new equilibrium, which can only be achieved by a further relaxation of the internal stresses. As you continue to cut a section shallower, it becomes more flexible, and therefore can and has to bow more to restore equilibrium. This same process happens during turning: the more waste you turn away, the greater the bowing.

Problems due to internal stresses are not restricted to spindle blanks. When you saw to create the fingers of a wooden spring chuck, you can find that the free ends of the fingers are no longer concentric about the lathe axis. Internal stresses are also a major cause of distortion in thin-walled bowls. As Peter Child so graphically puts it "An abdominal operation . . . causes some doubling up in most humans!"[3] These distortions in bowls due to stress relaxation are often confused with the distortions due to seasoning.

If you have an internally-stressed workpiece, the ideal solution is to abandon it, and replace it with one which is unstressed. However as the supply of long, straight-grained wood from mature forest-grown trees tightens, this becomes less feasible. Turners therefore need to be able to cope with internally stressed wood. The solution described in the previous section of assembling a turning from components is an option, but you will usually find it better to overcome the bowing with a steady or similar. While you can temporarily restrict bowing by using rigid steadies, once the steadies are removed the full bowing will occur. This can mean that you have been able to produce a turning which is then rejected.

Another means to minimize the effects of bowing is to use non-axial mounting as described in figure 3.30. This technique is often used with steadying.

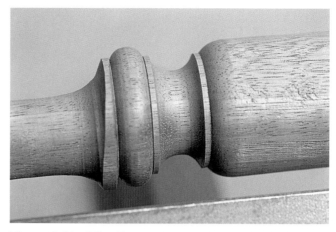

Figure 3.24 **Misalignment of sections turned at different times** due to the spindle bowing while it was being turned.

Figure 3.25 **Branch section ABCD.** Branch wood has high internal stresses.

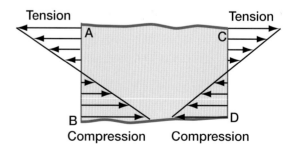

Longitudinal Section

Figure 3.26 **The bending-induced stresses in the fibers across AB and CD in the living tree.**

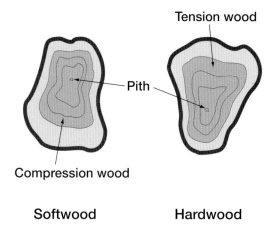

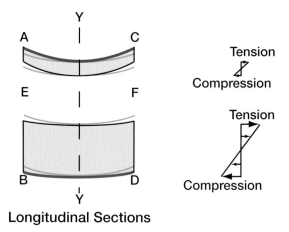

Figure 3.27 Branch cross sections showing reaction wood. *Left*, softwood trees grow compression wood beneath the pith; *right*, hardwoods grow tension wood above the pith[4].

Compression wood is harder, denser and more brittle than normal wood. Tension wood is difficult to differentiate from normal wood, but its sawn surface is usually woolly.

Figure 3.29 Stresses after ripping. After ripping the log **ABCD** along **EF**, the internal stresses can relax further. In doing so the thinner **ACEF** bows more whereas **EFBD** tends to straighten. The green lines show the profiles before **ABCD** was ripped along **EF**.

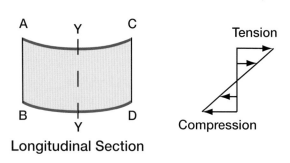

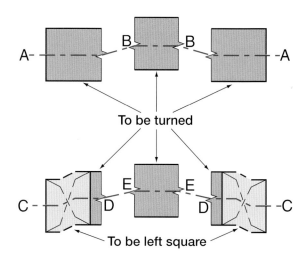

Figure 3.28 The stresses in wood after felling are substantially lower than in the living tree. Once the branch length **ABCD** does not have to support the rest of the branch, the length bows upwards, albeit imperceptibly, as the stresses within the wood across cross section **Y-Y** relax into a new equilibrium.

Figure 3.30 Mounting a bowed workpiece.

Top, mount a workpiece which will be fully turned on an axis halfway between **A-A** and **B-B**.

Bottom, if the workpiece will have squares left unturned at its ends (colored pale), center the workpiece on axis **D-D** or on an axis halfway between **D-D** and **E-E**.

When turning bowed and internally-stressed workpieces, turn from the center towards the ends, sanding each section before starting to turn the next. You may have to adjust the centering during the turning if the workpiece bows significantly while being turned.

3.11 DOWELLING

Dowels are short cylinders, often crosscut from long lengths of dowelling or dowel. You can produce dowelling on a hand woodturning lathe by:

1. Hand turning using a roughing gouge, a skew, calipers, and perhaps steadies (figure 3.31). The difficulty increases as the length and slenderness increase.
2. Using a hand plane to refine the profile of both stiff and slender workpieces (figure 3.32).
3. Using a headstock-mounted dowelling cutter (figures 3.33 and 3.34) if your headstock spindle has a sufficiently-large through hole. You can also buy or make hand-held dowelling cutters called rounders: their use is described in the next section.

Commercially dowelling is produced on special-purpose machines (figure 3.35). It may also be run on single- or double-headed molders which when incorrectly set up yield dowelling with non-circular cross sections.

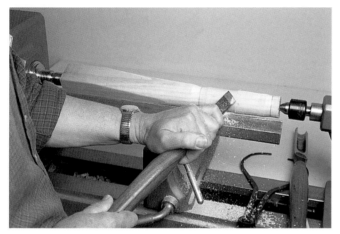

Figure 3.31 Turning dowelling by hand. Here the finished dowelling will be stiff enough to be turned without a steady. The steps are:

1. Rough, starting from the right-hand end of the workpiece. Start each cut to the left of the previous one, traversing the roughing gouge from left to right from larger diameter to smaller. For amply-stiff workpieces you can rough the whole length before starting to set and caliper the finished diameter at intervals.

2. Once the diameter of a roughed section is close to the required finished diameter, set that finished diameter using a roughing gouge and calipers. Each new section you caliper might be 4 to 6 in. (100 to 150 mm) to the left of the previously-calipered section.
3. Finish-turn by planing with a skew if the grain is axial, or if not, with a roughing gouge presented with 45° side rake.

The length and diameter of the dowelling may dictate that you use slender turning techniques. The preferred techniques in order of increasing slenderness include:

1. Hold the left-hand end of the workpiece rigidly in axial alignment in a chuck. You may need to preturn the end to be chucked with the workpiece held between centers. Work from right to left so that you make maximum use of the increased stiffness imparted by the chuck.
2. Turn a short length at the center of the workpiece to the finished diameter. Then finish-turn the remainder, working from the center towards the ends.
3. Rough a short length in the center of the workpiece to a diameter a little larger than the required finished diameter with hand steadying if required. Mount a steady on the cylindrical section. Rough and finish-turn the right-hand half of the workpiece . Move the steady a little to the right—the area on which you relocate the steady should still be a little oversize. Then rough and finish-turn the left-hand half of the workpiece, again working from right to left, so that the last section to be finish-turned is immediately adjacent to the drive center or chuck. Hand finish or carefully turn the area where the steady was last relocated to the finished diameter.
4. Work from right to left using multiple and/or mobile steadies.

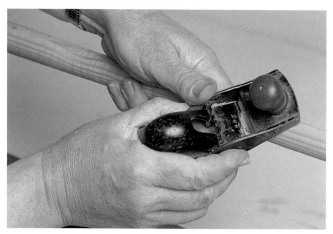

Figure 3.32 **Hand planing dowelling.** Because a plane's sole acts as a mobile steady, the technique is especially useful for slender workpieces.

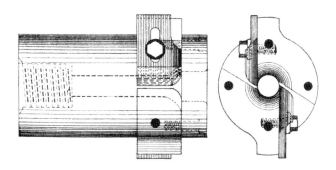

Figure 3.34 **A superior design of doweller** which screws onto a headstock-spindle nose.[5] Some versions had one curved cutter instead of the two shown here. The cutters *cut* to leave a better surface than that produced by the Devil doweller.

Figure 3.33 **The Devil doweller.** You can only use such devices with hollow headstock spindles because the machined dowelling has to pass out to the left through the spindle's through hole.

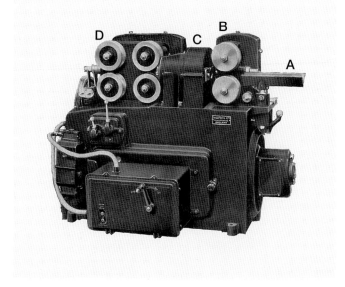

Figure 3.35 **A serious doweller**, the LDE by W.A. Fell Ltd of Windermere, England. A 6 ft. (1800 mm) long, 20 hp (15 kW) machine which will produce dowelling of any diameter from 3/4 in. to 4 in. (19 to 100 mm) at between 20 and 60 ft. (6 and 18 m) per minute. The blanks, usually in the form of squares, are pulled in along the vee cradle **A** by vee-grooved rollers **B**. The blanks need to be fed in without gaps between to avoid tear-out at their ends. The cutterhead is housed under guard **C**, and is similar to a four-jaw scroll chuck, except that a curved cutter is fixed to each jaw. The diameter of dowelling produced is thus governed by revolving the scroll which moves all four cutters in or out in unison. After being cut to diameter, the dowelling passes through the chuck, through a sleeve, and between the outfeed rollers **D**.

The dowelling is then sanded using a special form of belt sander which works on the principle of a machine tool called a centerless grinder.

3.12 ROUNDING

You can produce dowelling, both of uniform and varying diameter, with rotary planes called rounders.[6] Although hand held, a rounder incorporates its own steady and automatically cuts the diameter set.

Rounders traditionally have wooden bodies (figures 3.36 and 3.37), but metal-bodied rounders are available for prolonged and heavy use (figure 3.38). Standard rounders cut fixed diameters. An adjustable rounder called a trapping plane (figure 3.39) is available to cut varying diameters. The preferred geometry for rounder cutters is detailed in figures 3.40 and 3.41.

As the reduction in dimension which a rounder can cut is limited to about 3/8 in. (10 mm), you may first need to rough your blank using a roughing gouge or one or more larger rounders (figure 3.42). You can hand-rotate a rounder (figure 3.43) to produce a cylindrical pin. This pin can be held in a chuck, located in a steady, or be glued into a hole.

A rounder can only cut in one direction. Most only cut when you push them from right to left along a workpiece held in a lathe rotating forwards. Therefore although not essential, you will find a lathe with reverse more convenient for rounding. The rounding process is shown in figures 3.42 to 3.46.

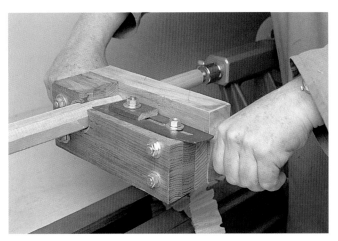

Figure 3.37 A wooden rounder that you can easily make.

The pink wood is drilled with an outfeed hole which has the same diameter as the required dowelling. The same diameter hole was drilled through the three browner pieces of wood at the same time. I then tapered the hole through the browner wood so that the hole was 3/8 in. (10 mm) larger in diameter at its left-hand end. I designed the nearside of the rounder long to accommodate the plane blade, but having the mass of wood more symmetrical about the hole would have made this in-lathe hole tapering easier.

The plane bade is both skewed in plan and tilted (as are the blades in the rounders shown in the next figure). The reason and geometry are detailed in figure 3.41.

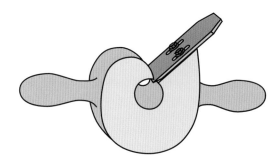

Figure 3.36 A traditional-style, wooden-bodied rounder. Versions are currently manufactured in England by Bristol Design and by Craft Supplies.

As a rounder is pushed forwards it is guided in a straight line by its outfeed hole. There should be a light interference fit between the wall of the outfeed hole and the just-cut dowel. If the fit is too tight considerable frictional heat will be generated and the rounder may jam. Too loose and the rounder will wobble and cut dowelling which is undersize, not straight, and with an inferior surface.

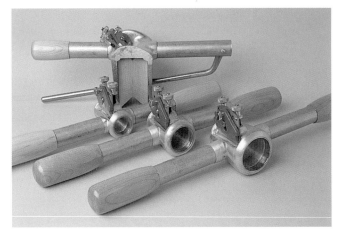

Figure 3.38 Metal-bodied rotary planes. *Front to back*: 1 3/4 in. to 1 3/8 in., 1 3/8 in. to 1 in., 1 in. to 5/8 in., and a lathe trapping plane 1 3/4 in. to 1/4 in. (see next figure).

These planes were developed from wooden rounders by the late Fred Lambert. They are now manufactured by Peter Hindle of Ashem Crafts, 2 Oakleigh Avenue, Hallow, Worcestershire, England.[7]

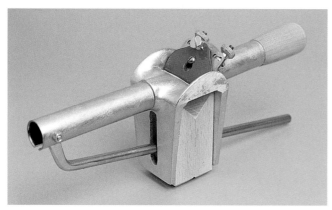

Figure 3.39 A trapping plane is used for producing straight and curved tapers. The wooden anvil has shallow and deep vee grooves, the appropriately-sized groove is positioned upwards according to the range of diameters being cut. Varying the pull on the lever varies the diameter being cut.

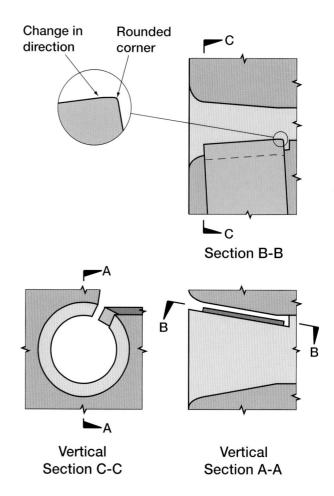

Section B-B

Vertical Section C-C

Vertical Section A-A

Figure 3.41 The design and mounting of a flat rounder blade. Tilting the blade allows the clearance angle to be constant along the whole length of the blade's cutting edge. If the clearance angle is also low, chatter is avoided. A blade sharpening angle of about 23° and a clearance angle of about 2° gives smooth cutting and leaves a superior surface on the dowelling.

 The magnified right-hand corner shows the short, straight section which cuts the finished diameter: the rounded corner prevents tear-out.

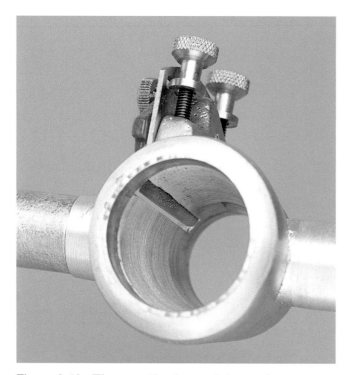

Figure 3.40 The mouth of a metal rounder.
At the small end of the taper a short length of cutting edge is sharpened at an angle to the main length. This short length smoothly cuts the finished diameter. Because the main length of the cutting edge follows the internal taper of the swallow down, the clearance angle can be small and constant along the cutting edge's whole length thereby ensuring smooth cutting. The geometry is detailed in the next figure.

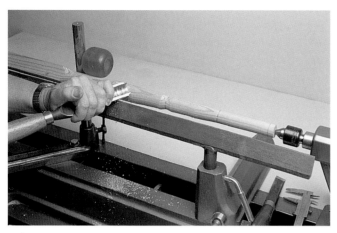

Figure 3.42 Roughing between centers using a roughing gouge and a two-wheel planetary steady to bring the workpiece down so that it can be fitted into a 1 3/8 in. (35 mm) rounder.

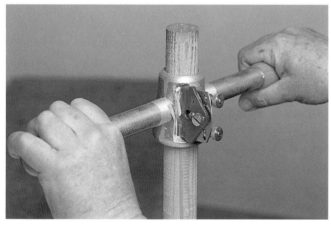

Figure 3.43 Rounding with the workpiece fixed in a vice. Turners can use this technique to prepare an end to go in a chuck or in a steady.

Figure 3.44 Rounding between lathe centers towards the tailstock with the lathe running in reverse. These rounders will reduce the workpiece diameter by a maximum of 3/8 in. (10 mm). If starting from a square, use a roughing gouge or successively smaller rounders to bring the square down close to the required finished diameter.

The workpiece should ideally be rotated at between 60 and 450 rpm depending on the finished diameter of the dowelling to be produced. If your lathe's lowest speed is somewhat higher than the ideal for the particular rounder, no appreciable harm seems to result. Ashem produce an electrically-powered turning head and a handcrank/twizzler for those who do not have a suitable lathe to rotate the wood.

Do not round from both ends—the two parts are unlikely to meet accurately.

Which end do you start from—either if the workpiece is stiff, usually the headstock end if the workpiece is slender. If rounding from the headstock, you have to first bring the headstock end down in diameter. For this you can use the rounder by hand as shown in the preceding figure. Avoid grabbing at the start of a traverse by bracing a rounder handle against your lathe bed. When the workpiece is slender, you should steady it as detailed in the next two figures.

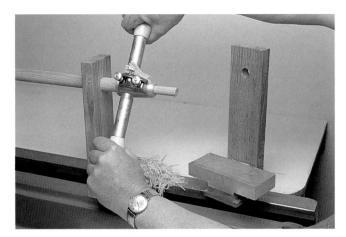

Figure 3.45 Cutting dowelling with a rounding plane. The workpiece's left-hand end is held in a chuck.

Although a rounding plane is largely self-centering, you should restrain the workpiece near the cutting with a steady and the tailstock, or with two steadies. You may need extra steadies for very slender dowels or for wood which is internally stressed and therefore bows during the rounding. Fortunately the steadies need only to be slightly oversize holes through wood because the lathe speed is low.

If your workpiece is longer than your lathe's capacity, you can rig a simple timber bed extension, or mount a steady at the right-hand end of the lathe bed if the workpiece will not project too far beyond it.

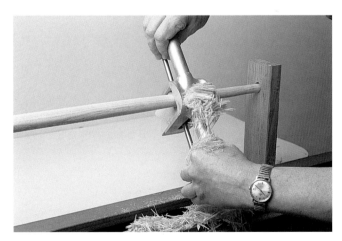

Figure 3.46 Tapering a spindle with a trapping plane. Although you can produce a better surface by hand planing with a skew which cuts the wood with side rake, trapping comes into its own on very slender lengths.

This adjustable rounder is especially useful for producing the long, tapered spindles used in Windsor-type chair backs. Before using the trapping plane, bring the workpiece down to close to the maximum finished diameter with a fixed-diameter rounder. To narrow the dowel, slowly squeeze the handles together as you traverse the plane along the rotating workpiece.

3.13 TURNING TREMBLEURS

The turning of trembleurs (figure 3.47) has a long history (figures 3.48 and 3.49), but has been neglected in recent decades.[8] Trembleurs (I favor retaining the French spelling) are especially slender and totally-useless spindles, or more positively, notable displays of patience and skill.

The turning of trembleurs is described in figures 3.50 to 3.52.

Figure 3.47 Your author holding his first trembleur. The trembleur's length is 38 in. (970 mm), the maximum diameters are 1 1/4 in. (32 mm), and the minimum diameters are 1/8 in. (3 mm).

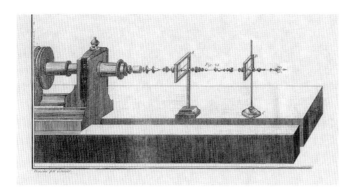

Figure 3.48 Trembleur turning with string steadies pictured in Plate XX of the 1816 second edition of *Manuel du Tourneur* revised by Pierre Hamelin-Bergeron.

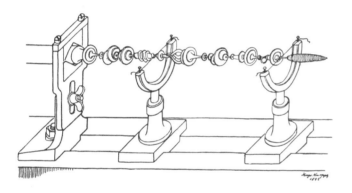

Figure 3.49 Tembleur turning pictured in figure 23 of the 1926 edition of *Meistertechniken der Drechslerkunst* by Hugo Knoppe. The steady on the left is moved to the left in steps as explained in figure 3.51.

Figure 3.50 Roughing to a constant diameter, the first step in turning a trembleur unless you can buy suitable, straight, axially-grained dowelling. The best first step is to produce a long dowel because it is then far simpler to move a steady along the workpiece from right to left as you finish-turn.

Use wood which is tough, straight-grained, and free of internal stresses. I first turned a short length in the centre of the workpiece to a circular cross section using hand steadying. I then mounted a three-wheel planetary steady to support this short length while I finish-turned the right-hand half of the workpiece. I then moved the steady a little to the right, and finish-turned the left-hand half of the workpiece. Figures 3.51 and 3.52 show the rest of the process.

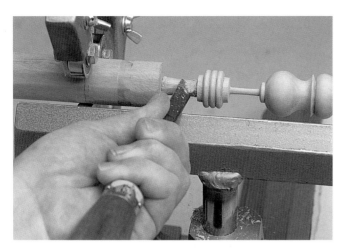

Figure 3.51 Finish-turning the trembleur. All the turning can be done with a 1/2 in. (13 mm) skew and 1/4 in. and 3/8 in. (6 mm and 10 mm) detail gouges. The 1/8 in. (3 mm) diameter cylindrical sections are turned solely with the skew.

You finish-turn a trembleur in short sections. Each fresh section lies immediately to the left of the section just completed, and is typically 2 to 4 in. (50 to 100 mm) long. The completed part of the trembleur is too slender to provide any support to the short section that you are finish-turning. You have to support the section you are turning with a closed steady mounted just to that section's left. At frequent intervals during the finish-turning you therefore have to shift the steady a short distance to the left. This process is far easier if the workpiece is in the form of a long dowel. A three-wheel planetary steady is the preferred type because only the top wheel of the three has to be slackened before each shift to the left.

You should turn each short section working from right to left (for this you plane from left to right). A lathe speed of about 700 rpm seemed ideal. String steadies are added from right to left as required to restrain the amplitudes of any vibration of the completed length.

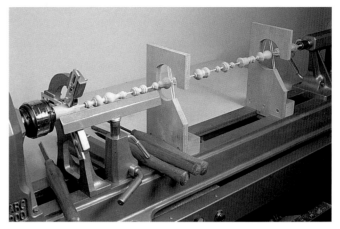

Figure 3.52 Nearly finished. Two string steadies were needed for this 38 in. (965 mm) long trembleur. The trembleur was then parted off just to the right of the chuck with a skew's long point in the normal way.

3.14 ENDNOTES

1   The same process is shown in *The Fundamentals of Woodturning*, p. 130, fig. 7.2.

2   A similar design is shown in: James Lukin, *The Lathe and its Uses*, p. 8, fig. 16.

3   Peter Child, *The Craftsman Woodturner*, p. 23.

4   Keith R. Bootle, *Wood in Australia* (Sydney, Australia: McGraw-Hill, 1983), p. 14.

5   von C.A. Martin, *Der Drechsler*, p. 269, fig. 558b.

6   R.A. Salaman in his *Dictionary of Woodworking Tools* (Mendham, New Jersey: Astragal Press, 1997) gives eighteen alternative names for rounders, one commonly used being *stail* engine. Jack Hill's *Country Chair Making* informs that stail is an archaic name for a long, straight, round handle; and *engine* is derived from the Latin meaning ingenious device.

7   Peter Hindle holds chairmaking courses in England and America. Ashem Crafts have written instructions and a video on chairmaking which detail the sharpening and use of their rotary planes.

8   The only recent references are: in a feature on Luc Caquineau of Les Roches, France, in *Woodturning in France* by Gerard Bidou and Daniel Guilloux; and Mike Darlow, "Turning Trembleurs," *Woodwork* (June 1999): pp. 40–43.

Chapter Four

TURNING SPHERES

Figure 4.1 Turning a sphere in the 16th century.
A woodcut from *Panoplia Omnium* by Hartman Schopper, published in Frankfurt-on-the-Main in 1568. The turner is using a pole lathe with the cord between the pole and the treadle wrapped around a driving mandrel located between the sphere and the headstock.

Over the centuries many turners have been drawn to the challenge of producing spheres even when there has been no functional imperative. Sphere turning is therefore included in most early turning texts (figure 4.1) and several recent ones.[1]

Spheres can be the starting points for a range of weird and wonderful turnings (figures 4.2 and 4.3). Spheres are also incorporated into spindles, finials, and other turnings.

Sphere turning is difficult to describe clearly, in part because the workpieces are often turned on two or more axes. To refer to locations on a workpiece being turned to a sphere I shall use terms associated with the sphere on which

we live, Earth. I also hope to avoid confusion when referring to axes by using a new term *turning-axis*. I define a turning-axis as: *the path of the lathe axis relative to the workpiece for each different workpiece mounting*. Each time you reposition the workpiece in the lathe to turn a particular part of the workpiece, you put a different turning-axis (the one used to turn that part) coaxial with the lathe axis. And the positions of turning-axes are related only to their workpieces.

Consider the cube in a sphere, top left in the figure below. Each of the circular holes in the outer shell was turned. Each hole could only be turned by positioning the workpiece so that the lathe axis ran through the center of that hole. You could also say that to turn each hole you must position its turning-axis along the lathe axis.

The first step in turning a sphere is almost always to turn the workpiece to a cylinder which has the same diameter and length as the intended sphere. You then have a choice of methods. This chapter describes thirteen, and advises how the quantity, size, accuracy, and appearance of the spheres you wish to produce should influence your choice of method. This chapter concludes by describing techniques and equipment used when drilling and decorating spheres.

Figure 4.2 Sphere-based turnings by Englishman David Springett. *Top row, left to right*: a cube in a sphere, a pierced sphere, Chinese lattice balls,[2] a spiked star in a sphere. *Bottom row, left to right*: a lattice pomander, a Singapore ball, a lattice pomander.

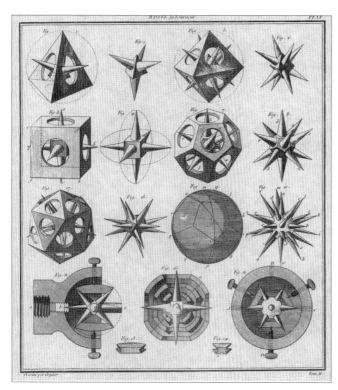

Figure 4.3 Sphere-based star turnings shown in plate XX of Pierre Hamelin-Bergeron's 1816 edition of *Manuel du Tourneur*. Fig. 11 (*left bottom*) and Fig. 12 (*right bottom*) illustrate how a star workpiece is held in a screw-bell chuck.

4.1 THE FIRST STEP

Figures 4.4 and 4.5 describe the usual first step in turning a simple sphere, that of mounting the blank in the lathe with its grain axial, and turning it to a cylinder of diameter equal to the designed diameter of the sphere.

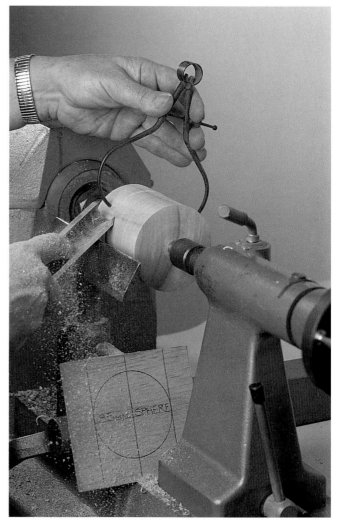

Figure 4.4 Cutting the cylinder to the diameter of the sphere using a roughing gouge and calipers. When you want the finished sphere to have a specified diameter, turn the cylinder to a diameter about 1/32 in. (1 mm) greater than the specified diameter to allow for later sanding.

The length of the blank need not exceed the diameter of the intended sphere plus a short length of waste at each end. The waste need only be sufficient to prevent the crushing caused by the drive and tail centers penetrating into the finished sphere.

4.2 THE SECOND STEP

Before you start to finish-turn the spherical surface, you should turn the cylindrical step-one workpiece either to a cylinder having a length equal to the sphere's intended diameter, or to a polygonal profile.

I recommend the polygonal profile in preference to the cylinder for all but small spheres. The polygonal method is described in section 4.3. However if you choose to turn the spherical surface directly from a cylinder, trim the cylinder to length leaving one or two supporting pins (figures 4.6 to 4.8). Leave two small pins if the workpiece is held between centers. If the workpiece is cantilevered from a chuck, flush the right-hand face of the cylinder and leave a substantial pin on the left.

Figure 4.5 Marking equator 1 and the polar latitudes of the intended sphere. I have marked equator 1 red, and the latitudes of the poles green.

Figure 4.6 Parting away the waste "outside" the right-hand pole. I don't part down immediately outside the latitude of each pole because it leaves a poorly-defined and porous end-grain surface. Instead I leave a thin layer of waste which I then face off with a skew as shown in the next two figures.

Figure 4.7 Starting to face the right-hand end of the cylinder with the long point of a skew chisel.[3] The skew's left-hand (facing) bevel should lie almost flush to the face being cut, and the skew's cutting edge should be tilted clockwise from the vertical just enough to give clearance. The cut is powered by a swing-push with the left hand. If you power the cut with your right hand, the facing bevel's heel is pushed against the face which the long point has just cut. This causes the skew to vibrate and rattle, which causes bruising and rippling on the end of the cylinder. If the facing cut is long, take your left-hand grip further back on the chisel than usual before you start the cut.

The waste pin(s) you leave at the pole(s) should be as small as possible while still providing a sufficiently-strong mounting. If the workpiece is cantilevered from a chuck, the left-hand pin should be reduced progressively as you finish-turn the left-hand half of the sphere working from right to left.

Figure 4.8 Completing the facing cut. The left hand has swung bodily forwards so that the bottom edge of the left-hand bevel remains almost parallel to and just clear of the just-cut surface throughout the cut.

The other methods for finish-turning a sphere from a cylinder are shown in sections 4.4, and 4.6 to 4.8.

4.3 THE POLYGONAL METHOD

The geometry of the polygonal method and its extension to very large spheres are described in figures 4.9 and 4.10. Figures 4.11 to 4.16 then show the simplest and most used version of the method in which you first produce a workpiece with an octagonal silhouette. The procedure is straightforward and accurate. From the octagonal silhouette you can then produce a sphere by several methods. You could finish-turn freehand, and monitor the profiles of the bands between the circles which lie on the sphere by frequently comparing each band's profile with a template. To narrow the width of the bands you could increase the number of sides on the silhouette to 16, or even 32 for a huge sphere. This is why John Jacob Holtzapffel termed this method polygonal rather than octagonal.[4]

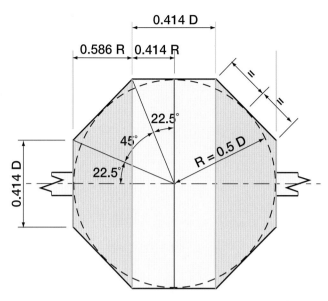

Figure 4.9 The geometry of a circle's enclosing octagon. You can establish the equator (red), the tropics (blue), and the polar circles (green) by drawing or by calculation—the latter is now easier because we have inexpensive, electronic hand-held calculators. In your calculations use a diameter about 1/32 in. (1 mm) larger than the sphere's designed diameter to allow for sanding.

Figure 4.11 Planing a cylinder to the sphere's designed diameter with a roughing gouge.

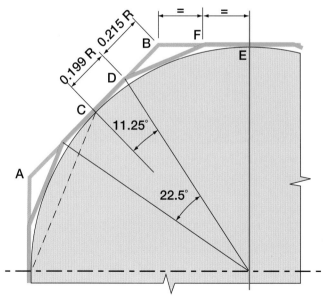

Figure 4.10 Increasing the polygon's sides to 16. The greater the designed diameter of the sphere, the more sides your polygon needs to keep the arcs of freehand turning and profile monitoring short. Points like **C**, halfway across any side of the surrounding octagon, are on the sphere. However if you equally divide **BE** to get **F**, the centers of bands joining neighboring **F**s are just outside the sphere. The accurate version of **F** is **D**: a circle halfway between two adjacent **D**s is on the sphere.

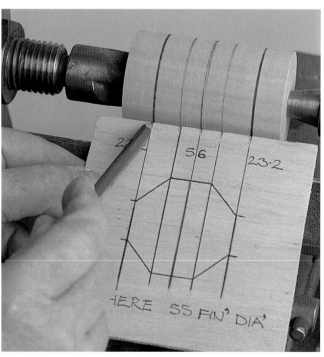

Figure 4.12 Marking the reference latitudes on the cylinder. I have colored the latitudes of the two tropics blue.

Figure 4.13 Parting "outside" the polar latitudes to leave pins of diameter equal to 0.414 of the sphere's diameter. This multiplier is the same for any size of sphere.

Figure 4.15 Cutting the chamfered bands from the tropics down to the polar circles using a skew's short point.

Figure 4.14 Facing the ends of the cylinder down to the diameter of the polar circles. Take these cuts with the skew's long point down a little deeper than the surface of the pins to more clearly define the junctions of both surfaces.

Figure 4.16 Cutting an end face of the octagonal profile with a skew's long point as shown earlier in figures 4.7 and 4.8. The pin left at the pole should not be so narrow that it shears.

From this stage you have several choices, you can:

1. Finish-turn the sphere by eye.
2. Finish-turn the sphere freehand using a template to monitor the profile as you turn (see next section).
3. Use the billiard-ball method described in section 4.6.
4. Remount the workpiece on a second turning-axis at 90° to turning-axis 1-1. You can mount the workpiece on this second turning-axis 2-2 between normal drive and tail centers (section 4.7), or between special cup centers which will not damage the sphere's surface (section 4.8).

4.4 USING TEMPLATES

If your previous step was to turn a cylinder, you can then turn off the remaining waste in onion-like layers. Use your skew's short point, cut from larger diameter to smaller, and to the left and the right alternately so that you finish both halves together. If you finish-turn one half before starting the other, you are less likely to get a good shape. You can finish-turn the sphere entirely by eye, but this is usually unwise. The larger its diameter, the greater the probability and cost-penalty of a noticeably non-spherical result, and the more beneficial it is to use a template as described in figures 4.17 to 4.19. However monitoring with a template still gives a less-accurate result than the methods described in sections 4.6 to 4.8.

After finish-turning, sand. If the workpiece was cantilevered from a chuck, you can part the sphere off. If the workpiece was mounted between centers, demount the turning, and saw off the waste pins. You can then hand-finish the polar areas, or finish-turn and sand them with the sphere held in a jam or sphere chuck (figures 4.70 to 4.72).

Figure 4.18 **A 90° template allows more accurate monitoring** than a near-semicircular.

To use templates which are "shorter" than 90°, you must first turn the workpiece to a polygonal profile as shown in the previous section.

Figure 4.17 **Using a near-semicircular (180°) template** to monitor a workpiece's profile.

You will find it almost impossible to monitor accurately with a near-semicircular template. The "shorter" the template, that is the smaller the angle between the radiuses from the sphere's center to the template's ends, the more accurate the finished turning tends to be. And the shorter the template, the more reference circles you have to mark beforehand on the sphere's surface to monitor between. These reference circles should be equally spaced around the sphere's profile.

Figure 4.19 **Monitoring with a turned ring.** Here the internal diameter of the ring should be a touch greater than the designed diameter of the sphere.[5] This monitoring method gives greater coverage over the sphere's surface when the workpiece is cantilevered from a chuck than when the workpiece is held between centers.

4.5 THE POLYGONAL METHOD FOR A SPHERE ON A SPINDLE

If you want to turn a sphere with one or two axial pins, you could turn the sphere, bore it (figure 4.64), turn a dowel or dowels, and glue the dowel(s) in. You could similarly produce a spindle or finial incorporating a sphere from components. But the stronger and easier solution is to adapt the polygonal method. You will need to establish the equator, tropics, and polar latitudes, plus the junction(s) of the spherical surface with the projecting pin(s), or the adjacent parts of the spindle or finial (figure 4.20). The remainder of the turning is straightforward and is illustrated in figures 4.21 to 4.23.

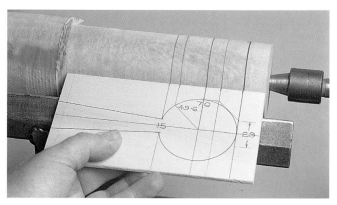

Figure 4.21 Marking out the sphere from a pencil gauge. The right-hand end of the workpiece has been turned to the finished diameter of the sphere.

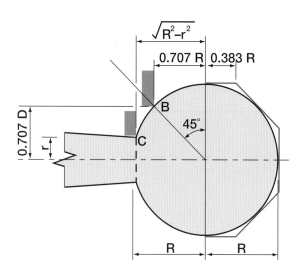

Figure 4.20 The geometry of a sphere at the end of a finial. The right-hand half of the sphere is turned using the polygonal method. Before rolling the left-hand half, points **B** and **C** can be established, here with the parting cuts shown red.

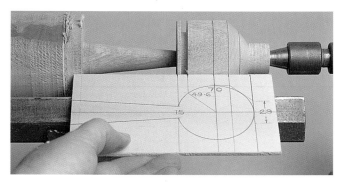

Figure 4.22 Ready for rounding. The specified diameters have been calipered and the waste between the right-hand tropic's latitude and the polar circle has been cut away. Halfway down the right-hand sloping band I have pencilled another reference circle which is on the surface of the sphere.

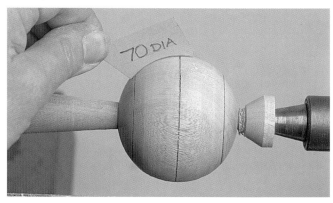

Figure 4.23 Checking with a template.

4.6 THE BILLIARD-BALL METHOD

This method is at least three centuries old (figure 4.24), and was used for hand turning ivory billiard balls.[6] It depends on the fact that if you rotate a cylindrical or octagonally-profiled workpiece about a diameter across equator 1, the solid core that you see is circular and generates a sphere as it rotates (figure 4.25). This method is the best for hand turning spheres of small and medium size.

I recommend that you first turn the workpiece between centers to an octagonal silhouette by the polygonal method (figures 4.9-4.16). You could however as in figure 4.24 start from the cylinder produced after figures 4.4 to 4.8.

After preparing the jam chuck, you turn one hemisphere on each workpiece in turn as shown in **C** and **D** of figure 4.24. You then shorten the jam chuck to reduce its internal diameter so that it will grip each workpiece in turn close to the already-turned equator 2. You then turn the waste off the other hemisphere as shown in **F** of figure 4.24. Finally you should rechuck each sphere at least twice to sand it. The method is described in figures 4.25 to 4.33. You will find this method surprisingly easy once you have turned the first couple of hemispheres.

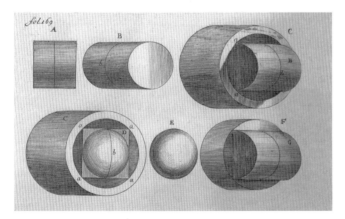

Figure 4.24 Chucking in the billiard-ball method, plate 47 from Charles Plumier's *L'Art de Tourner* of 1701. The cylinder **A** and **B** in **Fig. 1** is forced almost halfway into the jam chuck **C**. The waste "outside" the half sphere protruding from the chuck is turned off as in **D**. Finally, as shown in **F**, the finish-turned half sphere is held in a smaller jam chuck to allow the waste outside the other half of the sphere to be turned off. It is however preferable to start from the banded spheroid you produce by the polygonal method because you are less likely to hook the workpiece out of the jam chuck. This is because the banded spheroid has a greater area of contact with the chuck, and because the workpiece's projections are smaller and less likely to catch on your gouge.

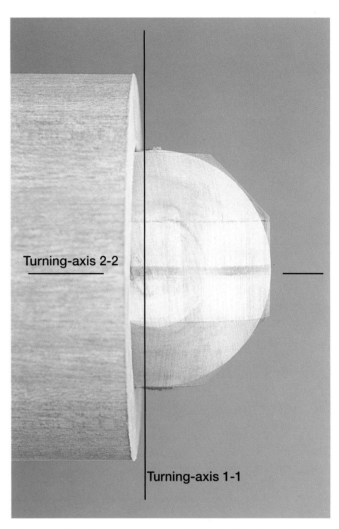

Turning-axis 2-2

Turning-axis 1-1

Figure 4.25 The geometry of the billiard-ball method.
You first turn a cylinder or banded spheroid about turning-axis 1-1 and mark equator 1. You then remount the workpiece in the lathe on turning-axis 2-2. which is at right angles to axis 1-1, and runs diametrically through equator 1. As the workpiece rotates about turning-axis 2-2, the rotation of equator 1 generates a spherical surface. Any wood outside that spherical surface is waste, appears as a blur, can be felt as an unevenness, and can therefore be turned off. A more accurate way to monitor turning off the waste is to take the cuts just up to but not across equator 1 (see figure 4.32).

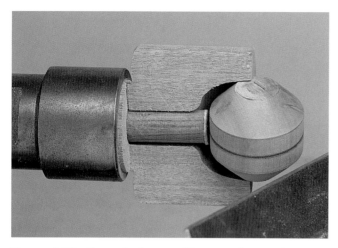

Figure 4.26   A workpiece with an octagonal silhouette held in a wooden jam chuck (here cut in half). You should size the jam chuck so that a little more than half the workpiece projects. Use a softer wood for the chuck as it will have more "give" and better accommodate minor variations in workpiece geometry. A knockout bar with felt on its end is shown here, but it is a luxury not normally used or needed.

Figure 4.28   Starting a cut. Use a medium-sized detail gouge (here 3/8 in. (10 mm)), and present it to cut with considerable side rake.

Figure 4.27   A workpiece chucked. To leave the best surface, angle the toolrest and start radial-skimming cuts with the shoulder of the cutting edge of a detail gouge. Feel with your left forefinger—any unevenness signifies waste. As you cut closer to the face of the chuck you will need to raise your gouge's handle to maintain large-rake-angle and good-side-rake cutting.

Figure 4.29   Continuing the cut. Keep the handle down, and the blade presented so that the cutting is performed by the left shoulder of the cutting edge.

Figure 4.30 **Raise the handle a little** to keep the ideal cutting edge presentation. You need to do this if your toolrest is straight, although angling the toolrest as here minimizes the need.

Figure 4.32 **A cut which is too deep.** The cut surfaces should almost meet, but not cross, equator 1.

If your cuts are too deep on one side only, the recess in your chuck is not axial, or more likely, you did not turn the banded sphere symmetrically, and it therefore seats asymmetrically in the chuck.

Figure 4.31 **The cut almost completed.** After turning each hemisphere, sand it.

4.7 TURNING ON TWO TURNING-AXES WITH HAND FINISHING

This method is simple and effective for larger spheres, say above 4 in. (100 mm) in diameter. It is described in figures 4.34 to 4.41. You will need to fill and hand sand two polar areas.

Figure 4.33 **Ready to turn off the waste from all the second hemispheres.** Below are two more workpieces ready for this next turning operation.

After turning off the waste to reveal each second hemisphere, sand. Then rechuck each sphere twice to sand across the conjunction between the two turned hemispheres. You could rechuck and sand in other orientations, but excessive sanding lessens sphericity.

Figure 4.34 **A blank turned to a cylinder.** The blank is for a 230 mm diameter sphere, and was made by gluing together disks of 3/4 in. (19 mm) thick plywood. I used high side rake peripheral skimming to minimize tearout, and allowed an extra 1/32 in. (1 mm) for sanding. The cylinder has been marked out for turning to an octagonal profile because that is the most accurate way to rough the sphere.

Figure 4.35 **Using radial skimming to define a polar circle** and produce the short pin seen in the figure below.

Figure 4.37 **Further defining the sphere.** The black pencil lines in the centers of the sloping bands between the tropics and the polar circles are on the surface of the finished sphere.

Figure 4.36 **Cutting away the waste between a tropic and a polar circle.**

Figure 4.38 **The waste has been largely cut away.** I took care though to leave the shape a little full.

If you turn the areas alongside equator 1 so that they form part of the final spherical surface, you will not need to mount the workpiece between centers for a third and final turning operation. If you leave the area around equator 1 cylindrical, you will need to finish-turn the poles 2 areas, which will lie on equator 1, in a third turning operation.

Figure 4.39 **Marking two poles on equator 1 with dividers.** Turning-axis 2-2 will pass through these two new poles 2. Alternatively you could use your lathe's indexing facility and mark the two poles with your pencil supported on the toolrest positioned close to equator 1.

    If you will be finish-turning the poles 2 areas in a third turning operation, ensure that the small holes at poles 1 formed by the points of your drive and tail centers penetrate below the final spherical surface so that you can relocate the centers in them for the third turning operation.

Figure 4.40 **Turning off the waste** with the workpiece mounted on turning-axis 2-2.

    If you started from an axially-grained blank, you should now use radial and peripheral skimming cuts with high-side-rake traversing from the poles 2 towards equator 2 to minimize tear-out. As your cuts approach the original red-pencilled equator 1, check that the workpiece is evenly centered. If so the cuts will approach equator 1 symmetrically. Adjust the centering if necessary. After turning just up to equator 1, fill any holes at poles 1 unless you intend to use them to locate the workpiece for a third turning operation, then sand.

    Demount the workpiece, fill and hand sand the poles 2 areas, or if they need to be finish-turned remount the workpiece between the original centers. Then turn off the excess at poles 2, and sand. After removing the sphere from the lathe, fill the holes left in poles 1, and hand sand.

Figure 4.41 **The finished ball after sanding and polishing.** All diameters were within 0.4 mm of the specified 230 mm.

4.8 TURNING ON TWO TURNING-AXES WITHOUT HAND FINISHING

The previous method is not suitable for larger spheres which are required to be without blemish. To avoid having to fill and hand finish the polar areas at the ends of turning-axis 2-2, you hold the workpiece on turning-axis 2-2 between non-damaging cups instead of between a conventional drive and tail center. You also use the cups if you need to mount the workpiece on more than two turning-axes (see figure 4.66). The turning procedure is detailed in figures 4.45 to 4.53.

Elaborate cup constructions are described in figures 4.42 to 4.44. The cups are best made from materials which will not split. The tail cup can however be simply and satisfactorily located on your cone or ring live tail center, although it is advisable to recess the right-hand, rear face of the cup so that your cone or cup tail center penetrates more deeply than usual.

Figure 4.42 **A tailstock cup screwed to a metal disk.** The metal disk has been bored and tapped, and is about to be screwed onto the threaded nose of a metal-spinning live tail center.

Figure 4.43 **Driving and tail center cups** made by Don Dickson of Sydney. The next figure details their construction. The overall diameters of the cups should each be a minimum of a fifth of the sphere's diameter to ensure a secure hold. The edges of the cups are rounded to prevent damage to the sphere's surface, and a resilient nonslip lining—car-tire inner tube or leather—further lessens the possibility of damaging the sphere's surface and increases the cups' grip.

The driving cup can be held in a chuck, or as here turned with a Morse-taper shank.

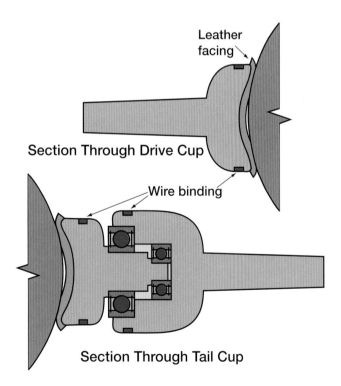

Figure 4.44 **The cups shown in the previous figure.** The sealed bearings have bores of about 3/8 in. and 3/4 in. (10 mm and 20 mm). Larger bore diameters and one bearing instead of two could be used. The use of such cups is detailed in figures 4.45 to 4.53.

Figure 4.45 **Turn your blank to a cylinder**, and mark equator 1 and the latitudes of the tropics and poles. Caliper the diameter of the cylinder about 1/32 in. (1 mm) larger than the sphere's designed diameter to allow for sanding. Then use the polygonal method.

Figure 4.46 **Cut the sloping bands** between the tropics' latitudes and the polar circles.

Figure 4.47 Roughly round the left and right hemispheres. Your objective is to create a rough sphere which is nowhere undersize. To aid in this, pencil circles in the centers of the sloping bands. These circles are on the surface of the sphere, and must not therefore be cut away as you round the hemispheres.

The next operation is to mark two poles (poles 2) on equator 1 using dividers or your lathe's indexing facility.

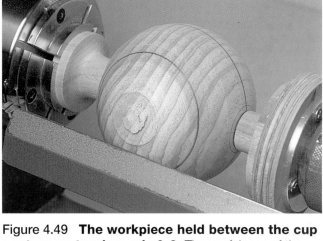

Figure 4.49 The workpiece held between the cup centers on turning-axis 2-2. The usefulness of the circles shown being pencilled in the previous figure is illustrated.

To trial and adjust the mounting:

1. Mount the sphere between the cups and rotate the sphere by hand. Check and adjust until the mounting seems true.
2. Run the lathe and take light cuts. If the sphere is truly mounted, each cut will start and end an equal distance from equator 1. How these cuts start and end will help you to adjust the mounting.

Figure 4.48 Drawing circles centered on poles 2. These circles speed accurate centering of the workpiece between the cup centers. The circle diameters should therefore be a little larger than the cups' diameters.

Next demount the workpiece, saw off most of the waste outside poles 1, and remount the workpiece on turning-axis 2-2, housing poles 2 within the two cups.

Figure 4.50 **Turn up to equator 2.** Because the grain is radial, turn from small diameter to large. Present your detail gouge with the minimum clearance angle and with a large side rake.

Turning up to all of the exposed equator 2 would be the final turning operation if you had earlier accurately finish-turned the sphere's surface adjacent to equator 1 when turning on turning-axis 1-1. You could have monitored with a template to achieve this. However in this case this has not been done. You therefore have to accurately establish equator 2 in order to then remount the workpiece accurately on turning axis 1-1 or on any diameter through equator 2. You can then finish-turn up to equator 2 to properly finish the pole 2 areas shown above housed in the cups.

To accurately establish equator 2, finish-turn one hemisphere first, say as here the left-hand one, just to the imprints left by the drive center and tail center center pins in poles 1. Through these two imprints pencil equator 2 onto the rotating wood. Turn the other, here right-hand, hemisphere, and sand the workpiece taking care not to lose equator 2 . The next step, shown in the next figure, is to mark a pair of cup circles at the ends of any diameter of equator 2. This diameter does not need to be turning-axis 1-1.

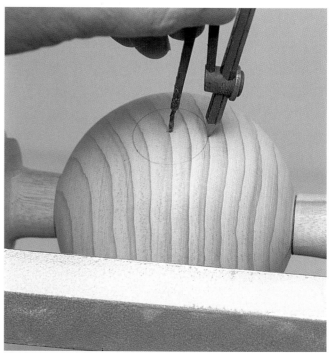

Figure 4.51 **Mark new cup circles** on equator 2 around what will be poles 3. Turning-axis 3-3 is at 90° to turning-axis 2-2

Figure 4.52 **Finish-turn the areas around poles 2, and then sand.**

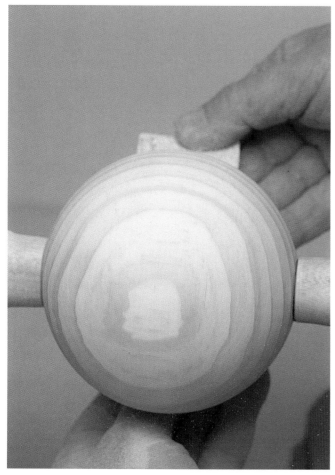

Figure 4.53 Sand again with the workpiece in different orientations.
You can sand further by remounting the sphere between the cups on different axes, but too much sanding will tend to produce an ovoid sphere because the side-grain area with be abraded faster than the end-grain areas.

4.9 THE LAYERS METHOD

Very big spheres or hemispheres are often face-to-face laminated from wood or wood-based board. (Two outboard-turned hemispheres can joined to create spheres which would be too big to turned between centers). If the joints in the sphere or hemisphere are clearly visible after laminating, you can readily calculate or obtain by drawing the maximum diameter of each lamination or group of laminations. Each maximum diameter can then be calipered to produce a stepped sphere as shown in figure 4.54. You can then produce a spherical surface by turning the steps off.

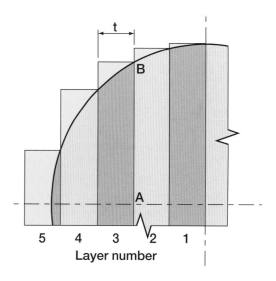

Figure 4.54 The geometry of the layers method.
The diameter which a layer has to be turned to is the diameter of the sphere at the face of that layer nearest to the vertical equator. If the number of the layer is **n**, the thickness of each layer is **t**, and **R** is the radius of the required sphere, each layer should be turned to a diameter which can be found by drawing or calculated by the formula

Layer diameter = $2 \sqrt{R^2 - [(n-1)t]^2}$

Therefore for layer 3, the required diameter is 2**AB** and (**n**−1) = 2

Once the layers have been turned to their diameters (shown yellow above), turn the waste steps off, ideally monitoring with a template as you do.

4.10 SPHERE TURNERS

Numerous and similar mechanical devices have been developed to overcome "the grave and unnecessary difficulties in the production of the true sphere by plain hand turning."[7] Described in figures 4.55 to 4.59,[8] their accuracy depends on having the vertical axis about which the device's cutter pivots passing exactly through the lathe axis. Although the *cutting* or scraping edge of the cutter need not be at lathe axis height, having it there simplifies cutting a sphere to a specific diameter..

There are two approaches to turning spheres mechanically. In the first the workpiece is usually held by and cantilevers from a chuck. The sphere cutter produces the whole sphere and parts it off through taking a series of arcing cuts. In the more elaborate versions such as that in figure 4.55:

1. The cutter is moved radially by a screw. This allows the depth of cut to be readily adjusted. It also allows the cutter to be backed off after completion of a cut with the grain, so that you can return the cutter to start the next cut without damaging the just-cut surface.
2. The device is constructed to slide precisely along the bedways so that its cutter's pivoting axis always passes up through the lathe axis whatever diameter of sphere is being turned.
3. The cutter and the upper body of the sphere cutter is rotated by a tangent screw operating on a wormwheel. The tangent screw is often disconnected, and the top half of the sphere turner rotated by hand.

The second approach to mechanical sphere turning replicates the billiard-ball method described in section 4.6. The workpiece projects a short way from a chuck, and the sphere cutter cuts a little more than half of a sphere. After all the first halves of a batch have been cut, the workpieces are in turn held by their first-finished halves while the other half is turned. This approach is used in the sphere-turning lathe shown in figure 4.57.

The optimum design of the cutter will depend on whether it has to just skim the sphere to final shape after preliminary hand turning, or remove all the waste from a cylindrical workpiece. Most sphere turners have scraping cutters, but for softer woods *cutting* cutters are preferred (figure 4.56). One *cutting*-cutter I recall was "Y"-shaped in plan, with a near-vertical cutting edge, slightly curved in elevation at the end of each arm of the "Y". It therefore *cut* whether it was being rotated clockwise or counterclockwise in plan.

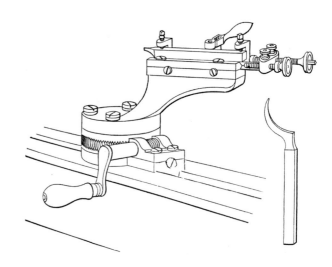

Figure 4.55 A 19th-century sphere turner. It has two cutters, that shown on the right being for parting off.

Figure 4.56 A sphere turner made from plywood, a large bearing (hidden) and a machine vice. The cutter is a detail gouge mounted in the *cutting* presentation to leave an excellent surface.

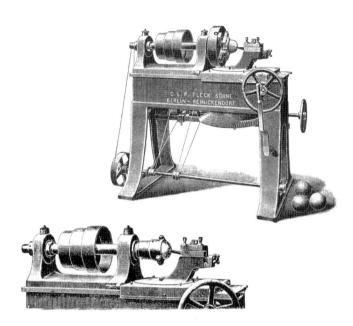

Figure 4.57 **A sphere-turning lathe**, German, late 19th century.[9] *Top*, a little more than a hemisphere is first turned on all the blanks in a batch; *bottom*, a collet-type chuck is then used to grip around the equator of each finished hemisphere while the other hemisphere is finish-turned.

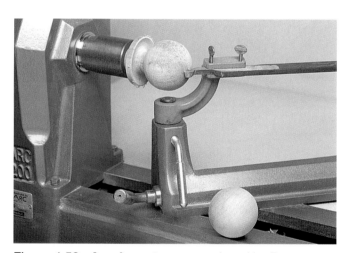

Figure 4.59 **About to part off with the Leadbeatter sphere turner.** The finish-turned surface of the sphere has already been sanded. As with many sphere cutters, the cutting tip is offset to the "left" so that the rotatable cutter-holding arm can part off a sphere without fouling the chuck, here a cupchuck.

Figure 4.58 **A sphere turner** produced by Bruce Leadbeatter of Sydney. It is inexpensive because it fits into a lathe's banjo, lacks radial-screw adjustment of the cutter, and requires the turner to align its pivoting axis transversely as well as longitudinally.

You should not reduce the diameter of the spigot supporting the sphere to below 40% of the sphere's diameter until the right-hand half of the sphere is completed. This prevents the sphere chattering as it is cut, and the rippled and torn surface which would result. Also take finishing cuts with the grain, from large diameter to small, to produce the optimum surface.

4.11   THE TUBE GOUGE

Although the tube gouge has long been promoted as a sphere turning tool in hand woodturning,[10] it is not the ideal you might imagine. Its sharpening and use are described in figures 4.60 to 4.61. A ring tool can do a similar job (figures 4.62 and 4.63).

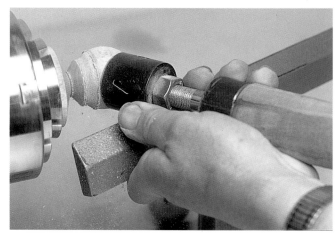

Figure 4.61   Turning a sphere with a tube gouge. If you attempt to cut a sphere with the same diameter as the internal diameter of the tube, the sphere tends to jam in the tube and shear its supporting spigot. Because of this it is better to use a tube gouge with an internal diameter which is a little less than the required sphere diameter. You then have to monitor the sphere diameter by calipering.

Figure 4.60   Ticketing a tube gouge. Despite commonly being called a gouge, the tool is used as a scraper in sphere turning. You therefore have to rough the workpiece first to an approximate and slightly-oversize sphere with conventional turning tools to reduce the waste that you have to scrape away with the tube gouge.

This tool was made from a HSS hole saw—a convenient solution described by Ray Hopper.[11]

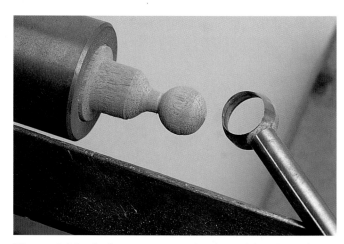

Figure 4.62   A ring gouge and sphere. Had the sphere been turned further, it would have jammed in the ring and sheared through the supporting pin.

Figure 4.63 Usi...   ...phere.
This Robert Sorb... ...ub inside
the ring which f...

4.12 ...HERE

Sa... ...ficult, and as wood is
l... ...obtain one perfect
... ...tion is to make a paper
... ...rough an equator. You
... ...propriate of the methods
... ...e to position the paper joint
... ...o rive the sphere into two down
the pape...

When you r...re one large hemisphere it is far less
wasteful to prepare, if necessary by laminating, a blank just
for the hemisphere. You then screw the blank to a faceplate,
and turn the hemisphere using the template, polygonal, or
layers method, or a sphere-turning device. These methods
can be used singly, or more often, in combination.

To turn hemispheres or spheres which are greater in
radius than your lathe's center height, turn hemispheres
outboard. As mentioned earlier, you can make very large
spheres by gluing two hemispheres together.

4.13 SPECIAL DEVICES AND TECHNIQUES

Figures 4.64 to 4.72 detail the texturing, chucking, and
drilling of spheres.

A method not illustrated is that described by Charles
Reed of Washington D.C. He recommended a method in
which sawn cubes of wood are power sanded, not turned,
into spheres.[12] He put 1/2 in. (13 mm) cubes of wood in a
lidded box which was without a bottom. The box was
mounted just clear of a sanding belt. The sanding of a dozen
spheres took about an hour—far longer than it would take
to turn them. I have not tried this method, but it could be
worth investigating if you need large numbers of small
spheres. You might also cut the cubes a little shorter in
length parallel to the grain to compensate for end grain's
greater abrasion resistance.

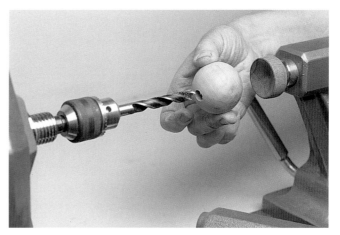

Figure 4.64 Boring a sphere by holding it against a
drill pad with a conical recess. You could also hold the
sphere in a sphere chuck; or use a drilling machine and
hold and locate the sphere in a conical recess in a
wooden plate centered under the drill.

Figure 4.66 A textured sphere is sometimes required—croquet balls are an example. The V-cuts were made with the ball mounted on three different turning-axes at right angles, and held between the drive and tail center cups shown in figure 4.50.

Figure 4.65 **V-cutting a sphere's surface.** Texturing by cutting closely-spaced V-cuts is best done with the long point of a skew.

If you had to texture many spheres it would be worthwhile making a multi-point tool, similar to an upside-down, outside, hand thread chaser. Ideally the points should be acute, sharp, and vertical not canted. The points should lie along a straight line rather than lie on a concave curve which mates with the sphere's surface.

You produce deep V-cuts, such as those shown in figures 4.67 and 4.68, in the same way that you V-cut before rolling beads on spindles.

Figure 4.67 **A hollowed sphere by Christian Burchard** showing V-cuts of even depth.[13] The osage orange wood is stained black in the fields between the bands of V-cutting. The diameter is 9 in. (230 mm).

Figure 4.68 **V-cuts of uneven depth** on a hollowed sphere by Christian Burchard. The wood is osage orange, the diameter 7 in. (180 mm). The hollowing can be done with the workpiece cupchucked, or with the sphere held in a sphere or cage chuck. The cage chuck would give the best access for calipering the wall thickness.

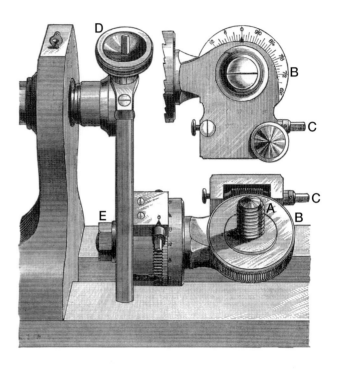

Figure 4.69 **The dome or spherical chuck**[14] is used in ornamental-turning to hold hemispheres and domes while they are being ornamentally machined. During this machining the headstock spindle is locked.

The workpiece is held in a chuck or on a faceplate which is in turn held on screw **A** which is integral with wormwheel **B**. Tangent screw **C** is used to axially rotate and index the workpiece. The eccentricity of the chuck's horizontal arm from the lathe axis can be varied using mainscrew **D**. Nut **E** is used to lock the horizontal arm at the desired eccentricity.

Figure 4.70 A sphere chuck with a collar which is screwed on. The red line is to ensure that the collar is fitted in its correct orientation.

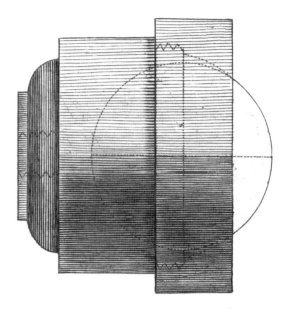

Figure 4.72 A sphere chuck with a collar which is screwed to the left to clamp a spherical workpiece, shown in plate 47 of Plumier.

Figure 4.71 The sphere chuck in the previous figure disassembled. The cardboard template aided accurately hollowing.

4.14 HOLLOWING A HEMISPHERE

Turning a hemispherical hollow in the right-hand end of a workpiece is a straightforward cupchuck job. To achieve high accuracy you would monitor your hollowing with a template. An alternative method would be to buy the invention of Andy Whyman of Hamilton, New Zealand, a simple sphere turner which can rapidly be converted to produce part-spherical hollows (figures 4.73 and 4.74).

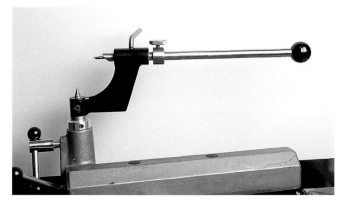

Figure 4.73 **Andy Whyman's device arranged for turning a sphere.** The conical projection on the vertical axis is used to help align the device's axis of rotation to pass through the lathe axis and through the desired sphere's equator.

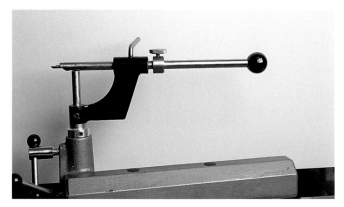

Figure 4.74 **The device converted for spherical hollowing.** The cone-ended round bar seen in the previous illustration is removed, inverted and locked back in its socket to support the cutting arm which has been repositioned so that it extends past the device's vertical axis.

4.15 ENDNOTES

1 Readily-available books with significant sphere turning content include: J.J. Holtzapffel, *Hand or Simple Turning*, pp. 288–293 and 406–445; and David Springett, *Woodturning Wizardry.*

2 The history of these is described in David Springett, "The Origins of the Chinese Ball," *The Society of Ornamental Turners Bulletin* No. 98, pp. 101–108. An introduction to the turning of Chinese balls is given in David Springett, "Heavenly spheres," *Woodturning*, No 68 (Oct 1998): pp. 65–69. For fuller instructions start with: J.J. Holtzapffel. *Hand or Simple Turning*, pp. 426–445.

3 This cut is detailed in *The Fundamentals of Woodturning*, p. 114, fig. 6.101.

4 J.J. Holtzapffel, *Hand or Simple Turning*, pp. 290–291.

5 J.J. Holtzapffel, *Hand or Simple Turning*, pp. 290–292 and fig. 378 recommends that the template ring's internal diameter be slightly less than the sphere's diameter. You can use either.

6 J.J. Holtzapffel, *Hand or Simple Turning*, pp. 406–425 includes advice on turning billiard balls.

7 J.J. Holtzapffel, *The Principles & Practice of Ornamental or Complex Turning*, p. 623.

8 These devices are also called spherical rests and are detailed in: J.J. Holtzapffel, *The Principles &Practice of Ornamental or Complex Turning*, pp. 623–644. That pictured is shown on p. 626, fig. 594. It is similar to that pictured in plate XVII of Hamelin-Bergeron.

9 von C.A. Martin, *Der Drechsler*, pp. 195 and 196, figs 449 and 450.

10 Park Benjamin, editor, *Appletons' Cyclopaedia of Applied Mechanics* (New York: D. Appleton & Co, 1889), vol 2, p. 251; L.H. Saury, *The Amateur's Lathe* (London: George Newnes Ltd, 1954), pp. 141–142; Ray Hopper, *Multi-Centre Woodturning*, pp. 124–128; and A. L. Hayes, "Ball Turning made Easy," *The Australian Woodworker* (March/April 1992): p. 67. Alan Hayes recommends a tube gouge with a castellated cutting edge for roughing.

11 Ray Hopper, *Multi-Centre Woodturning*, pp. 124–127.

12 Charles Reed, "Sanding little wooden balls," *Fine Woodworking* No. 23 (July/August 1980): pp. 10–11.

13 Christian Burchard, "Ways to have a ball," *American Woodturner* (June 1995): pp. 26–28.

14 J.H. Evans, *Ornamental Turning*, p. 164, fig. 168.

Chapter Five

ECCENTRIC TURNING

In eccentric turning, the workpiece's original axis of symmetry is not coaxial with the lathe axis. Situations in which there is only one eccentric mounting of the workpiece are considered in this chapter; multi-axis turning where a workpiece is turned on two or more different eccentric mountings is detailed in chapter 6. Chapter 7 describes elliptical turning in which the eccentricity of the workpiece's axis of symmetry varies continuously relative to the lathe axis.

When you turn an eccentrically-mounted workpiece your lathe will usually shake. This is caused by the dynamic imbalance of the workpiece. Section 5.1 describes how the shaking can be reduced by lowering the lathe speed and by counterweighting.

The simplest use for eccentric turning is to round or mold an edge or face (section 5.2). If the lathe axis runs within the workpiece and you continue turning until the workpiece cross section becomes circular, then you have rendered the process futile. Therefore implicit in the concept of eccentric turning is the assumption that the turning must not progress too far in some situations.

A now little-used application for eccentric turning is therming. It and its derivatives are described in sections 5.3 to 5.5.

A workpiece can usually be mounted between centers when its turning-axis and axis of symmetry are relatively close and near parallel. When, as in therming, the two axes are far apart, special equipment is needed, much of which you can make yourself as sections 5.3 and 5.4 show. Special chucks are manufactured for eccentric and multi-axis turning, and are described in section 6.1 of the next chapter (pages 125 to 127).

5.1 STATIC AND DYNAMIC BALANCE

Eccentric and multi-axis turning are more risky than most other forms. Lathes often shake, workpieces and counterweights want to fly off, and workpieces and fastenings project. These conditions demand greater caution and concentration, lower lathe speeds, and checking that the toolrest will not foul. You can further reduce risk through an understanding of static and dynamic balance and counterweighting. These are discussed in figures 5.1 to 5.4.

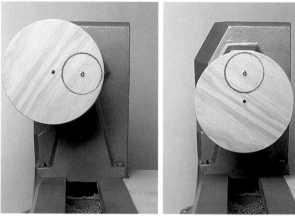

Figure 5.1 Static imbalance. The center screw of a screwchuck is screwed into the hole in the center of the red circle. If I release the disk from the position shown on the left with the driving belt loose and the lathe switched off, the disk will settle into the position of stable static balance shown on the right. If the disk's center were positioned vertically above the lathe axis, the static balance would be unstable. From all other positions except the two of static balance the disk will settle into the position of stable static balance.

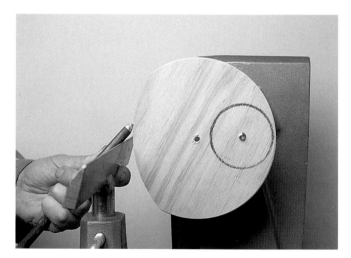

Figure 5.2 A workpiece in dynamic imbalance. If you turn the disk in the previous figure your lathe will shake because the workpiece is not in dynamic balance. The lathe shaking increases if you increase the lathe speed. As you continue to turn, the disk's periphery approaches the circular shape of the red circle, and lathe shaking lessens as the workpiece approaches dynamic balance.

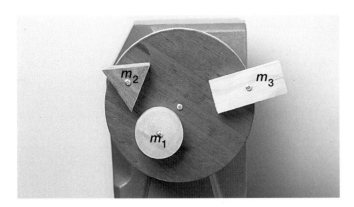

Figure 5.3 Calculating static and dynamic balance. Disk m_1, triangle m_2, and rectangle m_3 represent workpieces, counterweights, or off-center mounting components. The weight of each can be thought to be concentrated at a point (its center of gravity). The distances from the lathe axis to the centers of gravity are h_1, h_2, and h_3 horizontally; and r_1, r_2, and r_3 radially.

For static balance the sum of the weights multiplied by their horizontal distances from the lathe axis (their lever arms) must equal zero. Therefore for static balance:

$$m_1h_1 + m_2h_2 + m_3h_3 = 0$$

If lever arms to the left of the lathe axis are considered positive, those to the right will be negative .

Note that at different headstock-spindle orientations the static imbalance varies. However, as is explained in the next figure, the achievement of static balance does not necessarily signify dynamic balance.

For dynamic balance the sum of the rotational forces caused by the rotation of the workpiece(s), counterweights, and mountings must equal zero. To experience a rotational force twirl an object on the end of a string. When you twirl you feel a tension in the string. Twirl faster and the tension increases. Let go the string and the object flies off in a straight line. The tension you feel in the string is a radially-inwards, centripetal force pulling on the object to keep it moving in a circular path.

The tension in the string is balanced by the radially-outwards centrifugal force which the object exerts as it seeks to fly off in a straight tangential path. It is these revolving centrifugal forces caused by the revolving eccentrically-mounted workpieces, etc. which produce lathe shaking. The magnitude of a centrifugal force is proportional to the weight of the object, the radius from the lathe axis to the object's center of gravity, and the square of the object's speed measured in rpm.

Because the centrifugal force is proportional to the lathe speed squared, you can greatly lessen the shaking due to dynamic imbalance by reducing your lathe's speed. But you can only eliminate such shaking by counterweighting.

Figure 5.4 A simple situation of static and dynamic balance. The rectangular workpiece m_1 needed to have a recess turned towards one end. To achieve dynamic balance, a counterweight m_2 was mounted along the same diameter. The counterweight was chosen as 112.5 mm long, and was cut from the same plank as the 225 mm long workpiece. Therefore $m_2 = 0.5 \, m_1$

For static balance the sum of the horizontal moments about the lathe axis must be zero. Therefore if the center of the workpiece m_1 is 67 mm from the lathe axis, the center of the counterweight m_2 needs to be 134 mm from the lathe axis on the opposite side of the diameter.

There is then also dynamic balance because m_1r_1 and m_2r_2 are equal whatever the lathe speed (the lathe speed squared being the same for both m_1 and m_2). You can therefore easily check whether you have dynamic balance when all the components lie on one diameter. Position that diameter horizontal and disconnect the driving belt so that the headstock spindle is free to settle. If there is no tendency to settle there is both static and dynamic balance.

Although the revolving workpiece and counterweight combine to create a system in dynamic balance, both objects are each acted on by a centrifugal force trying to tear them off the lathe. And if m_1 or m_2 flew off, the radially outwards centrifugal force on the remaining object would then cause the lathe to shake.

Turning continually lightens the workpiece. Therefore you will only be able to truly balance the system for one instant during the turning unless you make intermediate adjustments to the position(s) and/or the weight(s) of the counterweight(s).

Apart from switching on the lathe (with its speed set low), the simplest way to determine whether there is dynamic balance in a system where all the components do not lie on a diameter is to draw a polygon of forces (see next figure).

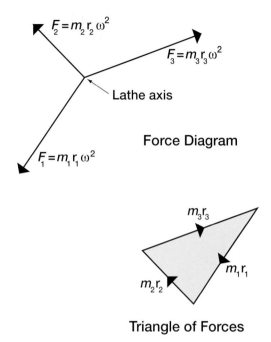

Force Diagram

Triangle of Forces

Figure 5.5 A polygon of forces.
The length of each arrow in the force diagram, *top left*, is proportional to one of the weights from figure 5.3 multiplied by the lathe speed squared multiplied by the weight's radial distance from the lathe axis. Each force arrow points in the direction of the radius from the lathe axis to the center of gravity of the weight. Because all the weights are revolving at the same speed there is no need to accurately calculate the force, the weight multiplied by the radius to its center of gravity will give arrows of the correct relative lengths.

The bottom diagram is equivalent to a polygon of forces. There is dynamic balance if the sides, here three, drawn in the correct directions and to the correct lengths, meet without gaps.

5.2 MOLDING AN EDGE

When profiling a face or edge, the workpiece is usually mounted with its axis of symmetry parallel to the lathe axis (figure 5.6).

In eccentric and multi-axis turning your tool's cutting edge may be cutting wood during only a fraction of each headstock-spindle rotation. This can lead to the back edge of each workpiece's outer surface splitting away if the lathe speed is low or the wood splintery. A second problem is that when *cutting* through wood your tool's cutting edge is supported, but when *cutting* air there is no support. And when just starting to *cut* wood after cutting air, the tool tip tends to be pulled down deeper into the wood. It helps to take fine cuts, minimize the clearance angle, and raise the lathe speed if this can be done safely. You should also, if practical, reduce the widths of the air gaps, either by increasing the number of workpieces (figure 5.7) and/or by introducing waste filler pieces.

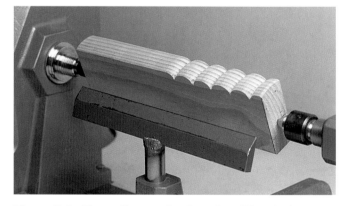

Figure 5.6 Rounding a single edge. The single turning-axis is here displaced about 3/4 in. (20 mm) from the workpiece's axis of symmetry.

You can produce a plain rounded edge or a more decorated longitudinal profile by this method. It is difficult to turn an accurate surface with this arrangement as during most of each headstock-spindle rotation your tool is cutting air. Turning against a background which contrasts with the workpiece will help you to see the core and the apparently-translucent outer parts of the workpiece.

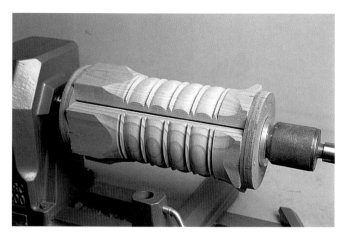

Figure 5.7 **Molding one face on four workpieces simultaneously.** Mounting four workpieces instead of one reduces the single large air gap to four short ones. This leads to truer turned surfaces and more efficient in-lathe sanding. Molding all the sides of a number of workpieces together in this way is called therming. In therming, when each workpiece face is being turned, that face's turning-axis is coaxial with the lathe axis.

5.3 THERMING

The turning of spindles to produce square cross sections with "flat" sides is called therming. The *Oxford English Dictionary* reveals that the term seems to be tortuously derived from the name of the Greek god Hermes, later called Mercury by the Romans. This son of Zeus and Maia was the messenger and herald of the gods, and the guide of travellers.[1] Usually portrayed as an athletic youth with a cap, winged sandals, and a staff, his statues were often mounted on pedestals which were square in cross section and tapered downwards from a large top to a small neck immediately above the base. Such pedestals, illustrated in figure 5.8, came to be called therms during the early 18th century. Square tapered legs, often with spade or Marlboro' feet, were sometimes described as themed,[2] although I suspect that the proportion of such legs which were thermed on a lathe was small.

The earliest major reference on therming is Bergeron's *Manuel du Tourneur*. Therming is well described in some German texts,[3] but is barely mentioned in English turning books.

Spindles with square cross sections are rarely hand turned now, but some rotating-knife automatic lathes can therm by varying the distance between the axis of the slowly-rotating workpiece and the parallel axis of the fast-rotating cutters with a rosette-and-rubber arrangement similar to that used in rose engines (page 152).

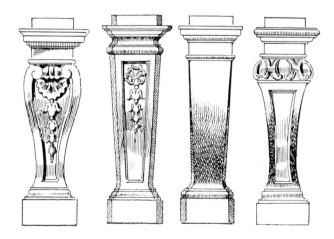

Figure 5.8 **Four therms** pictured by English architect James Gibbs (1682-1754).[4]

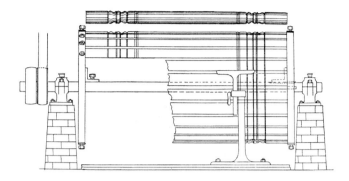

Figure 5.9 A 19th-century therming lathe.[5]
The square-cross-section workpieces were mounted
between and around the peripheries of two circular end
plates. These two end plates were rigidly connected by a
central spindle. They were also large, often about 6 feet
(1.8 m) in diameter, to reduce the convexity of the turned
faces.

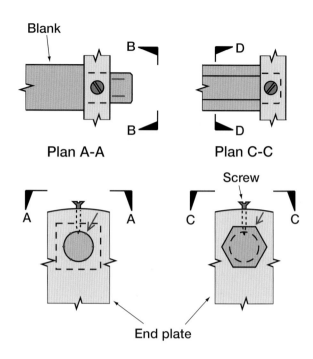

Elevation B-B   **Section D-D**

Figure 5.11 Indexing spindles is easy if you preturn a
circular mounting pin at each end of each spindle blank.[7]
These mounting pins are sized to house snugly in holes
drilled into or through the end plates. Before each
therming operation you rotate each spindle until you align
the next reference mark (colored magenta) pencilled on
the spindle or the next edge with the reference mark (also
magenta) on the end plate. You then lock each spindle
with the screw.

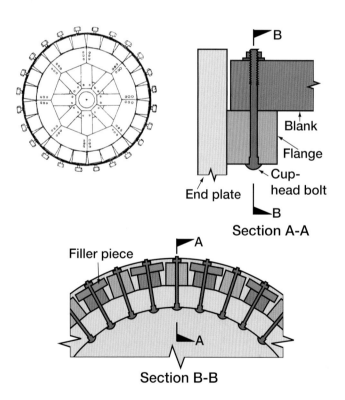

Figure 5.10 Fixing blanks for therming.[6] An end
plate of the lathe in the previous figure is shown top left. A
thick steel hoop is drilled and tapped so that blanks can
be screwed down against the end plate's periphery. *Top
right and bottom*, the blanks are bolted to a wooden
flange screwed and glued within each plate. The orange
temporary filler pieces are fixed to more-permanent
supports.

Figure 5.12 Mounting balusters prior to therming their second faces. Sigi Angerer of Luzern, Switzerland, has fixed short triangular spacers to both end plates to locate the ends of the balusters.

Sigi's has written on therming in "Angular Turning on the Lathe" which was translated by Alan Lacer and published in *American Woodturner* (Summer 1998), pp. 10-14.

Figure 5.13 Fixing the end of a baluster by screwing through an end plate. This is not the most secure method and requires the lathe speed to be kept low.

Figure 5.14 Therming the balusters' faces. Sigi Angerer is *cutting* not scraping to give a good off-the-tool surface. The *cutting* presentation also minimizes splitting away along the balusters' back edges.

If you therm on a lathe with a more typical inboard swing than Sigi's, the thermed faces will appear noticeably convex. Also the smaller the radius from the lathe axis to the turned faces, the larger the minimum-possible air gap between the outer faces of adjacent workpieces.

5.4 ANGULAR THERMING

Thermed spindles usually have four sides, but therming can be used to produce cross sections with any number of sides from two upwards. Two- and three-sided turnings were aptly christened angular in Sigi Angerer's article. The mounting of angular spindles is outlined in figure 5.15, and the therming of two-sided spindles is described in figures 5.16 to 5.18.

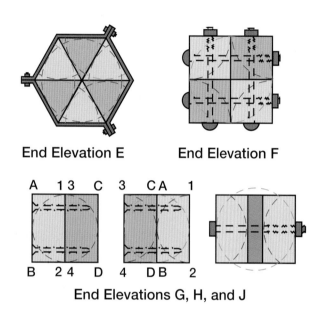

End Elevation E   **End Elevation F**

End Elevations G, H, and J

Figure 5.15 Mounting spindle blanks for angular therming. The blanks are first turned to produce the red faces, then the green, then the magenta. The lathe axis passes centrally through the assemblage for each turning operation.

The individual spindle blanks tend to be thrown outwards by the centrifugal force induced by the lathe's rotation. The blanks' ends must therefore be held securely; steel bolts, screws, or bands are most often used.[8]

End elevation **E**   The ends of the triangular-cross-section blanks are secured by three metal bands bolted together.

End elevation **F**   Each end of the assemblage is held together by four bolts. After the first turning operation (red), each blank is rotated 180° about its own axis of symmetry. The four blanks are then bolted together in the new configuration for the second turning operation.

End elevations **G** *and* **H**   After the first turning operation (**G**), the blanks are reassembled as in **H**. This therming is detailed in figures 5.16 to 5.18.

End elevation **J**   By sandwiching a filler piece (orange), the cross section of the two-sided angular spindle is made relatively narrower.

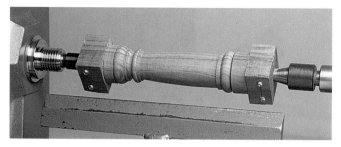

Figure 5.16 The first turning operation for two-sided angular therming completed. The blanks are screwed together as shown in figure 5.15, end elevation **G**. I am using a live cup tail center because it will hold the two workpieces together, unlike a tail center with a cone-shaped nose which will tend to wedge them apart.

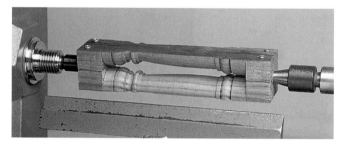

Figure 5.17 Ready to start the second turning operation. The blanks have been screwed together in the configuration shown in figure 5.15, end elevation **H**. When this combined workpiece is rotated the features turned during the first turning operation show clearly, making it easy to repeat the features in the second turning operation.

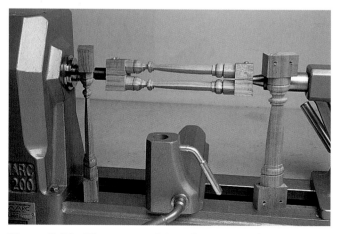

Figure 5.18 The second turning operation completed. The vertical spindles turned previously better illustrate the resulting angular spindles.

5.5 SKEWED THERMING

If you set up a drum of spindle blanks for conventional therming like that in figure 5.9, and then rotated one of the end plates say 20°, the blanks would then be "skewed" relative to the lathe axis. You could then therm the spindles in the usual way to produce sides which were slightly twisted, and had their design features running not square across the sides, but at an angle. I term this process skewed therming. An example is described in figures 5.19 and 5.20.

Although described in Bergeron's *Manuel du Tourneur* and Hugo Knoppe's *Meistertechniken der Drechslerkunst*, one of the few contemporary turners to have explored the technique is Frenchman Gerard Bidou.[9]

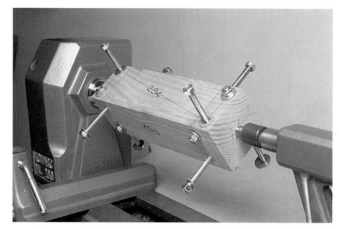

Figure 5.20 A four-sided mounting core, that used in the previous figure. Two rows of two holes are drilled through each end of the 4 in. x 4 in. (100 mm x 100 mm) core . The lengths of 3/8 in. (10 mm) diameter threaded rod can slide within the holes. Here the diagonal distance between two outside holes is 294 mm: between two inside holes the distance is 253 mm.

Two pairs of square-cross-section blanks (here 55 mm x 55 mm x 340 mm long) were used. The pair which will be held by the inner screwed rods has two 10 mm holes drilled 253 mm apart through from two adjacent faces. These blanks are then mounted on opposite sides of the core using the rods which slide within the inner holes through the core. The second pair of blanks has two pairs of holes 294 mm apart, and is mounted on the core using the outer rods.

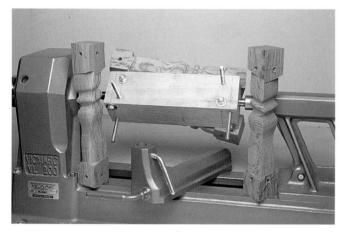

Figure 5.19 Skewed therming. The spindles to the left and right show the twisted faces produces by skewed therming.

Square-cross-section blanks were mounted on the mounting core detailed in the next figure. By reversing the skewing of the mounting the turned features can be angled the opposite way across the spindle faces. For example, if you wanted the features to join and change their direction of skewing at each edge you could go zig, zag, zig, zag like the spindle on the right. The skewing of the spindle on the left was changed only between the second and third turning operations; thus the features go zag, zag, zig, zig.

5.6   THERMED BOXES

This section illustrates the therming of items other than spindles by describing the turning of a batch of four three-sided boxes. The steps are outlined in figure 5.21, and detailed in figures 5.22 to 5.29.

Although not shown, you could mount a circle of blanks which are cantilevered from a faceplate. Then by turning using a process similar to cupchuck hollowing, you could therm concave faces instead of the usual convex.

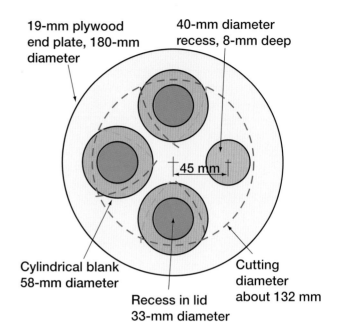

Figure 5.22   The design of the end plates and box cross sections. I did not want to make a large batch of boxes, and settled on four. The 45 mm radius chosen from the lathe axis to the axes of symmetry of the blanks ensured that the blanks were close together. The resulting periods when the tool was cutting air were thus relatively short, and not wide enough to make the turning at all difficult.

The cutting diameter is chosen to leave small edges of the cylindrical blank on the finished boxes, the resulting cross section was also large enough to accommodate the desired 33 mm diameter lid recess.

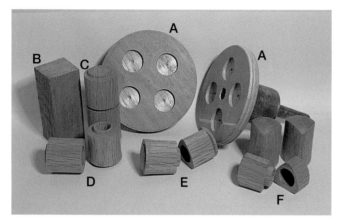

Figure 5.21   The box-therming process.

1. Design the boxes and end plates **A** (figure 5.22).

2. Turn four blanks like **B** to a cylinder **C** with a short spigot at each end. The spigots should be sized to fit neatly into the recesses in the end plates. The lengths of the four cylinders must be equal. Part each workpiece **C** into lid and base sections with a narrow parting-off tool.

3. Gripping the spigot of first the lid and then the base of each blank in a chuck, hollow the lid, turn the spigot on the base to a tight fit inside the lid, and hollow the base. Ensure that the net lengths of the four cylindrical boxes **D** are equal.

4. Turn the three side faces with the boxes gripped between the two end plates. After turning each face the boxes are indexed 120° to produce boxes **E**.

5. Hold each lid in turn by the spigot on its top. Finish-turn the top of each lid as far as possible, and then part it off.

6. Chuck each base in turn by the spigot on its bottom. Fit its correct lid, and finish-turn and sand the lid where it was parted off. Finish-turn as much as possible of the bottom of the base, and then part it off.

7. Reverse-chuck the bases by jamming their top spigots into a recess in waste wood. Finish-turn and sand the bottoms of the bases. In the photograph above the finished boxes are labelled **F**.

Figure 5.24 Cutting the box sides.
The left-hand end plate is screwed onto a small faceplate. The right-hand end plate is screwed onto a small metal plate which is drilled and tapped to screw onto the nose of a metal-spinning live center. You can locate a right-hand end plate with just your tail center's nose.

Figure 5.25 The therming "barrel".

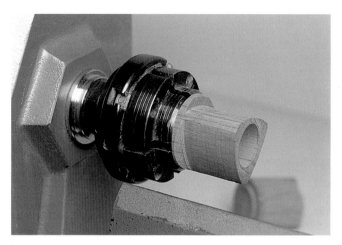

Figure 5.26 A lid held by the spigot at its top, ready for finish-turning as much of the top as possible.

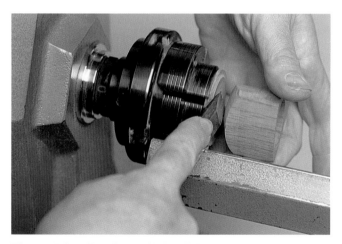

Figure 5.27 Parting off the lid after finish-turning as much as possible of its top. The stub left after parting off is turned off with the lid reverse chucked on the base (next figure).

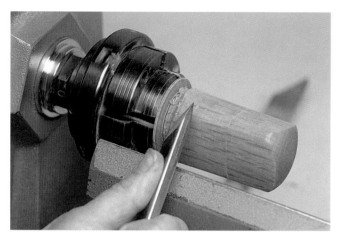

Figure 5.28 **Finish turning towards the bottom of the base.** The base is held by the spigot on its bottom. The lid was fitted and its top finish-turned and sanded before starting to finish-turn the bottom of the base.

5.7 INSIDE-OUT TURNING

Inside-out turning is vaguely related to therming, and is used to produce turnings with transverse through holes called windows (figure 5.30). You can create striking figurative associations by relating the subject(s) of the windows to the external form of the finished turning. The external form is usually left square in cross section or turned without detail in the region of a set of windows—the combination of much more detailed external forms in widow regions has yet to be explored.

The technique is straightforward (figures 5.31 to 5.38). It may be old, or may have been initiated in Canada by Stephen Hogbin, and travelled via Americans Albert LeCoff and Del Stubbs to English turner Tobias Kaye who developed and formalized it in late 1989.[10] American Mike Kehs has pushed the technique further by introducing asymmetrical windows (figure 5.39).[11]

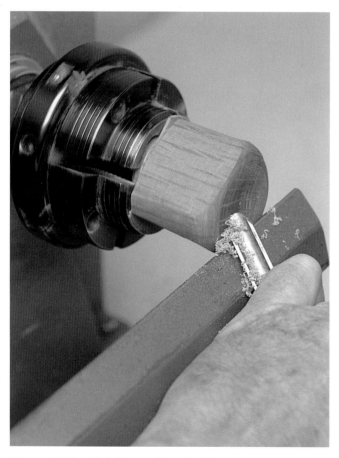

Figure 5.29 **Finish-turning the bottom of the base concave.** The spigot onto which the lid fits is held in a jam chuck, which is in turn here held in a Nova scroll chuck.

Figure 5.30 **An inside-out turning** with symmetrical windows.

The production of an inside-out turning with symmetrical windows requires two turning operations, T1 and T2, has five stages:

1. Prepare the design. The T2 turning of the outside affects the final silhouette of the windows, and this is discussed in figure 5.32.
2. Prepare the workpiece for the first turning operation T1. The workpiece may be assembled from four square-cross-section lengths, ideally cut from the same length of wood (figure 5.33). If starting from a single, large, square cross section, you can rip (saw along the grain) it into four square sections. An inferior alternative is to rip the large square into four later in stage 4. If you want the T2 workpiece to have a particular thickness, you need to allow for the wood thickness lost through sawing and any planing when sizing this large square workpiece. When assembling the T1 composite workpiece, orientate the annual or growth rings of the component squares so that the joints will be barely noticeable in the T2 turning. Note that each T1 component is axially rotated 180° before being reassembled into the T2 workpiece.
3. Turn the half windows (turning operation T1).
4. Disassemble or longitudinally saw the workpiece into four, and reassemble and glue the squares into the new configuration for the second turning operation T2.
5. Finish-turn the outside of the T2 composite workpiece.

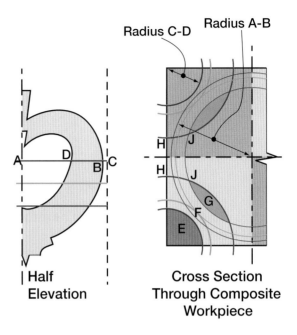

Figure 5.32 Window distortion. The wider you design a window in its T2 elevation, and the more you turn down the T2 workpiece in the region of that window, the greater the real width of that window is compared with its designed width.

An intended T2 elevation is shown on the left. Three horizontal cross sections will be taken through the red, green, and magenta planes.

On the right is a horizontal cross section through the T2 workpiece. The arcs **CD** with the thicker lines show the wood surfaces turned at the red, green, and magenta levels during the first, T1, turning operation. The arcs **AB** with the thinner lines show the wood surfaces turned in the second, T2, turning operation. The two sets of arcs show that:

1. At the level of the red plane no T2 turning is possible because the thick and thin red arcs do not overlap. After assembling the T2 workpiece there are only four outside corner columns **E**. By the time you have turned the square section at the level of the red plane just to a cylinder, the workpiece will have shattered.
2. At the level of the green plane, the situation is only marginally improved as the thick and thin arcs only touch.
3. At the level of the magenta plane, wood **G** is left after the second turning operation, but the window is wider (**J-J**) than designed in the simple T2 elevation (**H-H**).

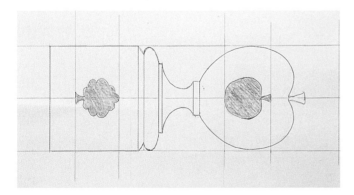

Figure 5.31 The design of an inside-out turning (that in the previous figure) in the form of the T2 elevation drawn on card. This drawing on card can be used as a template as shown in figure 5.35.

If a window will be in a flat face in the finished T2 turning, the window width on the drawn elevation will equal the width in the finished turning. If the window is in a turned surface in the finished turning, the drawn window width will be narrower than the actual. And as the next figure shows, it may be impossible to have a large window in a part of the final T2 turning which is to be turned to a relatively small diameter.

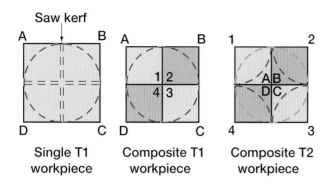

Single T1   Composite T1   Composite T2
workpiece   workpiece   workpiece

Figure 5.33 End elevations showing how the composite workpieces are assembled.

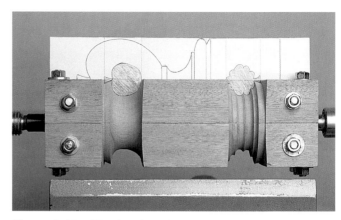

Figure 5.35 Monitoring the T1 window turning.
If the length of the T2 workpiece which will house a level of windows is to be left square, use the half-window template from the T2 elevation to monitor the shape and size of the window "cove". Monitor the cove by holding the half-window template along the center of a T1 face.

If the level of windows will lie in a section of the T2 workpiece which is to be turned, the half-window template will be, perhaps to a significant extent, too deep. You could do an accurate drawing of the required window profile based on figure 5.32, or just guesstimate how much shallower you need to turn the window coves.

Figure 5.34 A combined workpiece towards the end of the first turning operation. Here the four component square sections are bolted together with two staggered pairs of bolts at each end. You could also:

1. Glue the components together in extra waste left at their ends.
2. Mount the T1 and T2 workpieces in and between shallow, square, tapered recesses, akin to cupchucks.
3. Use strong straps or bands around the ends

Whichever mounting method(s) you use for the T1 and T2 workpieces, leave ample end waste, and ensure all components are exactly square so that you will be able to glue the T2 workpiece together without any gaps. The T1 workpiece must also be exactly centered or the half windows will not meet precisely in the T2 workpiece.

The T2 elevation drawn on the card has been folded along its center line. Waste has been cut away to leave two half-window silhouettes which are used to monitor the window profiles during the first turning operation.

Figure 5.37 **The T2 workpiece turned.** A spigot has been left at the right-hand end. This will enable the workpiece to be chucked so that the stalk and top of the apple can be finish-turned.

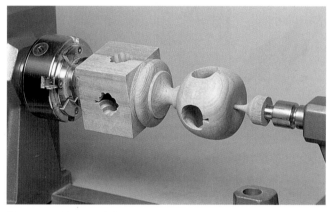

Figure 5.38 **Finish-turning the stalk and the top of the apple.** The spigot shown in the previous figure is here gripped in a scroll chuck. After the top of the apple has been finish-turned, the tail center will be retracted so that the stalk can also be finish-turned.

Figure 5.36 **A T2 composite workpiece being glued together.** The bolts which held the T1 workpiece together are here reused as temporary clamps. Compare the positions of the numbers and letters on the ends of the components with their configuration in figure 5.34.

5.8 ASYMMETRICAL INSIDE-OUT TURNING

The technique of inside-out turning can be extended by combining compatible components from different T1 composite workpieces to create asymmetrical windows as shown in figure 5.39. Different T1 and T2 workpieces can be further combined to create more-complicated effects as described in the article by Mike Kehs.[11]

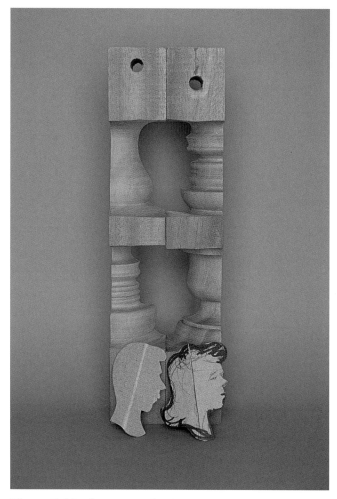

Figure 5.39 Asymmetrical windows. Half a T2 workpiece composed of one component from each of two different but complementary T1 workpiece components.

The two cardboard templates are folded in half longitudinally, each half being used to monitor the turning of a half window during the two T1 turning operations.

5.9 ENDNOTES

[1] *The Macmillan Encyclopedia* (London: Macmillan, 1983), p. 570.

[2] John Gloag, *A Short Dictionary of Furniture* (London: George Allen And Unwin, 1977), p. 338.

[3] Hugo Knoppe, *Meistertechniken der Drechslerkunst*, pp. 39–48; and von C.A. Martin, *Der Drechsler*, pp. 208–212.

[4] T.A. Strange, *English Furniture, Decoration, Woodwork, and Allied Arts* (London: McCorquodale and Company, 1950), p. 46.

[5] von C.A. Martin, *Der Drechsler*, p. 210.

[6] Knoppe, p. 40, figs 7 and 8.

[7] Knoppe, p. 40, fig 8.

[8] Knoppe, p. 40, figs 1, 2, 4 and 5.

[9] Gerard Bidou and Daniel Guilloux, *Woodturning in Fance*, pp. 177–183.

[10] Tobias Kaye, "Within Every Acorn an Oak Tree," *Woodturning* No. 11 (Nov/Dec 1992): pp. 38–41.

[11] Michael F. Kehs, "Turn Your Christmas "Inside Out,"" *American Woodturner* (September 1991): pp. 2–5.

Chapter Six

MULTI-AXIS TURNING

The turning described in this chapter has been called both multi-axis and multi-center. The number of different axes and centers involved in turning a multi-axis turning can make a description of the process confusing, but I hope to overcome this by using the compound noun *turning-axis* which I introduced at the start of chapter 4. Multi-axis turning could therefore be more accurately but less conveniently called multi-turning-axis turning.

In most turning the workpiece's axis of symmetry lies along the lathe axis: the workpiece's axis of symmetry is therefore its sole turning-axis. In multi-axis turning a workpiece is mounted and turned in succession on turning-axis 1, then on turning-axis 2, etc. The position of each turning-axis relative to the workpiece (and to the workpiece's other turning-axes) remains constant, although at each new mounting the positions of the turning-axes relative to the lathe axis alter.

Multi-axis turning may be forced upon you—section 3.10 showed that you may have to turn internally-stressed spindles on two or more turning-axes to overcome the increase in bowing during turning. There can be other purely functional reasons for multi-axis turning—some examples will be shown in this chapter. But in most cases, function, if there is any, is secondary or an excuse (figures 6.1 and 6.2), the desire to create special aesthetic effects being primary. The technique may also be used to create figurative turnings (figure 6.3).

Multi-axis turning is a long-established technique. In the last decade of the 20th century the technique's sculptural possibilities have come to the fore through the 1992 publication of Ray Hopper's *Multi-Centre Woodturning*, and the explorations of many turners including: Americans, Mark Sfirri and Stoney Lamar; Australian, John Wooller; Frenchmen, Jean-Francis Escoulen and Gerard Bidou; German, Hans Joachim Weissflog; and New Zealander, Peter Battensby.

In multi-axis turning you have an infinite number of choices for positioning turning-axes. You can:

1. Have all a workpiece's turning-axes parallel. Within this:
    a. A turning-axis can lie wholly or partially within or outside the workpiece.
    b. All the turning-axes can lie within one plane, or not.
    c. Between the turning operations or after all the turning is finished, the form of the workpiece may be altered, for example by dividing and reassembling it, or by carving.
2. Have some or all of the turning-axes not parallel to one another. The above choices a to c are again available.

But there is no grand, linear design theory for multi-axis turning. Instead there are many distinct but related ways that you can apply the technique. You can combine different ways, but too much technical complexity can reduce aesthetic clarity and impact.

You can design effectively on paper when all the turning axes lie in one plane. When they lie in different planes you may be able to draw cross sections along an axis; otherwise you would need to be an expert in three-dimensional computer-aided design. Sections 6.2 to 6.5 introduce a variety of applications through examples.

Figure 6.1 **A mirror and console by Mark Sfirri.**

The optimum sequence in which you mount a workpiece on its different turning-axes can be obvious; or may be dictated by the design, by efficiency, or by other factors. Sometimes the optimum sequence may not become apparent until you have started turning. The optimum sequence is interconnected with how you mount the workpiece to turn it about each turning-axis. Most multi-axis turning is done between centers, but turning-axes can lie wholly or partially outside a workpiece or emerge from an end too close to the edge to safely locate a center. Special chucking is then required, and is described in section 6.1 and later. The multi-axis technique can also be applied to disk-like and cantilevered workpieces.

Multi-axis turning sometimes involves an additional requirement, introduced in the previous chapter, that when the turning-axis lies within the workpiece, the workpiece's design might dictate that you must not continue to turn particular sections until their peripheries become circular.

In much multi-axis turning your tool will not be cutting wood continuously. For part or parts of each workpiece rotation or revolution your tool may be "cutting" air. When cutting wood you have to thrust. You cannot stop thrusting when cutting air, and your tool will then tend to move forwards. As your tool enters wood again, it will be pushed backwards. These involuntary tool movements adversely affect the off-the-tool surface. You can shorten the durations in which your tool is cutting air by:

1. Using a high, but still safe, lathe speed.
2. Mounting multiple workpieces rather than a single one.
3. Using filler pieces.
4. Gluing or fixing temporary waste onto the workpiece(s).

These actions also make sanding safer and more efficient.

When the periphery of a particular cross section varies greatly in radius, it is worthwhile to use a contrasting background to make the various parts easier to see.

Figure 6.2 **A bench commissioned from Mark Sfirri by Yale University.**

Figure 6.3 **Glancing figures by Mark Sfirri**, 4 to 6 feet (1200 to 1800 mm) high, and turned on four turning-axes with a little hand carving around the heads.

6.1 CHUCKS FOR MULTI-AXIS TURNING

You may be able to mount a workpiece safely between your usual drive and tail centers when the turning-axis lies wholly within the workpiece. But the greater the displacement between the axis of symmetry and a turning-axis, the higher the centrifugal forces generated by the revolving workpiece, and the greater the need for a lowered lathe speed, counterweighting, and special chucking.

Where the turning-axes are parallel to the workpiece's axis of symmetry, ornamental-turners often use the basic eccentric chuck (figure 6.4). When at least one of the turning-axes is not parallel to the workpiece's axis of symmetry, the chuck in figure 6.5 provides the necessary facility. These chucks must not be rotated at high speed. Figures 6.6 to 6.10 show less elaborate chucks. You can of course make your own chucks, and some will be shown in later sections of this chapter.

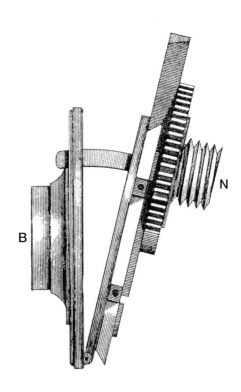

Figure 6.5 A tilting accessory pictured in Hamelin-Bergeron plate XXXVII. Its internally-threaded boss **B** could be screwed onto a headstock spindle nose or onto the nose of an eccentric chuck similar to that shown in the previous figure. The chuck or faceplate which held the workpiece was screwed onto nose **N**.

Figure 6.4 An ornamental-turning eccentric chuck pictured in figure 162 of *Ornamental Turning* by J.H. Evans.[1]

The workpiece is fixed to a faceplate or chuck which is in turn screwed onto nose **N**. The lateral eccentricity is varied using screw **S**. New turning-axes can brought coaxial with the lathe axis by rotating the workpiece relative to the chuck by using tangent screw **T**.

Figure 6.6 The Latalex eccentric chuck accessory has a radially-adjustable screw. The accessory has a circular recess in its rear face into which the jaws of a Nova scroll chuck can be expanded to grip.

Figure 6.7 **The Robert Sorby RS60 eccentric chuck.** This chuck provides a screwchuck and a small faceplate, the maximum eccentricity of each being 35 mm. The left-hand end of a spindle can be both offset and tilted by up to 20°. Workpieces can also be indexed.

Figure 6.9 **A prototype eccentric chuck by Kelton Industries** of New Zealand. The counterweights mounted on the rear of this heavy chuck can be revolved until dynamic balance is achieved. They are then locked in position.

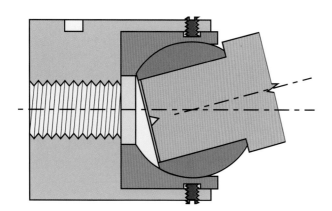

Figure 6.8 **A ball-and-socket chuck** developed by Jean-Francois Escoulen, and now commercially available.[2]

Figure 6.10 Gripping eccentrically with a scroll chuck.

If you feed the jaws of a scroll chuck into the chuck not in the proper order they will not be concentric. With a three-jaw scroll chuck, pictured here, all jaws will grip a circular cross-section; with four-jaw scroll chucks, usually only three jaws will grip.

An independent-jaw chuck can also be used to hold workpieces eccentrically.

Figure 6.11 Gerard Bidou with his eccentric chuck. This chuck allows offsets of up to 100 mm, and features sliding counterweights and indexing. The workpiece shown has been turned on five parallel turning-axes lying in one plane.

Photograph by Daniel Guilloux and previously shown on page 180 of *Woodturning in France*.

6.2 EXAMPLES WITH PARALLEL TURNING-AXES IN THE SAME PLANE

This most used multi-axis technique is demonstrated through examples each turned on two turning-axes:

1. Three chucking procedures are shown being used to turn two ducks and a stork. These examples were prompted by a duck pictured on page 131 of Gottfried Bockelmann's excellent book *Handbuch Drechseln*.
2. A leg with a club foot.

6.2.1 DUCKS AND STORKS

Figures 6.12 to 6.22 show three related methods that you might care to have a quack at. In all three the workpiece is mounted first on the body turning-axis A-A, then on the neck-and-head turning-axis B-B.

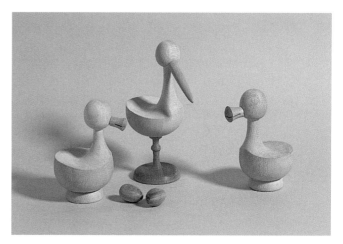

Figure 6.12 Two ducks and a stork. Their beaks are turned separately from mulberry wood. Each bird is turned on two parallel axes as explained in the next figure.

There are several chucking options. This section shows using both a proprietary chuck and a homemade wooden chuck.

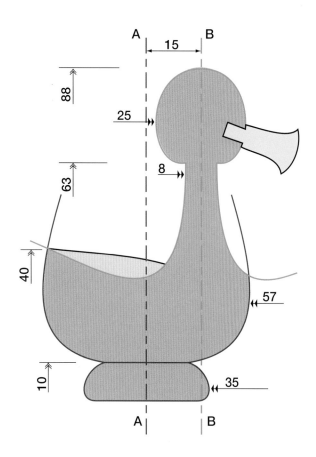

Figure 6.13 Duck section showing turning-axes.
The dimensions are in millimeters. The profile turned on
turning-axis **A-A** is outlined in red, that turned on turning-
axis **B-B** is outlined in green.

Here the head is turned with the top of the body. The
head can also be turned separately and glued onto a pin
turned at the top of the neck. In the first case the beak
has to be turned and carved separately and glued into a
drilled hole in the head. If the head is separate, the beak
can be integral with it, or be turned separately.

After any preliminary turning and drilling, the
workpiece is mounted on turning-axis **A-A** first because:

1. If you first turn the birds between centers on axis **B-B**,
    you will not be able to turn the top of the head
    because of the need to retain substantial waste to
    then turn the workpiece between centers on **A-A**.
2. You could not use a screwchuck to mount the body
    on turning-axis **B-B** because the pilot hole would mar
    the appearance of the finished bird. Also the blank
    would need to be mounted eccentrically to drill the
    pilot hole along **B-B** in the lathe—a tricky operation.
3. If you decide to drill a pilot hole along **A-A** in the lathe,
    it is more efficient to turn the body at the same time.

METHOD ONE

This method uses a simple homemade eccentric chuck and
explains the best way to position your toolrest and present
your gouge.

**Figure 6.14 Turning the duck body and feet on
turning-axis A-A.** The pad at the right-hand end of the
workpiece needs to be sized to fit neatly into the
eccentric recess in the plywood eccentric chuck shown in
the next figure.

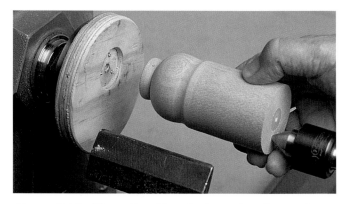

**Figure 6.15 Mounting the duck on turning-axis
B-B.** Three screw tips project from the bottom of the
eccentric recess to grip the underside of the duck's foot
pad.

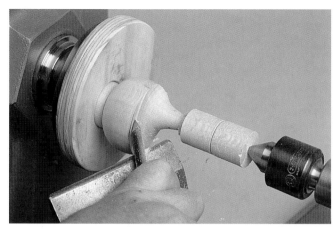

Figure 6.16 Turning the duck's upper body and neck on turning-axis B-B. I have positioned the toolrest so that I can present my detail gouge steeply, and thus *cut* with a large side rake and little clearance. A curved toolrest would be even better provided its top member was narrow so that the gouge could still be presented steeply. Even with these precautions it is difficult to avoid noticeable unevenness on the top of the body. If you were doing a batch of ducks it would be worth sharpening a gouge with a convex bevel or with a microbevel with a slightly coarser sharpening angle than that at which the full bevel is ground to enable the edge to be presented almost without clearance.

Less-cohesive woods may splinter away along the far side of the body. To overcome this you could turn the top of the body first about **B-B**, then turn the lower part of the body about **A-A**, then turn the neck and head about **B-B**.

METHOD TWO

Here an eccentric screwchuck is used to mount the workpiece to turn it on turning-axis **B-B**.

Figure 6.18 Boring a duck body after turning its bottom part on A-A. The hole will used to mount the body on an eccentric screwchuck along turning-axis **B-B**.

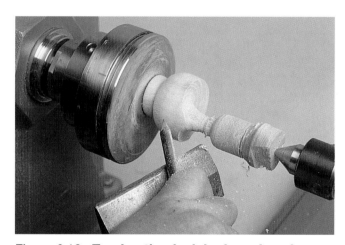

Figure 6.19 Turning the duck body and neck about B-B with the workpiece mounted on an eccentric screwchuck, here a Robert Sorby RS60. You could also simply screw through an off-center hole in a wooden plate which you then screw onto a standard faceplate.

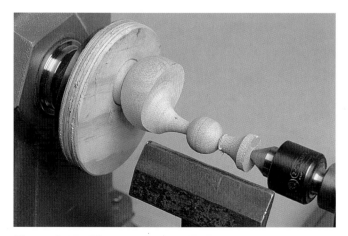

Figure 6.17 The turning on B-B almost finished. The top of the duck's head will have to be hand finished after the projecting waste is sawn off.

METHOD THREE

Again an eccentric screwchuck is used to chuck the body to turn it about axis **B-B**, but a concave supplementary backing plate is needed to retain the convex-bottomed workpiece in alignment.

Figure 6.20   Turning and boring a stork body mounted along turning-axis A-A. Because the feet are shallow and the legs slender, they are turned separately, with a pin which is later glued into the screw chuck's pilot hole being drilled here.

Figure 6.21   Mounting the stork body along turning-axis B-B using a Sorby RS60 eccentric chuck. A small concave backing plate has been first screwed onto the screwchuck to support the workpiece.

Figure 6.22   Turning on turning-axis B-B.

6.2.2   CORNER LEG WITH CLUB FOOT

Stretch the neck of one of the ducks just described and you almost have a leg with a club foot and a pad. Such legs are still needed by antique-furniture restorers and reproduction-furniture makers. Although the turning-axes (usually two) always lie in one plane, they are not necessarily parallel as in this example.[3]

On a long piece of furniture any intermediate club feet usually point forwards, while the corner feet point diagonally outwards (figure 6.23). Figure 6.24 shows the design of a corner leg. Making the leg is described in figures 6.25 to 6.28.

Figure 6.23   A whip and crop stand with diagonal club feet at each corner.[4] The ideal bedroom accessory for the friskier woodturner. Excluding the projections of the feet, the overall dimensions are: 1025 mm high, 350 mm wide, and 350 mm deep.

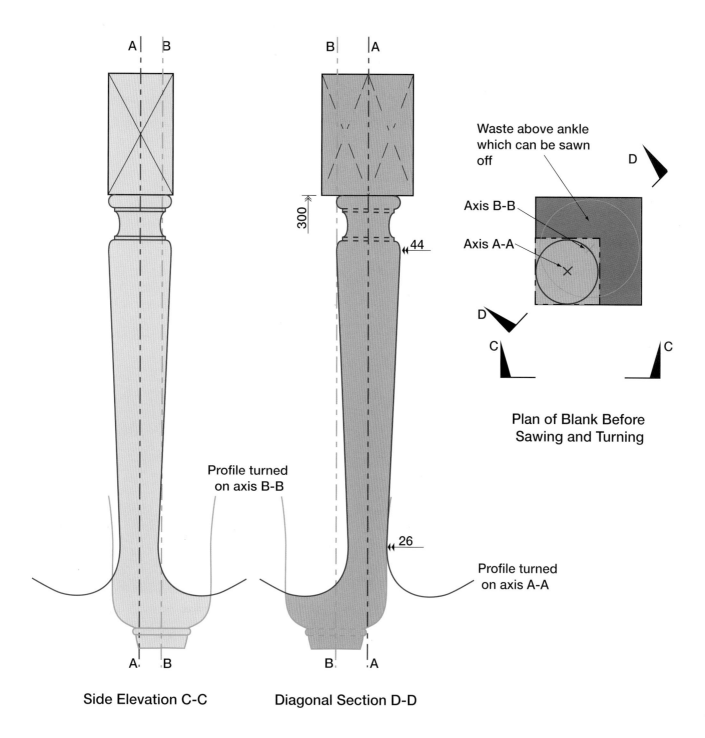

Waste above ankle
which can be sawn
off

Axis B-B

Axis A-A

Plan of Blank Before
Sawing and Turning

Profile turned
on axis B-B

Profile turned
on axis A-A

Side Elevation C-C

Diagonal Section D-D

Figure 6.24 Leg design showing turning-axes. To the left is a side elevation, to the right a diagonal section. To design a diagonal leg, draw the diagonal section to decide upon the junction between the profiles cut on the two turning-axes. The side elevation is used to determine the minimum size of the square blank required (the size can also be found by calculation or by drawing the plan).

You would only need to draw a side elevation for an interior leg with a forwards-pointing club foot.

Club foot turning is sometimes called cabriole-leg turning—inaccurately because all the shaping above the ankles of cabriole legs is done by bandsawing and carving. The word *cabriole* is derived from the 16th-century French term meaning a leap like that of a goat, and is now also the name for a ballet step in which, paradoxically, the dancer's legs are kept straight. The furniture term cabriole leg displaced the term bandy leg late in the 19th-century: it is properly applied to a leg which has a convex upper part and a concave lower part because of such a leg's supposed resemblance to the shape of the front leg of a leaping quadruped.

The starting blank for a corner leg is ideally square in cross section. This makes it easier to saw off most of the waste above the ankle. This upper waste shaded is red in the plan in the previous figure. Figures 6.25 and 6.26 show the sawing; figures 6.27 and 6.28 show the turning.

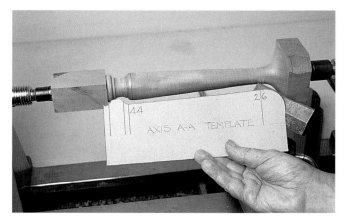

Figure 6.27 **Checking the turning on turning-axis A-A with a template.** The leg has been calipered at the two points shown, and these and the corner of the pommel provide the references which allow accurate monitoring with the template. Monitoring with a template is worthwhile, especially if you are only doing a small number of legs and want them to match.

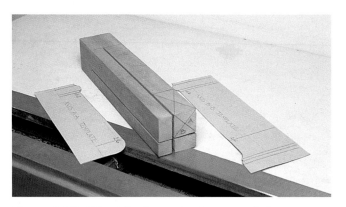

Figure 6.25 **The blank marked out and the waste partially sawn free.** Two cardboard templates are shown which are used to ensure that the legs are all turned to match.

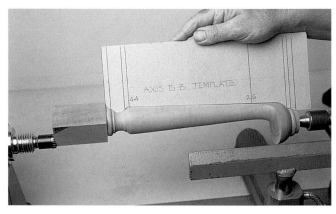

Figure 6.28 **Checking the turning of the underside of the foot** on turning-axis **B-B** with the second template.

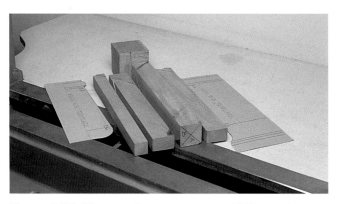

Figure 6.26 **The waste sawn away.** All the waste below the pommel could be turned off with the blank mounted on turning-axis **A-A**, but sawing the waste off is usually quicker and leaves it in usable sizes.

6.3 EXAMPLES WITH PARALLEL TURNING-AXES NOT IN THE SAME PLANE

The possibilities for turning on multiple parallel turning-axes which are not in the same plane are illustrated by four examples:

1. A column of eccentric disks turned between centers.
2. A cantilevered column of eccentric disks.
3. A lattice of eccentric rings.
4. A Saueracker shell.

6.3.1 ECCENTRIC DISKS

Spirals (or helixes) of eccentric disks are sometimes used as a quirky stems or columns by ornamental-turners:[5] they can also be turned by hand (figures 6.29 to 6.36). If the disks' turning-axes are relatively close to the axis of symmetry of the cylindrical blank there will be a continuous core which will permit turning between centers (figure 6.31). If the turning axes are relatively far from the axis of symmetry, the workpiece has to be cantilevered (figures 6.35 and 6.36).

Although not illustrated, you can extend the concept of the spiral by turning convex or concave profiles on the disks instead of the straight profiles shown. You could also vary the disk thicknesses and turn them on less-regularly positioned and sometimes nonparallel turning-axes.

Figure 6.30 **The eight turning-axes** are marked and punched on the ends of a cylindrical workpiece of 60 mm diameter. The parallel turning-axes are equally spaced around a circle of 9 mm radius.

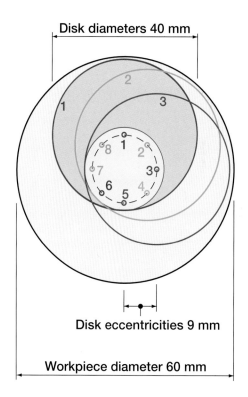

Figure 6.31 **The design of the eccentric disks.**
Only three disks are drawn to avoid confusion. The blue circle is the uninterrupted core of wood running through the helix which resists the force applied by the drive and tail centers. The eight turning-axes lie on the dashed circle within the blue circle .

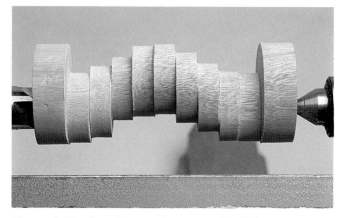

Figure 6.29 **A column of eccentric disks** turned on the eight parallel turning-axes shown in the next figure.

Figure 6.32 **Turning the center of the eccentric disk about turning-axis 7-7.** The wood, camphor laurel, is a softish hardwood, and would therefore tear on the endgrain if I used a parting tool. The discontinuous left- and right-hand faces of the disk also make a straight cut in with any tool difficult. I therefore cut the center to diameter first using a parting-off tool. I then cut the left- and right-hand sides of the disk as shown in the next two figures.

Figure 6.33 **Cutting the left-hand side of the disk with a parting-off tool.** The tool handle is held low so that the edge is *cutting* not scraping.

Figure 6.34 **Cutting the right-hand side of the disk**, again with a parting-off tool. The final stage is to clean up the periphery of the disk with a standard parting tool or a narrow skew.

6.3.2   CANTILEVERED ECCENTRIC DISKS

When the eccentricity of a helix of disks is too great for them to be turned between centers, the workpiece has to be cantilevered. Figure 6.35 illustrates the theory, figure 6.36 its realization.

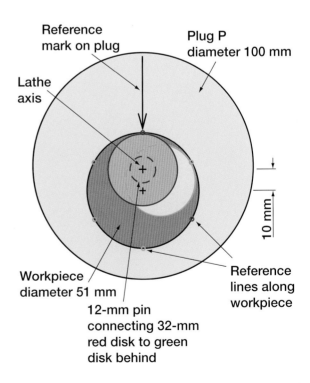

Figure 6.35 **Looking from the tailstock in the next figure.** The 51 mm hole through the plug is drilled 10 mm off center through the plug.

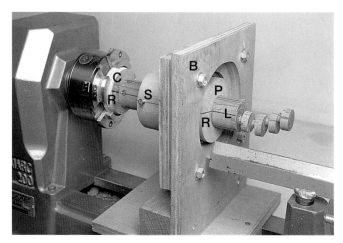

Figure 6.36 Turning eccentric disks with the workpiece cantilevering through an eccentric steady. This arrangement is similar to that pictured in plate XXXVIII of Hamelin-Bergeron.

The disks are connected by thin pins and could not therefore be turned between centers. To position and maintain the turning-axis for each disk coaxial with the lathe axis the cylindrical workpiece has to be held eccentrically. To achieve this:

1.   A split plywood collar **C** with an eccentric through-hole is located between the scroll-chuck jaws and the workpiece.
2.   A wooden plug **P** with a slight taper is wedged inside the inner race of the ball bearing housed in the boring collar **B**. An eccentric hole is drilled through the plug, and the workpiece is turned to be a very snug fit within that hole.
3.   A reference line **L** for each disk is drawn along the outside of the workpiece. Before turning each fresh disk the workpiece has to be indexed round within the collar **C** and the plug **P** so that the line **L** aligns with the appropriate reference marks **R** on the plug and collar. Screw **S** is then tightened to prevent the workpiece slipping within the hole through the plug.

6.3.3 LATTICE RINGS

Lattice rings are one of the classic exercises.[6] Among contemporary turners David Springett has written about the technique,[7] and Joachim Weissflog has used the technique in three- rather than the traditional two-dimensional pieces. An unlimited number of patterns are possible with two-dimensional clusters: a simple example is detailed in figures 6.37 and 6.38. John Wooller has taken the technique further (figure 6.39).

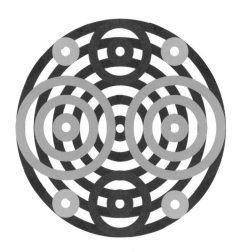

Figure 6.37 The design of the lattice rings shown being turned in the next figure.

Patterns of lattice rings are tricky to design. Ensure that:

1.   There are no long lengths of unsupported rib—they fracture too easily.
2.   All rings are integrated, and will not fall free because they are not joined to rings on the other face.
3.   All or almost all of the waste can be turned off—you don't want to have to carve much waste off.

The stages in turning this and other combinations of lattice rings are:

1.   Prepare the workpiece by bringing it to the finished thickness. Neatly bandsaw the periphery if non-circular, or turn it if circular.
2.   Drill a hole through the center of each nest of rings. The diameter of the holes should equal the clear distance between two adjacent rings. The holes must be exactly positioned and square to the faces of the workpiece.
3.   Mount a disk of scrap on a faceplate. True and flatten the disk's front face. The workpiece will be screwed onto this waste disk in various positions, each position centering the exact center of a nest of rings about the lathe axis. The best screws to use are conventional woodscrews. Choose the screws' gauge so that the cylindrical section next to the head fits neatly through the holes drilled through the workpiece. Use several screws to hold the workpiece, and do not force them or you can fracture ribs. You may need to file the screw heads to a smaller diameter to prevent them fouling your tools.
4.   Turn the red rings first working from inside to outside. Reverse the workpiece. The front rings were turned in the order: green, magenta, pale blue. Only the dark-blue areas have to be carved off at the end.

Figure 6.38 Turning lattice rings. The ribs here are 5 mm wide and thick, but in suitable woods they could be much thinner.

The wood I used was Tasmanian blackwood, a quality cabinetmaking timber rather than one suited to ornamental-turning . To avoid tear-out I have cut halfway down the sides of the ribs using pointing cuts with a 1/4 in. (6 mm) bowl gouge sharpened like a spindle gouge. The gouge is presented horizontally, at lathe-axis height, and with the flute pointing horizontally. For harder woods use single V-cuts at lathe-axis height with a skew's long point to define the rings and lessen the possibility of tear-out.

The sides and bottom of the grooves were cut with a scraper with a central tooth. To use the shoulders as depth stops is not as satisfactory as you may imagine, but rounding the top edges of the shoulders will minimize damage to the tops of the ribs if you do lose concentration or control.

Although the turning is not difficult, it and your drilling must be precise for the result to stand up to the intense examination which it will receive.

Figure 6.39 Two pieces by John Wooller of Melbourne.[8] The top piece is, like lattice rings, turned on several far-apart turning-axes. The bottom piece more closely recalls its heritage.

6.3.4   A SAUERACKER SHELL

J.E.H. Saueracker was an outstanding ornamental-turner. He died in 1942, aged 87, and during his lifetime donated much of his work to his home city of Nuremberg. These marvellous pieces seem to have been destroyed during WWII, but at least a pictorial record remains.[9] Hugo Knoppe has also described some of Saueracker's techniques in *Meistertechniken der Drechslerkunst*, and includes the shell on pages 54 to 55.

The design and turning of the shell in figure 6.40 is straightforward, and is described in figures 6.41 to 6.47. It requires the workpiece to be turned on a large number of different, but parallel turning-axes. The chucking and indexing arrangement shown is not the only one possible, but is perhaps the most convenient.

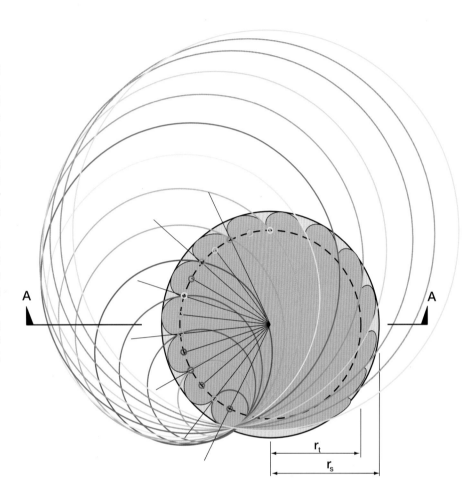

Figure 6.40   **A Saueracker shell bandsawn and ready for final carving.**

The shell's ribs were produced by turning a series of approximately-vee-shaped grooves into the top face of a disk-shaped workpiece. Each groove is turned with the workpiece mounted so that the corresponding turning-axis is coaxial with the lathe axis. This shell was turned on eleven different turning-axes which were parallel but not in the same plane. The shell's design is shown in the next figure.

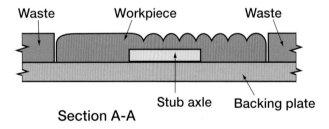

Figure 6.41   **A Saueracker shell's design.**

The first and smallest vee groove is represented by the small red circle. It has a radius r_1 which is about a sixth of r_s, the radius of the whole shell. The fewer ribs you want on your shell, the larger r_1 needs to be as a proportion of r_s. Radius r_t, the radius to the circle on which all the turning-axes lie is r_s–r_1, about $5r_s/6$.

The turning-axes are in the centers of the tiny circles, and are spaced around the black-dashed circle of radius r_t. Each turning-axis is perpendicular to the page, and a straight-line distance r_1 from its neighbor(s). The turning-axes and the circles representing the grooves turned about them are correspondingly colored.

Figure 6.42 The workpiece in preparation. It has been preturned to a radius of 80 mm, a third greater than the minimum value of r_s specified in the previous figure. The finished thickness is 18 mm.

The marking-out consists of:

1. The larger circle of radius r_t (here 50 mm).
2. The smaller circle of radius r_1 (12.5 mm) drawn with its center on the larger circle.
3. Two diametrical lines passing through the center of the workpiece. One passes through the center of the small circle (the turning-axis for the first vee groove). Where this diameter meets the nearside edge of the disk is marked **1**. The other diameter passes through the lower intersection of the large and small circles which is the turning-axis for the second vee groove (the smallest green circle in the previous figure). Where this diameter meets the nearside edge of the disk is marked **2**.
4. A series of marks, one for every vee groove, is continued clockwise around the nearside edge of the workpiece using dividers and a pencil. The distance between successive marks is equal to that between marks **1** and **2**. The distance between these marks is related to the distance between adjacent turning-axes, and is used to index the workpiece to bring successive turning-axes coaxial with the lathe axis.

Figure 6.43 A 7 mm deep recess of radius r_t (50 mm) has been turned in the workpiece pictured in the previous figure. As shown in the next figure, this recess fits over and rotates about a stub axle.

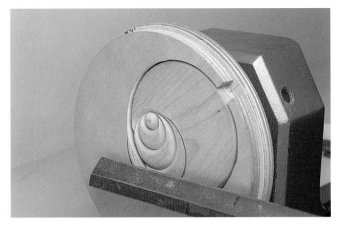

Figure 6.45 **Vee groove 4 just started.** Through the slot in the waste disk the number **4** indexing mark on the workpiece has been aligned with the radial reference line on the backing plate.

Figure 6.44 **The chucking arrangement.**

A large plywood backing plate **B** is here mounted on an outboard faceplate.   A waste disk **W** about 2 1/4 times the diameter of the shell is mounted onto the backing plate. The waste disk is the same thickness as the workpiece, and has a circular area cut out within which the workpiece can be indexed (rotated by the preset amounts). A narrow slot **C** is cut through the waste disk. This enables the numbered indexing marks shown in figures 6.42 and 6.43 to be seen, and in turn aligned with the reference line drawn on the backing plate through slot **C**. This line is projected from the lathe axis through the center of the stub axle. Two screws **S**, used to hold the workpiece, pass through the backing plate, and if necessary through the outboard faceplate.

In the center of the cutout area a 6 mm thick plywood disk which acts as stub axle **A** is fixed. The lathe axis runs past the edge of the stub axle.

Before starting to turn, I indexed the workpiece around on the stub axle by successively aligning the indexing marks on the edge of the workpiece with the reference line in the slot. At each alignment I pushed the screws **S** in sufficiently to mark where to drill pilot holes for the screws. I then drilled all the pilot holes in the back of the workpiece.

To start turning the ribs, hold the workpiece over the stub axle, align indexing mark **1** with the reference mark in the slot, tighten the two screws **S** to clamp the workpiece in place, and turn the first vee groove. You then repeat the process for each vee groove and indexing mark in the series. How to best turn a vee groove is detailed in figure 6.47.

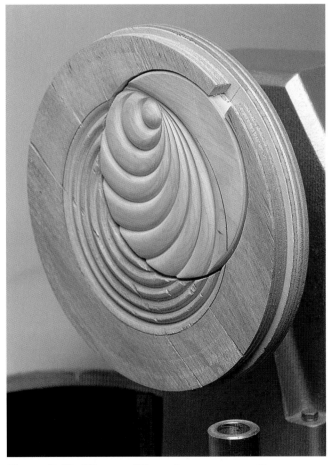

Figure 6.46 **The position of vee groove 9 pencilled onto the front face of the waste disk and the workpiece.** Again the indexing reference number is visible through the slot.

Figure 6.47 Turning a vee groove. Here I am using a 6 mm bowl gouge sharpened with a ladyfinger nose which is a little longer in proportion than usual. This sharpening allows the tool to cut a groove with a tight vee in the bottom.

There are five stages in turning a vee groove:

1. Undo the two screws **S**, rotate the workpiece until the next indexing mark on the workpiece edge aligns with the reference line, and tighten screws **S**.
2. Mark the position of the center of the vee groove lightly with a pencil. Stop the lathe and check that the pencilled circle is just tangential to the bottom of the first vee groove of radius r_1. If necessary repencil the circle.
3. V-cut on the pencil circle with a skew's long point. The long point must first contact the waste and workpiece at lathe-axis height to minimize any possibility of the skew skating sideways.
4. Deepen, widen, and profile the groove with a small, stiff, detail gouge. Take care not to cut away any of the small dome produced by cutting the first vee groove.
5. Remove the toolrest and sand the groove.

After turning all the vee grooves, remove the workpiece from the chuck. Finally, sketch the convex ends of the ribs; and bandsaw, carve, and sand them. The shell is then ready for polishing.

6.4 EXAMPLES WITH NON-PARALLEL TURNING-AXES IN THE SAME PLANE

To illustrate the methods used, I shall discuss turning:

1. An oval-cross-section tool handle turned on three nonparallel turning-axes lying in the same plane.
2. Chair backs turned on two nonparallel turning axes lying in the same plane.
3. A spoon.

6.4.1 A TOOL HANDLE

Figures 6.48 to 6.51 show how to turn a handle of oval cross section. The cross section of the handle trends from oval at its headstock end to circular at its tailstock end.

Figure 6.48 The finished handle. I neither sand nor polish tool handles. The off-the-tool surface feels pleasing, gives a better grip, and develops an attractive patina with use.

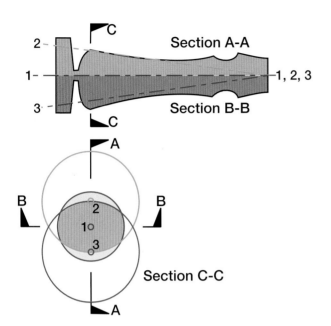

Figure 6.50 **The workpiece turned on axis 1-1** to a circular cross section. If you wanted to fit a ferrule, you would turn the right-hand end only on axis **1-1**.[10]

Figure 6.49 **The tool handle's design.** Turning on the three turning-axes creates a roughly-elliptical cross section at the left-hand end. As the turning-axes converge towards the right, the handle's cross section becomes nearer to a circle.

The turning method is:

1. After marking and punching the centers, the blank is roughed to a cylinder before being turned to the red circular profile. Do not reduce the left-hand waste's diameter, leave it fairly long, and leave the pin joining the waste to the handle fairly thick.
2. Locate the drive center's center pin into punched hole **2** or **3** in the left-hand end of the workpiece, and turn one facet on the long part of the handle.
3. Repeat step 2 about the other eccentric turning-axis.
4. Remount the workpiece on turning-axis **1-1** and part off.

You could bore the hole for the tool tang before starting to turn, after roughing to a cylinder, after turning the profile on turning axis **1-1**, or at the end.

Figure 6.51 **Turning on turning-axis 3-3.**
To part off at the left-hand end of the handle the workpiece needs to be relocated on turning-axis **1-1**.

6.4.2 CHAIR BACK UPRIGHTS

Some chair back uprights are straight and turned on one turning-axis. From the 17th century, back uprights turned on two or more axes became more common. This enabled more-comfortable chairs to be produced, but made turning the uprights more difficult. Two of many similar chucking and steadying solutions are shown in figure 6.52. They overcome the slenderness problems by:

1. Rigidly fixing the headstock end of the workpiece to a faceplate or similar.
2. Increasing the effective stiffness of the left-hand section of the workpiece.
3. Allowing a steady to be mounted at the left-hand end of the section being turned.

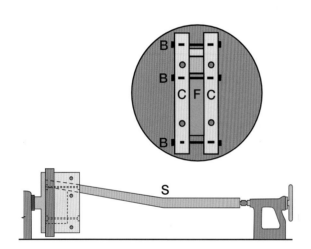

Figure 6.52 Chucks for cranked chair uprights.
In the top drawings[11] the leg is rigidly clamped between two cheeks **C** using bolts **B**. A filler piece **F** ensures consistent positioning for a batch of uprights. It may be worthwhile mounting a steady at **S**.

The long chuck, *bottom*,[12] greatly increases the effective stiffness of the left-hand half of the upright. How the upright is rigidly fixed into the chuck will depend on the upright's design. The steel collar on the right could be extended so that a steady could be mounted around it.

6.4.3 SPOONS

A slow and wasteful way to make a caddy, salt, or other spoon would be to turn a bowl with a small central hollow and a wide rim, bandsaw off most of the rim except for a radial strip which becomes the spoon's handle, and complete by hand finishing. The method shown below in figures 6.53 to 6.55 is only one of several variations which are far more efficient.[13] It involves turning the workpiece on two turning-axes almost at right angles in the same plane.

Figure 6.53 Four salt spoons, 4 in. (100 mm) long, turned on two axes in the same plane.

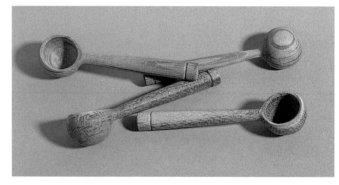

Figure 6.54 A spoon workpiece turned on turning-axis A-A, and ready for sanding. The pencil gauge behind shows the dimensions and the two turning-axes.

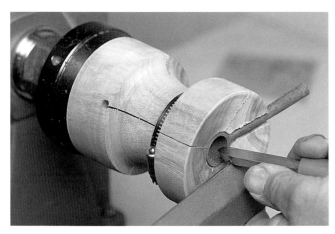

Figure 6.55 **Hollowing the spoon's bowl with a small scraper.** The inclination of the handle groove in the front face of the spring chuck automatically positions the workpiece's turning-axis **B**-**B** along the lathe axis. The chuck is tightened using a hose clamp. A Woodfast Multi Grip contracting step collet chuck is here used to hold the wooden spring-chuck body.

6.5 CONTEMPORARY SPINDLES

In traditional multi-axis turning there is usually some blending of the surfaces turned on the different axes. In contemporary studio turning the desire is often to create and highlight disjointedness (figures 6.56 and 6.57). With two or three turning-axes in the same plane, a side elevation is easy to sketch (figure 6.58). You can create similar turnings which have nonparallel turning-axes in different planes, but it is not possible to readily determine exactly how they will look in advance.

Once you have turned a few multi-axis forms you will start to become much more comfortable with both their turning and design. When designing:

1. The surfaces turned on different turning-axes cannot meet smoothly except along a small fraction of the length of the junction. It is easier to design an abrupt junction.
2. It is easier to leave the surface at the end of a zone of turning fairly square to the turning-axis. The surface turned next can then be turned into the earlier-turned surface(s).
3. The intersection of surfaces turned on different turning-axes is more extreme the further away it is from the intersection of those turning-axes.
4. It is generally better to turn the central section of spindles first, working towards the ends.

Figure 6.56 **Two candlesticks by Mark Sfirri.**[14]

Figure 6.57 **A maquette for three-legged stool.** The design for the left-hand leg is shown in the next figure.

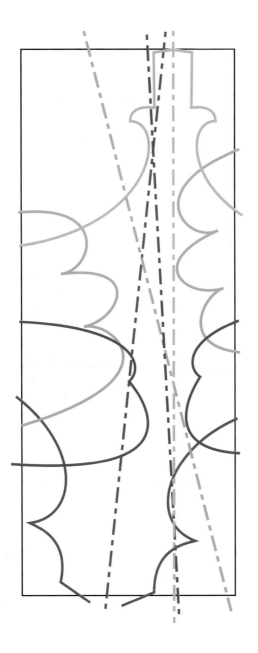

6.6   EXAMPLES OF NON-PARALLEL TURNING-AXES NOT IN THE SAME PLANE

STACKED AND SQUASHED BOWLS

Figures 6.59, 6.60, and 6.64 show apparently simple bowls and platters turned by New Zealander Peter Battensby.[15] Figures 6.61 to 6.63 and figure 6.65 illustrate the designs and mountings for these fascinating pieces.

Figure 6.59   A stacked plate and a stacked bowl, both turned on two nonparallel turning-axes which intersect.

Figure 6.58   The design of the left-hand "cabriole" leg of the stool in the previous figure. On this central longitudinal section parallel to a side of the square blank, the profile turned on each of the four turning-axes is outlined in the same color as the axis.

   The turning on the red and green turning-axes must be completed before that on the blue, and that on the blue before that on the magenta. Although all the turning-axes are drawn here in the same plane, you can readily turn similar designs with the axes in different planes.

Figure 6.60   A four-stack bowl turned on four intersecting turning-axes in different planes.

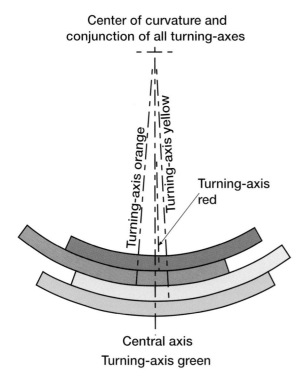

Figure 6.61 **The design of stacked bowls.** The turning-axes for the four component bowls all meet at one point. That point is also the center of curvature for the inside and outside surfaces of all the component bowls.

Although this drawing shows the four turning-axes lying in one plane, they need not as the next figure shows. Nor does the central axis need to be a turning-axis (also explained in the next figure).

Each mounting of the workpiece with a particular turning-axis coaxial with the lathe axis must be precise. You could use an eccentric chuck with a tilting facility, but there are cheaper alternatives which include:

1. The workpiece could be mounted with screws or glue, etc., to a timber backing wedge particular to each turning-axis. The backing wedge would then be fixed, at the appropriate eccentricity, to a faceplate.
2. Turn the inside of the top bowl with the blank held on a faceplate or by a chuck. Turn a mandrel which has its right-hand face convex and of the same curvature as the inside of the top bowl (figure 6.63). To mount the workpiece on a particular turning-axis, force the top bowl against the mandrel with the tail center positioned where that turning-axis issues from the right-hand face of the workpiece. The last turning operation would be to finish-turn the bottom of the bottom bowl, holding it between the mandrel and the tailstock or in a cage chuck. Alternatively you could finish-turn the bottom of the bottom bowl earlier, and use a profiled pad to locate the right-hand end of the workpiece as shown in the figure 6.63.

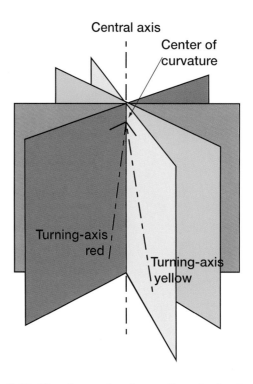

Figure 6.62 **Turning-axis planes for stacked bowls.**

The turning-axes for the component bowls need not lie in one plane as in the previous figure. Instead each turning-axis can lie in a plane which crosses and contains a common central axis. Each plane resembles two opposite leaves of a revolving door, the central axis being the axis of rotation of the door.

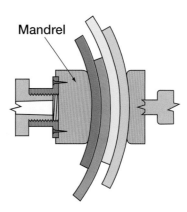

Figure 6.63 · **Turning a stacked bowl between centers.** Before turning on a fresh turning-axis, the workpiece merely has to be realigned. The mandrel and tailstock pad should be lined with a resilient material such as leather to give more grip and prevent damage to the workpiece. You will need a narrow, curved-bladed, square-ended scraper to remove the channels of waste between component bowls.

Figure 6.64 Two folded bowls. Their design is described in the next figure.

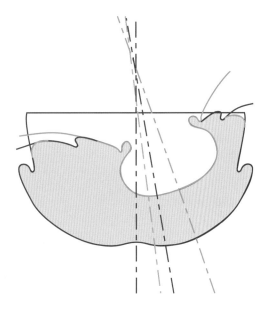

Figure 6.65 The design of folded bowls. Here four turning-axes all lie in the same plane. If the turning-axes lie in different planes, the junctions between adjacent surfaces turned on different turning-axes will tend to be more abrupt.

The workpiece can be turned either first or last on the red turning-axis. The three other turning operations are best performed in the order green, purple, blue. Some folded-bowl designs may be able to be turned between centers by the method shown in figure 6.33, except that the positioning of the mandrel on its faceplate or in its chuck will need to be adjusted between the turning operations on some turning-axes.

6.7   ENDNOTES

1 Most books on ornamental-turning include sections on the eccentric chuck, for example: J.H. Evans, *Ornamental Turning*, pp. 121–134; J.J. Holtzapffel, *The Principles & Practice of Ornamental or Complex Turning*, pp. 348–368; and T.D Walshaw, *Ornamental Turning*, pp. 35–37 and 125–128.

2 Based on a drawing on page 84 of *Woodturning in France*.

3 Mike Darlow, *The Practice of Woodturning*, pp. 202–208.

4 This stand is based on a photograph in a book by R.W. Symonds.

5 Hugo Knoppe, *Meistertechniken der Drechslerkunst*, pp. 58–61; J.H. Evans, *Ornamental Turning*, plate 7; J.J. Holtzapffel, *The Principles & Practice of Ornamental or Complex Turning*, p. 355, plate XXXII; and T.D Walshaw, *Ornamental Turning*, pp. 125–128.

6 Hugo Knoppe, *Meistertechniken der Drechslerkunst*, pp. 25–31.

7 David Springett, *Woodturning Wizardry*, pp. 97–102. This book also describes how to turn a lattice box lid (pp. 103–114), and a lattice pomander (pp. 137–146).

8 More of John's work is described in: John Wooller, "Celebrating Jarrah and Overcoming the Circle," *American Woodturner* (June 1996): pp. 25–27.

9 Paul Bass, editor, *Ornamental Turning Work of J.E.H. Saueracker The Master Turner of Nuremberg*, Society of Ornamental Turners, 1985.

10 Fitting a ferrule to a handle is described on page 116 of *The Fundamentals of Woodturning*.

11 Based on Fritz Spannagel, *Das Drechslerwerk*, p. 102, fig. 457.

12 von C.A. Martin, *Der Drechsler*, p. 189, fig. 440.

13 Three different methods are described in: Richard Raffan, *Turning Projects*, pp. 160–167; Ray Hopper, *Multi-Centre Turning*, pp. 128–132; and Gottfried Bockelmann, *Handbuch Drechseln*, p. 138.

14 Articles by Mark Sfirri on multi-axis turning include: "The Simple Turned Table leg and a Variation," *American Woodturner* (June 1993): pp. 2–5; and "Multi-Axis Candlesticks," *American Woodturner* (March 1994): pp. 36–38

15 Peter Battensby's work is introduced in: Ken Sager, "Wacky Work," *Woodturning* (April 1995): pp. 36–38.

Chapter Seven

ELLIPTICAL TURNING

Elliptical turnings such as those in figures 7.1 and 7.2 are much less common than circular. You need complicated special equipment to fully explore elliptical turning (figure 7.3), but simplified equipment can be made and used by hand turners.[1] The tools used to turn ellipses are often held mechanically in a compound slide. Elliptical turning is therefore usually considered as a specialty within ornamental-turning.

Elliptical turning has been a sometimes-important specialty since shortly after the birth of ornamental-turning in the early 16th century. The high period for elliptical turning was the second half of the 19th century and the early part of the 20th when there was a strong demand for elliptical frames for mirrors, pictures, and photographs. Since that time the elliptical woodturning lathe has been largely superseded by spindle-molders working off templates, by template-guided or computer-controlled overhead routers, by casting in reinforced plaster, and by molding in plastic.

Elliptical turning is commonly called oval turning, but elliptical is the preferred adjective. An ellipse is a mathematically and geometrically defined shape; an oval is any shape resembling the longitudinal silhouette or outline of an egg.[2]

Johannes Volmer[3] of Chemnitz, Germany, has kindly collaborated on the text for this chapter. He has inspired or supplied figures 7.17 to 7.20 and 7.27 to 7.34. His work on elliptical turning includes several publications and many articles.[4] He has developed a new type of elliptical lathe which can be run much faster than a lathe fitted with the traditional type of elliptical chuck shown in figure 7.3. The faster speed of the Volmer lathe greatly increases the ease and efficiency of using both hand-held and mechanically-held tools.

Elliptical turning is far easier to do than to understand. Many readers will find the explanations of the geometry and mechanisms heavy going because they are complicated. However once you have the appropriate equipment, elliptical turning is straightforward. I suggest that you graze through this chapter as you need.

Figure 7.1 A nutmeg grater, English, 17th century, in lignum vitae. *Length* 122 mm, *width* 90 mm, *height of body* 145 mm. *John Hawkins Antiques.*

Figure 7.2 **An elliptical vase in ash** shown at the Ornamental Turners Group of Australia seminar in Frankston, Victoria, in 1999.

7.1 THE ELLIPSE

Cut obliquely through a cylinder and you reveal an ellipse (figure 7.4). But the ellipse is more commonly regarded with the circle, the parabola, and the hyperbola, as one of the four conic sections (figures 7.4 and 7.5).

The geometry of the ellipse is fascinating, at least to some, and is introduced in figure 7.6.

There are several ways to draw ellipses–if you drew an ellipse at school it was probably with the string method shown in figure 7.7. You can also draw ellipses using trammels (figures 7.8 and 7.9).

Figure 7.4 **Ellipses revealed by cutting oblique sections.** *Front*, through a cylinder; *rear*, through a cone. The cut planes which reveal these elliptical sections are called section planes.

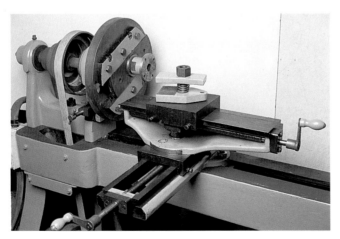

Figure 7.3 **An elliptical-turning lathe** showing its elliptical chuck and compound slide. This lathe was manufactured by the German company Alex. Geiger in the late 1930s. The chuck and compound slide can be removed, and the lathe then used for normal hand turning.

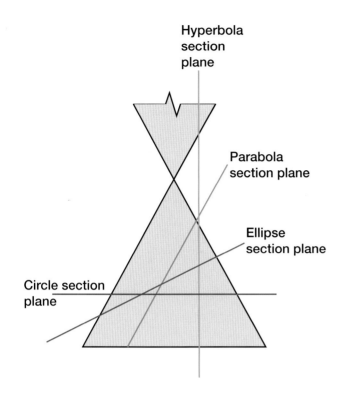

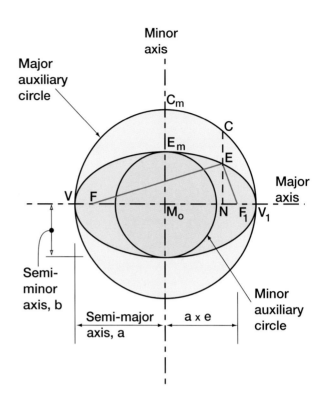

Figure 7.5 **The section planes for the four conic sections** drawn on a vertical section through the axis of two cones.[5]

The word ellipse came into use in the mid-18th century, supplanting the word ellipsis. Both derive from the Greek word meaning "a coming short." In this diagram the inclination of the ellipse section plane "comes short of", that is less steep than, the inclination of the left-hand side of the cone.

Figure 7.6 **The auxiliary circles and properties of an ellipse.**

$FE + EF_1 = $ constant $= V V_1 = 2a$
$EN:CN = E_mM_o:C_mM_o$
Area within an ellipse $= \pi ab = 3.1416ab$

Perimeter of an ellipse $= \pi\sqrt{\{ 2(a^2 + b^2) - (a-b)^2/2.2\}}$

$FM_o = M_oF_1 = ae$, the linear eccentricity of an ellipse, where **e** (sometimes represented by ε, the Greek letter epsilon) is the eccentricity, or more specifically the numerical eccentricity, of the ellipse, and is less than 1. The relationships between **a**, **b**, and **e** are given by:

$b^2 = a^2(1 - e^2)$
$e^2 = 1 - b^2/a^2$

Another property is that a radius of length **a** drawn about E_m crosses the major axis at **F** and F_1.

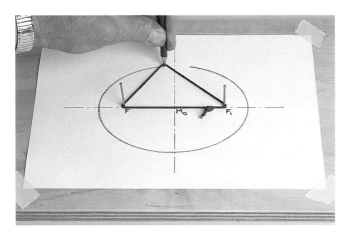

Figure 7.7 Drawing an ellipse with a ring of string. This is a crude, but convenient form of ellipsograph (device for drawing ellipses). It utilizes the property stated in the previous figure that $FE + EF_1 = 2a$. The two nails are at the two focuses.

To draw an ellipse with major and minor axes of $2a$ and $2b$ respectively, the length of the ring of string should be $2a(1 + e)$, and the two nails should be $2ae$ apart, with $e = \sqrt{\{1 - b^2/a^2\}}$.

Here a = 80 mm, and a/b = 4/3

Therefore b = 80/1.33 = 60 mm
$e = \sqrt{(1 - 60^2/80^2)} = 0.66$

Distance FF_1 = 0.66 x $2a$ = 0.66 x 160 = 106 mm

Length of string ring = $2a(1 + e)$
= 160 x 1.66 = 266 mm

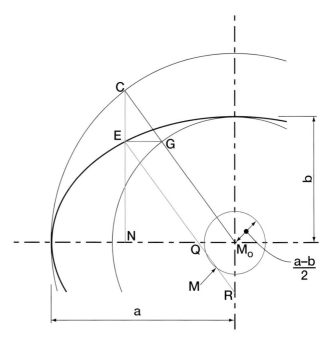

Figure 7.9 The principles of the two trammel methods.

The short trammel. M_oGC is any radius from the centre of the ellipse M_o. It crosses the minor auxiliary circle at G, and intersects with the major auxiliary circle at C. If you drop an ordinate from C it crosses the ellipse at E and joins the major axis at N.

EQR is parallel and equal in length to CGM_o.

Irrespective of the inclination of CGM_o, $QR = CG$ = radius major axis – radius minor axis = $a–b$.

Therefore if you make a trammel with the lengths a and b marked on it as shown in the previous figure, at any inclination provided Q is positioned on the major axis and R on the minor axis, E will be on the ellipse.

An important property of the short trammel for elliptical turning is that as the trammel is moved to draw an ellipse, the centre point M midway between points Q and R on the trammel describes a circle of radius $(a – b)/2$.

The long trammel. This is more accurate than the short trammel for drawing near-circular ellipses. Its theory is similar to that of the short trammel, but is not detailed here because it is not directly relevant to elliptical turning. To use a long trammel (see figure 7.8), end Q_1 must be positioned on the major axis and end R_1 on the minor axis. The point on the long trammel midway between R_1 and Q_1 describes a circle of radius $(a+b)/2$, while E is describing the ellipse.

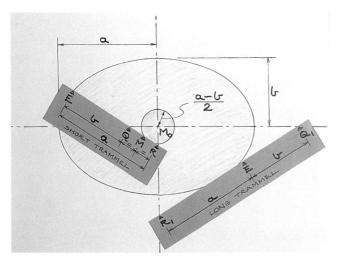

Figure 7.8 Drawing an ellipse using long and short trammels. How trammels work is explained in the next figure. Here a = 85 mm, and b = a/1.5 = 56.7 mm.

7.2   TURNING ELLIPSES

There are five pieces of equipment that you can use to turn ellipses:

1. A screwchuck or faceplate allows you to turn a workpiece on several turning-axes to yield a vaguely-elliptical form.
2. A rose engine .
3. An elliptical chuck.
4. The Cardan-circles-based elliptical lathe developed by Johannes Volmer.
5. An elliptical cutting frame.

   Their uses are described in sections 7.3 to 7.7.

7.3   MULTI-TURNING-AXIS TURNING

Figure 7.10 shows how by turning a workpiece, either of plate or spindle form, you can produce an ellipse-like oval. The sharp discontinuities left by turning can be reduced and blended by carving and heavy sanding.

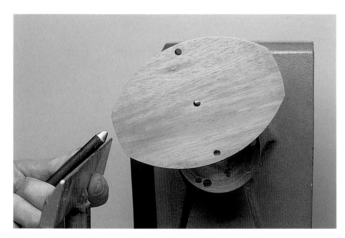

Figure 7.10   **An oval produced by turning a workpiece on three centers.** The centers are each a turning-axis and are defined by the three drilled holes. The workpiece was held on a screw chuck, its screw going into the centers' holes, starting with the middle one. Extra screws (not visible) were added through the faceplate for additional security.

7.4   THE ROSE ENGINE

Elliptical rose-engine turnings are especially prized (figures 7.11 and 7.12). Figure 7.13 shows the principle of a rose engine in its commonest form, and figure 7.14 its manifestation. Cutting with a rose engine has inherent difficulties as figure 7.15 shows.

Figure 7.11   **A miniature case turned on a rose engine**, lignum vitae, 17th century. *Length* 93 mm, *width* 75 mm, *height* 14 mm. *John Hawkins Antiques*.

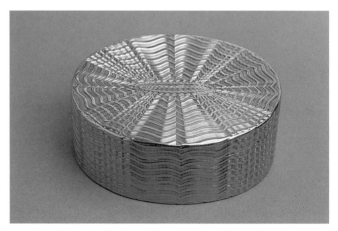

Figure 7.12   **A rose-engine-turned gold box.** French. Presented to Edvardo Baroni in 1821. *Length* 73 mm, *width* 52 mm, *height* 31 mm. The decoration on the lid is produced by rosettes alone, that on the sides is produced by the headstock spindle pumping to-and-fro longitudinally, this movement being controlled by the addition of a crown facility (see pages 57 to 59). *John Hawkins Antiques*.

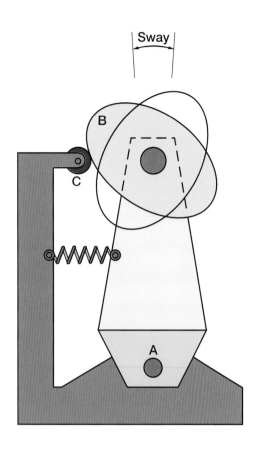

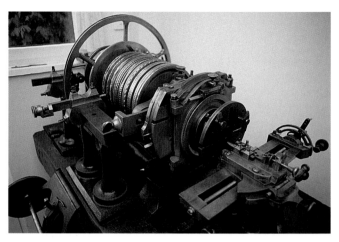

Figure 7.14 **A pivoted-headstock rose engine** by John Bower, manufactured in about 1845 in Clerkenwell, London. *Photograph by David Wood-Heath.*

Figure 7.13 **The principle of the pivoted-headstock rose engine.**[6] The headstock is in two parts, the upper part pivots about axis **A**, the lower part is rigidly fastened to the lathe bed. A rosette **B** is fixed onto the headstock spindle. The wheel **C** is known as a rubber, probably because most forms do not incorporate a rotatable component.

As the headstock spindle rotates, the rosette's periphery revolves past and is kept in contact with the rubber by the tension spring. This causes the spindle to rock, and a fixed cutting tool to cut an ellipse on the face or periphery of the workpiece.

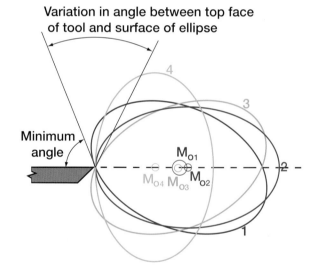

Figure 7.15 **The motion of an ellipse being turned on a rose engine.** The angle between the top, horizontal face of the tool and the periphery of the ellipse varies greatly during a single workpiece rotation. This can lead to a variation in surface finish. The traditional type of elliptical chuck described in the next section is preferred for elliptical turning because there is less variation in rake angle as a comparison with figure 7.20 shows.

7.5   THE ELLIPTICAL CHUCK

The mechanism shown in figure 7.16 and the traditional elliptical chuck both utilize the short-trammel principle in figures 7.8 and 7.9. But in the elliptical chuck, instead of the trammel and a pencil or cutter mounted on it moving, the trammel and cutter are fixed and the elliptical workpiece moves (figures 7.17 to 7.20).

The elliptical chuck is said to have been invented by Leonardo da Vinci (1452-1519). It is first shown in 1701 in Plumier's *L'Art de Tourner*, and thereafter appears in most ornamental-turning texts.

The elliptical chuck shown previously in figure 7.3 and in figures 7.21 to 7.26 is made from cast iron and steel and is heavy. Even without a workpiece aboard, run the chuck at more than the lathe's minimum speed and the lathe shakes. The shaking increases with the weight of the workpiece and as **a/b** increases. Lightening the chuck's construction and reducing its size helps. Various complicated designs to reduce the shaking have been developed, but none have been truly effective. Turners often therefore opt to achieve an improved off-the-tool finish by using fixed cutters instead of hand-held tools, or by using cutters which rotate at high speed and are mounted, like the fixed cutters, on a compound slide. But there is now a way of achieving a high, safe lathe speed for elliptical turning—the Volmer lathe described in the next section.

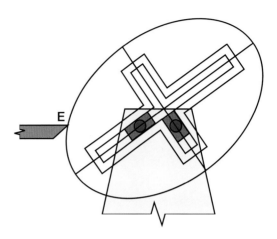

Figure 7.17   The converse of the short trammel.
To turn an ellipse with a "fixed" cutter using the short-trammel principle, you would have to use its converse. You would have to fix the trammel, here horizontally, while rotating the workpiece. You could mount two pivoting sliders on the front of a headstock. The workpiece could be fixed to a faceplate with two grooves milled at right angles into its rear face. The scriber at **E** in figure 7.8 would be replaced by a tool tip. The only problem then is how to rotate and revolve the workpiece.

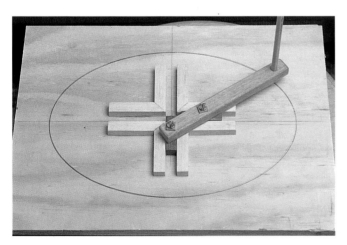

Figure 7.16   A short-trammel mechanism which exactly mimics the arrangement shown in figure 7.8.[7] The slides pinned to the underside of the trammel are free to pivot. Here **a** = 150 mm and **b** = 107 mm.

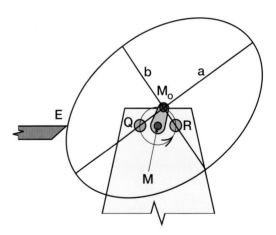

Figure 7.18   Driving an elliptical workpiece.
Figure 7.8 showed that the midpoint between **Q** and **R** on a short trammel moves in a circular path of radius (**a**–**b**)/2 around M_o. The converse could be used to drive an elliptical workpiece. A crank MM_o of length (**a**–**b**)/2 could be rigidly fixed to a headstock spindle **M** and pivotly fixed to the center of the workpiece at M_o. Rotating spindle **M** would, in liason with the sliders at **Q** and **R**, cause a fixed cutter mounted distance (**a**+**b**)/2 to the left of **M** to cut an ellipse. I am conveniently ignoring how crank MM_o could be combined with the pivotted sliders mounted at **Q** and **R** in a real machine.

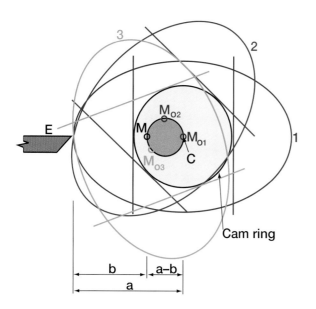

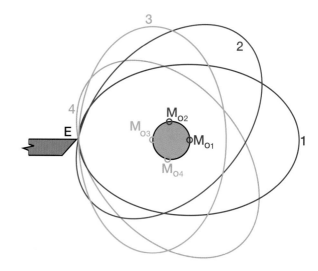

Figure 7.20 **The rotation and revolution of a workpiece mounted on an elliptical chuck.**

As the workpiece is rotated bodily, its center M_o is revolved around a small circle of radius $(a–b)/2$. The position of M_o corresponding to different instants in the rotation of a workpiece is indicated by **1**, **2**, etc.

This figure shows that while the elliptical workpiece rotates through 180°, the center of the workpiece M_o revolves around the small circle once, that is through 360°. This phenomenon is used in Johannes Volmer's elliptical lathe shown later.

The horizontal distance of the cutter **E** from the lathe axis is **b**.

Figure 7.19 The operating principle of the elliptical chuck.

The simple converses of the short trammel shown in figures 7.17 and 7.18 are impractical. The solution employed in the elliptical chuck gives identical workpiece movements, but drives the chuck by locating the headstock spindle **M** at the position of the left-hand slider **Q** in the previous figure.

To make the center of the elliptical workpiece M_o revolve in a circle of radius $(a–b)/2$, the elliptical chuck uses a cam-ring which is fixed to the headstock (the construction of an elliptical chuck is detailed in figures 7.21 to 7.26). When an elliptical chuck is used to turn a workpiece circular, the center of the cam-ring **C** and the headstock spindle **M** are coincident, and $M_oM = 0$.

For an elliptical chuck to turn an ellipse the center of the cam-ring **C** has to be displaced (usually horizontally to the right) from the headstock spindle **M**. The magnitude of this displacement is $(a–b)$, where **b** is determined by the horizontal distance of the cutter **E** to the left of **M**. The diameter of the cam-ring is irrelevant, only the displacement of its center **C** from **M** matters. The center of the cam-ring **C** is always coincident with **R**, the right-hand slider in the previous figure.

The workpiece is fixed at its center M_o onto a rectangular plate which slides on a circular plate mounted concentrically onto the headstock spindle nose at **M**. The sliding of the sliding plate is dictated by straight rubbers fixed to its rear. These rubbers, represented by the straight colored lines, circle around the outside of the cam-ring. As the workpiece rotates, its center M_o revolves around a circle of radius $(a–b)/2$, the requirement previously confirmed in figure 7.9. This "rotating/revolving" movement of the workpiece is more fully described in the next figure.

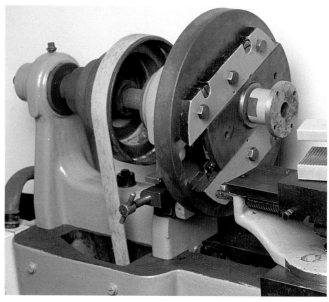

Figure 7.21 The elliptical chuck shown in figure 7.3. The detailed construction and working of the chuck are described in figures 7.22 to 7.26.

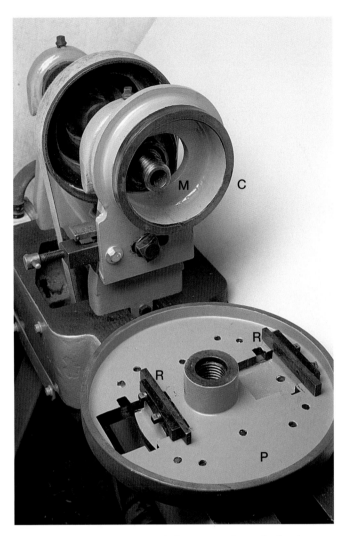

Figure 7.22 The lathe with the cam-ring about to be screwed on. A rib in the rear of the cam-ring **C** casting mates with and slides in the horizontal groove machined along the right-hand face of the headstock casting. The knob on the left of the headstock is used to adjust the displacement of the cam-ring **C** which can be read on the adjacent scale. Adjusting the displacement of the cam-ring **C** varies the eccentricity of the ellipse. The required displacement of the cam-ring is (**a–b**). The square-headed screw on the right-hand face of the headstock is tightened to lock the cam-ring at the required displacement.

Figure 7.23 The front of the cam-ring. A circular periphery is machined on the cam-ring **C**. The headstock spindle nose **M** projects through a slot in the cam-ring casting. Onto nose **M** is screwed the center plate **P**, with the sliding plate, etc. mounted upon it, as shown in the next two figures.

Here the center plate **P** is face down with the sliding plate underneath. The two rubbers **R** which are fixed to the back of the sliding plate and revolve around and in contact with the cam-ring project through the center plate. Some elliptical chucks have a plate with a hole machined in it with the same diameter as the cam-ring instead of the two separate rubbers shown here.

Figure 7.24 A rear view of the elliptical chuck.
The large circular center plate **P** screws onto and rotates concentrically with the headstock spindle. A sliding plate is mounted (see next figure) on the center plate's right-hand face. Two lugs on the back of the sliding plate project through the two slots in the center plate. To the lugs are fixed the straight rubbers **R** which revolve around and in contact with the machined periphery of the cam-ring **C**. If the center of the cam-ring is displaced from the lathe axis, as the center plate rotates the sliding plate is oscillated transversely by its rubbers.

Figure 7.25 The front of the elliptical chuck. Two faceplates which can screw onto the threaded nose M_o rest on the lathe bed. The workpiece is fixed to either of these faceplates.

    S is the sliding plate which is held onto the front face of the center plate **P** by the two dovetail guides **D**. The sliding plate has an integral screwed nose M_o onto which is screwed a faceplate or chuck which in turn holds the workpiece.

    On the underside (rear) of the sliding plate **S** are cast two lugs onto which the rubbers **R** are screwed. There is some adjustment between the rubbers and the lugs so that the rubbers can revolve around the cam-ring **C** without any slop. It is the oscillation of the sliding plate **S** and whatever is mounted on it which causes the shaking. Therefore the lighter this assemblage is, the better.

Figure 7.26 Turning an elliptical box. The wood is oak. By using a gouge I can present an edge at a large rake angle and with considerable side rake to achieve a superior finish. I could also grind a special cutter to achieve a similar presentation.

7.6 THE VOLMER LATHE

The shaking associated with traditional elliptical chucks greatly restricts the safe lathe speed, and makes turning with hand-held tools difficult. Johannes Volmer has overcome this problem by using the Cardan circles (figure 7.27) as a basis for a new and superior type of high-speed elliptical lathe. The construction and use of the Volmer lathe are shown in figures 7.28 to 7.34.

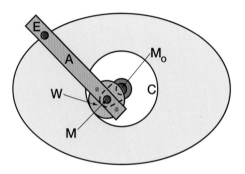

Figure 7.27 The Cardan circles. Girolamo Cardano (1501-1576), an Italian physician and mathematician, discovered that every point firmly connected to a circle rolling in another circle of twice the diameter of the first describes an ellipse. Using this relationship, a mechanism can be constructed for drawing or cutting ellipses. This mechanism causes the workpiece to rotate and revolve in exactly the same way as with an elliptical chuck.

A rotating spindle at M_o has fixed to it a crank of effective length M_oM. A wheel **W** is able to spin freely on a stub axle fixed into the crank at **M**. An arm **A** is fixed diametrically onto the wheel. The wheel **W** has an effective outside diameter of $2M_oM$. The outside of the wheel must roll without any sliding around the inside of a circle **C** of internal diameter $4M_oM$ as if both circular surfaces were toothed

As the spindle at M_o is rotated clockwise, a scriber **E** fixed to the arm will revolve counterclockwise and draw an ellipse. The ellipse has half-major and half-minor axis lengths of $(EM + M_oM)$ and $(EM - M_oM)$ respectively.

The Volmer lathe is described in the next figure. It inverts the Cardan circles by fixing **E** and **M** in space. **E** becomes the cutting tool tip. **M** becomes the headstock spindle axis. M_o, the center of the elliptical workpiece, rotates about **M** just as in figure 7.18.

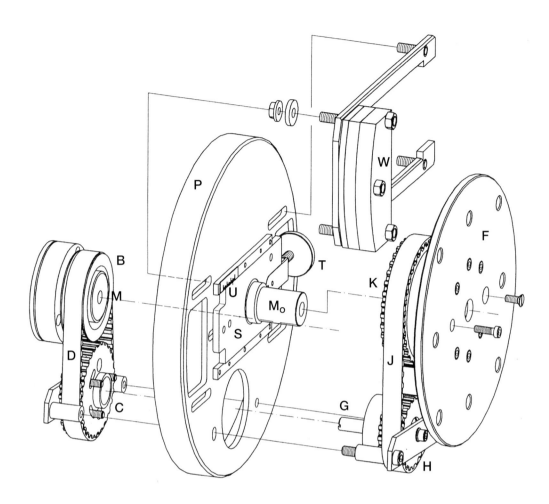

Figure 7.28 The construction of the Volmer elliptical lathe.

M is the headstock spindle nose. Surrounding it but rigidly fixed to the headstock structure is an externally-toothed wheel B. A center plate P is centrally screwed onto the spindle nose M by a threaded boss on its rear (not shown). A toothed wheel C is fixed to the back of the center plate P, but is free to rotate. Toothed wheels B and C have the same effective diameters. Therefore as the center plate P is rotated clockwise by the headstock-spindle nose M, toothed wheel C is also rotated counterclockwise by the toothed belt D.

Wheel C is rigidly mounted on an axle G which passes through a hole in the center plate. On the right-hand end of axle G a toothed wheel H is rigidly mounted. As H is rotated by C, it in turn rotates via a toothed belt J a toothed wheel K. The effective diameter of K is double that of H. To the front of K is rigidly and concentrically fixed a faceplate F onto which the workpiece is fixed. Therefore as the lathe spindle M rotates, the workpiece is rotated at half the speed, but in the same direction.

In order that the workpiece can be turned to an ellipse the workpiece axis has to be displaced from the headstock-spindle axis M. The toothed wheel and faceplate assemblage K and F are free to spin concentrically on stub axle M_o. M_o is fixed to a plate S. The displacement of plate S (and stub axle M_o and assemblage K, F, and any workpiece) from the headstock spindle M is adjusted by screw T, and can be read on the scale U. In the Volmer lathe the plate S does not oscillate to-and-fro on the center plate P as the chuck rotates, but is firmly screwed, after being offset, onto center plate P.

The final ingenious feature of the Volmer lathe is its counterweight system. As described in figure 7.20, the centre of gravity of the turning and its immediate mounting revolve twice as fast as the workpiece. Therefore dynamic balance can be achieved by fixing an offset counterweight to center plate P which is rotating twice as fast as F. And as lathe axis M lies between counterweight W and M_o, it is possible to calculate by how much a counterweight of a given weight should be displaced to make the lathe run almost without shaking. The weight of counterweight W can be varied, however it is usually set at 625 g and dynamic balance obtained by adjusting its displacement.

The Volmer lathe will be manufactured from late 1999 by Vicmarc Machinery, Queensland, Australia.

Figure 7.29 Preparing to turn a large elliptical bowl. The 100 mm thick spruce blank has been bandsawn to an ellipse 330 mm x 280 mm in plan, dressed flat on its top face, and weighed.

The 625 g counterweight has to be fixed at the appropriate displacement if lathe shaking is to be minimized. Johannes Volmer is here reading the required displacement from a graph. Values of the combined weight of the workpiece and the faceplate onto which it is mounted are marked along the graph's horizontal x-axis; values of a quarter of the difference between the workpiece's major and minor axes are marked along the vertical y-axis. Each of the series of lines sloping down to the right represents a particular value of counterweight displacement. Therefore the required workpiece displacement can read at the intersection of the vertical ordinate from the combined weight and the horizontal abscissa from the axes' difference.

Figure 7.37 shows that if the cutting-tool tip is not applied at lathe-axis height, the orientation of the resulting ellipse is skewed. The projector, left, provides a shadow line on the workpiece at lathe-axis height. All cutting should take place within this shadow line.

Figure 7.31 Turning the outside of the bowl. Note the projected black shadow line which the tool tip should cut within. A shallow recess is being turned in the base to jam fit onto a shallow elliptical spigot. Before the workpiece is demounted, its outside is sanded.

Figure 7.32 Hammering the workpiece onto an elliptical jam-spigot chuck which has just been turned. The bowl and the jam chuck have just been weighed for a second time, and the counterweight displacement reset.

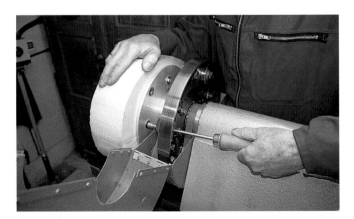

Figure 7.30 Screwing the workpiece onto the faceplate.

Figure 7.33 Turning the bowl's inside. The projected dark band clearly shows the inside shape as well as enabling cutting to be accurately performed at lathe-axis height.

7.7   THE ELLIPTICAL CUTTING FRAME

This rare attachment for an ornamental lathe is described in figures 7.35 and 7.36. It was invented by a Major James Ash. Although its use is described in most ornamental-turning books,[8] in its usual form it is only suited for engraving and light work on the faces of turnings.

Figure 7.35 An elliptical cutting frame. The engraving is from page 252, figure 181, of *Ornamental Turning* by J.H. Evans.

The elliptical cutting frame is fixed to an ornamental lathe's compound slide, and the stepped pulley is driven from the overhead gear. The frame's construction is explained in the next figure.

Figure 7.34 Johannes Volmer with the finished elliptical bowl, just removed from the jam-spigot chuck to the right.

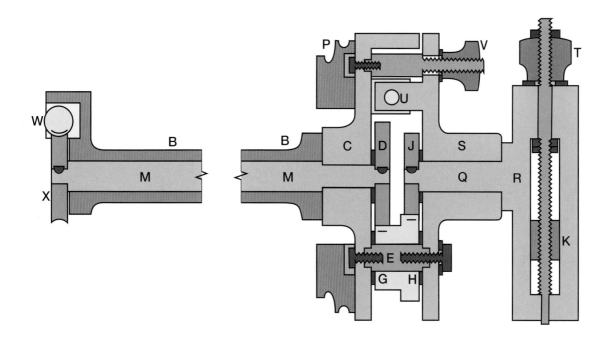

Figure 7.36 A longitudinal section through an elliptical cutting frame.

B is a square section stem which is used to hold the frame in an ornamental lathe's compound slide. A spindle M runs through stem B. N, the right-hand section of spindle M, is machined to act as a stub axle. A circular center plate C is free to rotate on the stub axle N. A single pulley or a stepped pulley P which is driven by a continuous belt from the lathe's overhead gear is fixed onto the rear, left-hand, face of C. A gear wheel D with 48 teeth is rigidly fixed onto the right-hand end of spindle M.

In an arrangement which resembles the Volmer lathe, a stub axle E is fixed into plate C. Sector plate S can pivot about the right-hand end of E. A gear G with 24 teeth is free-to-spin on stub axle E. Alongside and fixed to gear G is the 36-tooth gear H, which is also free to spin on axle E. Gear H in turn engages with gear J.

The front of the stub axle E locates but is not rigidly fixed to the sector plate S. On the front of sector plate S is an integral boss, bored to accept spindle Q. Gear J, which has 36 teeth, is fixed to the left-hand end of spindle Q. R, an eccentric cutter device, is fixed to the right-hand end of spindle Q. The further the cutter, mounted in block K, is displaced from the axis of Q using knob T, the larger is the ellipse.

When the position of the sector plate S is set at zero, spindle Q aligns with spindle M. To increase the ratio a/b of the ellipse being cut (to make the ellipse more squashed), the sector plate S has to be adjusted away from the zero setting to increase the displacement between spindles M and Q. This is done using screw U. Knurled knob V is used to lock the sector plate S in position.

When the overhead gear drives the pulley P and center plate C, sector plate S also rotates. Stub axle E revolves, and gear G, which is meshing with the stationary gear D, rotates at twice the speed of center plate C and in the same direction. Gear G directly rotates gear H, and through gear J and spindle Q the eccentric cutting device R. Thus the elliptical cutting frame replicates the Cardan circles principle.

A tangent screw W is mounted at the back (here left-hand) end of stem B. This tangent screw can be rotated by engaging a suitable key with the screw's square end. It is used to rotate wormwheel X. X is rigidly mounted on the spindle M which passes through and is free to rotate within stem B. This adjustment is used to position the cutter at the start of a cut, and to compensate for any changes which may be made to the position of the sector plate S as the pattern is cut.

7.8   TURNING AN ELLIPTICAL WORKPIECE

The importance of cutting at lathe-axis height when turning ellipses has been stressed. Figure 7.37 shows the consequences of erring.

The geometry of ellipses readily allows a variety of patterns to be turned. Some are shown in figures 7.38 to 7.41.

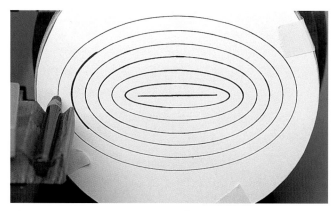

Figure 7.38   A nest of ellipses with a constant cam ring displacement appear parallel to one another.

The displacement of the cam-ring of an elliptical chuck is always (**a**–**b**). If do not alter that displacement as you turn a series of concentric ellipses with increasing or decreasing values of **b**, the half-axes' difference (**a**–**b**)/2 for every ellipse is the same irrespective of the lengths of **a** and **b**. But if, say, you increase **b** in steps, that is move the cutter to the left in steps, the ellipses grow and become rounder.

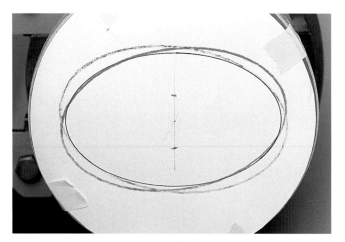

Figure 7.37   Cutting not at axis height. The cutter (the term cutter in the next five figures includes pencil) was 3/4 in. (20 mm) above lathe-axis height for the pink ellipse and the same distance below for the blue ellipse. If you cut above or below lathe-axis height, the ellipse produced, while still being a true ellipse, will be orientated slightly clockwise, and vice versa. The angle of the orientation from horizontal increases as the cutter's distance above or below lathe-axis height increases.

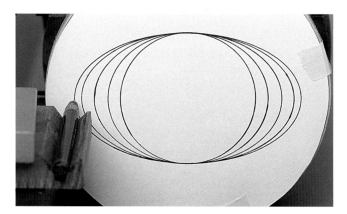

Figure 7.39   Ellipses produced by keeping the cutter fixed in position while varying the cam-ring's displacement.

The central ellipse was marked first. I then increased the cam-ring's displacement in increments of length **x**. This also increased **a** each time by **x**, but the "heights" of all the ellipses remained unchanged because **b** remained constant.

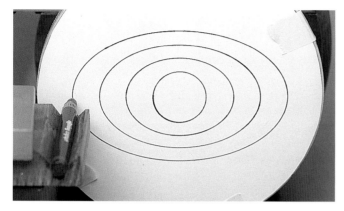

Figure 7.40 Ellipses produced by altering the cam-ring and cutter displacements in steps of the same length.

The circular ellipse was turned first with the cam-ring concentric with the lathe axis. Before turning each new ellipse I moved the cutter to the left and the cam-ring to the right, both by equal amounts (**x**). For the nth ellipse:

$$b_n = b_1 + x(n-1)$$

and $a_n = a_1 + 2x(n-1)$

Figure 7.41 A nest of ellipses which each have the same ratio of a/b. I first marked the outer ellipse . I then moved the cutter distance **x** to the right before cutting each new ellipse in the nest. To maintain the same ratio of **a/b** for all the ellipses, for every cutter movement of **x** to the right I had to reduced the cam-ring's displacement by moving it **x(a–b)/b** to the left.

There is an infinity of combinations of tool positionings and cam-ring displacements which will produce worthwhile patterns. These are further explored in specialist ornamental-turning texts.[9]

7.9   DIVIDING ELLIPSES

You may wish to ornament an elliptical turning's periphery or an internal elliptical band with an evenly-spaced ornamental detail (figure 7.42). This would require the ellipse to be divided into a whole number of arcs or chords of equal length. Figure 7.43 demonstrates that there is a difference between dividing into equal arcs and equal chords, with the latter usually being preferred. There is no simple means to calculate the divisions for equal chord lengths, but complicated mechanisms have been developed.[10] Much fruitful work has been done recently, but it is too complicated to be detailed here.[11] Two simple methods for dividing an ellipse are shown in figure 7.44.

Figure 7.42 A fluted elliptical box by Bernard Oke of Mont Albert, Victoria, Australia. The periphery had to be divided equally for the flutes to be spaced evenly.

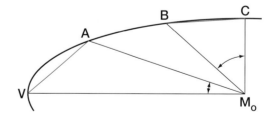

Figure 7.43 Equal division of the ellipse. VC is part of the perimeter of an ellipse. Chords **VA** and **BC** are of equal length. By inspection, arc **VA** is longer than arc **BC**, while angle **VM$_o$A** is smaller than angle **BM$_o$C**. There are no simple relationships between the angles, chord lengths, or arc lengths involved in the equal division of an ellipse, nor are there any simple, relevant relationships with an ellipse's auxiliary circles.

Figure 7.44 Hand methods for dividing an ellipse.
The paper-tape method involves first winding a tape around the periphery of the elliptical workpiece, or around an ellipse of the appropriate size turned in waste, to find the length of that periphery. (The length of a periphery can also be calculated by the formula given in the legend of figure 7.6). The peripheral length is then laid on a flat surface and divided into the appropriate number of parts. After winding the tape back around the appropriate part of the workpiece, the divisions are marked onto the workpiece from the divisions on the tape. This method gives divisions of equal arc length.

For most carved or machined details, dividing an ellipse into lengths of equal arc is not the ideal—the correct divisions would have equal chord lengths. Using dividers around an ellipse gives equal cords.

7.10 ENDNOTES

1 David Springett, *Adventures in Woodturning*, pp. 177–225.

2 E.W. Newton and J.W. Volmer, "Another Note on Ovals and Oval Generators," *The Society of Ornamental Turners Bulletin*, No. 98 (March 1998): pp. 125–131. This paper defines an oval as "plane, closed, and completely convex, between a circle and [one of] its diameter[s], having this diameter as an axis of symmetry." The paper also demonstrates how different ovals can be generated.

3 Born 1930. Studied mechanical engineering at the Technical University, Dresden. He worked and designed in both metal and wood, and from 1962 to 1995 was the professor for the theory and design of mechanisms at the Technical University of Chemnitz in Germany.

4 Johannes Volmer's articles in English include: "The Oval Lathe," *American Woodturner* (June 1990): p. 20; (September 1990): pp. 26–27; and (December 1990): pp. 26–28; "Turning a Deep Oval bowl," *Woodturning*, No. 5 (Autumn 1991): pp. 64–68; and with E.W. Newton, "Learning curves," *Woodturning*, No. 71 (January 1999): pp. 76–80.

5 Much of the geometric information on ellipses in this chapter is distilled from W. Abbott, *Practical Geometry and Engineering Graphics* (London: Blackie & Son Ltd, 4th ed, 1946), pp. 20–29.

6 Drawing based on Fritz Spannagel, *Das Drechslerwerk*, pp. 129, fig. 558.

7 A fully-adjustable version is shown in Hamelin-Bergeron, *Manuel du Tourneur*, plate III.

8 J.J. Holtzapffel, *The Principles and Practice of Ornamental or Complex Turning*, pp. 246–276; J. H. Evans, *Ornamental Turning*, pp. 252–259; and T.D. Walshaw, *Ornamental Turning*, pp. 47–48.

9 Evans, *Ornamental Turning*, pp. 138–142; and Holtzapffel, *The Principles and Practice of Ornamental or Complex Turning*, pp. 379–396.

10 Evans, *Ornamental Turning*, pp. 149–154; Holtzapffel, *The Principles and Practice of Ornamental or Complex Turning*, pp. 396–403; and Walshaw *Ornamental Turning*, pp. 132–135.

11 E.W. Newton and J. Volmer, *The Improved Compensating Index* (England: The Society of Ornamental Turners, March 1995); E.W. Newton and J. Volmer, *The Equal Division of the Ellipse* (England: The Society of Ornamental Turners, March 1995); and John Edwards, "The Ellipse Chuck," *The Society of Ornamental Turners Bulletin*, No. 97 (Sept 1997): pp. 73–77.

Chapter Eight

DRILLING

Stand a lathe vertically on the right-hand end of its bed and the lathe resembles a drilling machine. A lathe might lack a drilling machine's table, but it allows you to drill in more ways. This chapter describes those ways, the associated equipment, drill sharpening, and how to hold a bored workpiece for finish-turning.

The terms used to describe drills and drilling overlap and confuse:

Drill is the general term for a tool which is typically held in chuck jaws or in a socket, and in a process called drilling is rotated and forced forwards to cut a circular hole.

Augers are long, have one or more spiral grooves to remove the waste from the hole, and have a specially-formed end incorporating extra metal and sometimes spurs. The tip often has a central conical point which in hand-operated augers is threaded to pull the auger deeper. A long-series twist drill is not an auger because it does not have an end incorporating extra metal.

Bit is a term related to bite, and would be best reserved for the cutting edges or tip of a drill. Bit is sometimes unnecessarily used in place of drill; for example: in *brace and bit*, and in *drill bit* when the words are referring to the whole drill.

Boring is the axial drilling of a workpiece, often to produce a cylinder or similar. Boring is also enlarging a drilled hole, usually with a single cutter which is typically the bit of a tailstock- or carriage-mounted boring bar.

Reaming is the process of refining the diameter and sometimes the shape of a drilled hole, usually with a tool called a reamer.

Run-out, the deviation from the true alignment, is often measured at the bottom of the hole.

Spurs, also called nickers, are small sharp blades projecting from the edge of a drill tip: they cleanly cut the wall of a hole.

Figures 8.1 to 8.6 and table 8.1 detail the drill types most used in woodturning.

Drill cutting edges may be HSS, tungsten carbide, or carbon tool steel. HSS and tungsten carbide retain their hardness at high temperatures. Carbon tool steel loses its ability to take and hold an edge if you cause its temperature to exceed its tempering temperature. This softening of the steel is not instantaneous but progressive. Carbon-tool-steel drills are tempered at between 460°F and 510°F (240 °C to 265°C), depending on the intended use.[1] Within this temperature range, straw-colored to reddish-brown oxides form on the steel's surface. To avoid softening carbon-tool-steel cutting edges:

1. Don't run your lathe too fast while drilling, and feed at a comfortable rate. Recommended drilling speeds are listed in table 8.1. In general it is better to rotate a drill too slowly. When boring by rotating the workpiece, use the lower of the safe recommended turning speed for the workpiece and the speed recommended for the drill.
2. You must feed the drill while the lathe is running or frictional heat will build.
3. Clear the chips frequently. If you do not, frictional heat will build rapidly, the drill will jam in the hole, and shortly afterwards damage is likely to occur to the workpiece, to the drill, and perhaps to you.

8.1   DRILL TYPES

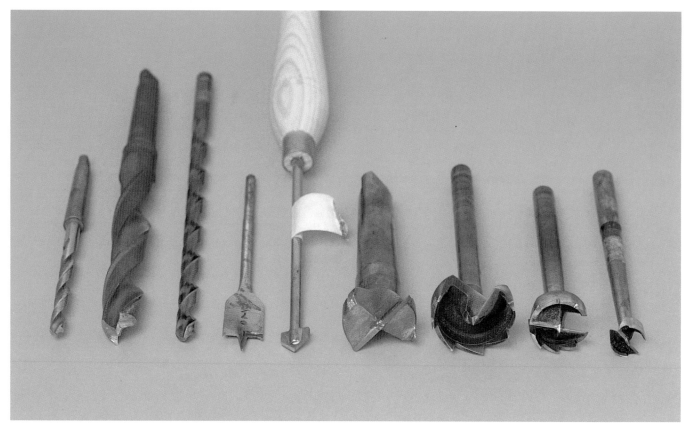

Figure 8.1 **Drills used in woodturning to drill shorter holes.** *Left to right:* a twist drill with a tapered shank, a brad-point-sharpened twist drill with a tapered shank, a long-series twist drill with a straight shank, a spade drill, a spear-point drill, a boring drill with tungsten-carbide cutters and spurs, a sawtooth drill with a single radial cutter, a sawtooth drill with two radial cutters, and a Forstner drill.

The twist drill was developed in New England during the 1850s. It was superior to the spear-point drill previously used to drill metals, but was tedious to manufacture. Frederick W. Howe discussed the problem with Joseph R. Brown of Browne & Sharpe who in response designed and built the first universal milling machine to mill the drills' spiral grooves.[2]

The spurs produced by brad-point sharpening give a cleaner entry and hole wall in wood than does a conically-sharpened twist-drill tip.

Spade drills are too delicate for boring into end grain, especially for larger-diameter holes into harder woods. Always stop the lathe before starting to withdraw a spade drill.

This spear-point drill is by Robert Sorby. It is hand fed, and drills effectively through both end grain and side grain. You should preturn a cone-shaped recess with a detail gouge to provide an axial start.

The Forstner drill was invented by Benjamin Forstner of Ogden, Utah in 1886.[3] It allows you to cleanly start and drill a hole which does not descend squarely from the wood's surface.

Drill Type	Diameter, inches	Diameter, millimeters	Recommended Speed, rpm
HSS twist, brad-point, and boring	$^1/_8$ to $^3/_8$	3 to 10	3000
	$^1/_2$	13	2300
	$^3/_4$	19	1550
	1	25	1150
Spade	All diameters	All diameters	2500
Shell	$^1/_4$ to $^1/_2$	6 to 13	1000
Gun	$^1/_4$ to $^1/_2$	6 to 13	2500
Sawtooth and Forstner	$^3/_8$	10	1000
	$^1/_2$	13	750
	$^3/_4$	19	500
	1	25	400
	1 $^1/_2$	37	250
	2	50	200

Table 8.1 Drilling Speeds

Figure 8.2 The tips of three gun drills and a shell drill. The drill diameters from left to right are: 20 mm, 9.1 mm, 15 mm, and 1¼ in.

The drills pictured in figures 8.1, 8.5 and 8.6 are unsuitable for boring long holes. Long versions of them would be unlikely to bore true because their tips would tend to follow the grain direction or any bands of softer wood. Long twist drills with conically-sharpened tips are both tip steered and partially held in alignment by their shanks. A twist drill will therefore bind if its tip veers off-line.

No drill is self-centering, but shell drills and gun drills wander least because their tips do not steer. Instead these drills are held in alignment by being a snug fit within the wall of the hole they have just drilled.

The shell drill is so called because of its resemblance to the razor shells of the family *Solenidae*. Alternative names for the shell drill include long-hole-boring bit and lamp-standard auger. Although shell drills were available in a range of diameters up to 2 in. (50 mm), the usually-available diameters are now 1/4, 5/16, 3/8, and 1/2 in. (6, 8, 10, and 13 mm).

Gun drills are superior for high-accuracy, high-speed, high-volume, long-hole boring. Gun drills are tungsten-carbide tipped and considerably dearer than shell drills, but they can be run at much higher speeds which aids drilling accuracy. When gun-drilling metal, speeds of up to 10,000 rpm are used, and an accuracy of alignment of 0.4 mm per meter of hole length is achievable.[4] In wood the sacrifice in drilling accuracy of using speeds of 1000 to 2500 rpm is negligible. As with the oil-hole drill shown in the figure 8.6, compressed air is used to cool and to expel the chips backwards out of the hole. Gun drills do not therefore have to be withdrawn during boring. Gun drills are routinely manufactured to client-specified diameters.

Note that only the edge to the right of center of both drill types cuts. The short carbide tip of the left hand gun drill will tend to run out more than the longer tips of the other two.

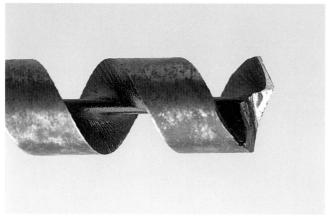

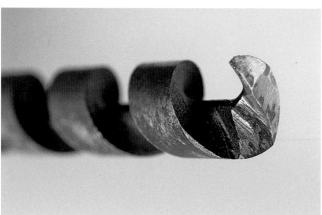

Figure 8.3 A combination auger sharpened for long-hole boring.

Shell drills are no longer made for larger hole diameters. Alternatives can be substituted, although their run-outs will usually be greater. Here a combination auger has been modified to minimize tip steerage. The central screw and spur have been ground away, and the cutting edge has been ground, filed, and honed to resemble that of a shell drill.

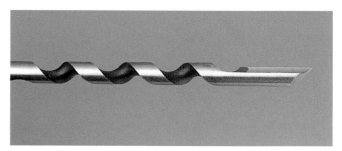

Figure 8.4 A HSS long-hole-boring auger by Crown Hand Tools, England. It has what Frank Pain calls a parrot nose.[5] The nose on this drill can be resharpened easily and many times.

Figure 8.5 An adjustable-diameter drill, the WR 20/2 by Record Power, England. The drilling diameter can be adjusted to be between 7/8 and 2 in. (22-50 mm); the separate cutter being used for smaller-diameter holes. The recommended drilling speed is inversely proportional to the drill-tip diameter, and is 850 rpm for 2 in. (50 mm) diameter.

Figure 8.6 An oil-hole drill has oil pumped through the two holes to the twist-drill tip when drilling metal.[6] The oil lubricates and cools, and expels the metal chips back along the flutes so that there is no need to withdraw the drill while drilling. Compressed air is used instead of oil when drilling wood.

8.2 DRILL CARE AND MODIFICATION

Drills can be protected from rust by brushing them with light oil or wax. Keep drills separated to prevent them damaging each other. Tungsten-carbide cutting tips are particularly brittle and liable to impact chipping. There are many proprietary drill holders, or you can easily make your own (figure 8.7).

A new drill should have been correctly shaped and sharpened for its intended purpose by its manufacturer. Where that intended purpose may not have been drilling wood, it may be worthwhile modifying the original tip geometry (figures 8.8 and 8.9). Particularly for batch production of cupchuck turnings, you can find it worthwhile to reprofile a drill (figure 8.10).

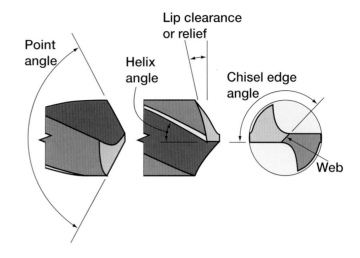

Figure 8.8 **Twist-drill geometry** showing the lip clearance angle and point angle. Ideally the clearance angle should increase slightly towards the axis of the drill, but is typically 15°. For optimum performance the clearance angle is increased as the drill diameter and workpiece hardness fall. The recommended point angles are: 130° for hard steels, 118° for general-purpose metal drilling, 105° for mild steels, 80° for soft grey cast iron, and 60° for wood.[7] Woodworkers do not need to be too particular, will usually use the same twist drills for metal and wood, and therefore usually retain the original 118° point angle and a clearance angle of about 15° when they resharpen.

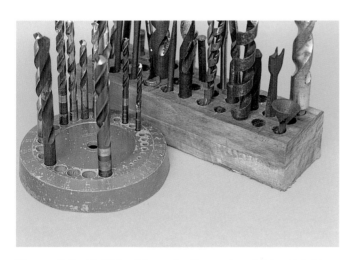

Figure 8.7 **Drill holders**, in die-cast metal by P & N, Australia, and homemade in wood.

Figure 8.9 **Variations on a twist drill.** *Left to right*: for general-purpose metal drilling with a 118° point angle; brad-pointed for drilling dowel holes in wood; and with a 60° point angle and a large cross-sectional-area single flute for drilling wood.

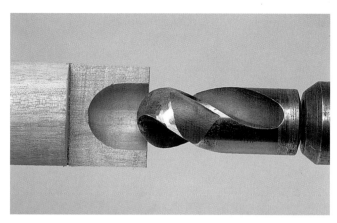

Figure 8.10 A profiled twist drill. You can drill profiled holes with suitably-modified drills. To monitor the hole shape accurately you may have to drill a trial hole into scrap wood, and saw the scrap in half longitudinally. This will also enable you to judge whether all the (usually two) cutting edges are actively cutting. The forces exerted during drilling should be reasonably evenly distributed between and along the cutting edges: if not the drill will chatter.

Ideally all the cutting edges should be identically shaped. If grinding freehand, such accuracy is improbable. The alternative is to have only parts of each cutting edge actively cutting. Regrind so that all cutting edges apply an approximately-equal cutting force and moment (force multiplied by distance from the drill's axis) about the drill's axis. To check which sections of the cutting edges are actively cutting, ink the bevels immediately alongside the cutting edges with a felt-tipped pen, and make a very brief cut into a piece of slowly-rotating scrap wood. The ink will be rubbed off where there is active cutting.

8.3 DRILL SHARPENING

Some drills, for example twist drills, can be resharpened many times; others, such as shell drills, only a few. Unless there is a good reason otherwise, opt to buy drills which allow many resharpenings.

Drills should obviously be kept sharp, but if stored and used correctly the need for resharpening is minimized, drill life is maximized, and the risk of softening any carbon-tool-steel cutting edges is reduced. Remove the minimum metal when resharpening. Therefore hone rather than file, and file rather than grind. When resharpening, assess which faces you can hone, file, or grind without affecting the hole diameter which the drill drills, and the drill's efficiency and geometry. If, for example, you increase a drill's clearance angle(s), you increase the chip thickness and corresponding feed speed. The drill may then pull in too fast to be controllable, may demand too much power, may run out more, and will leave an inferior surface on the hole wall. The sharpening of the major drill types is described in figures 8.11 to 8.25, starting with the twist drill.

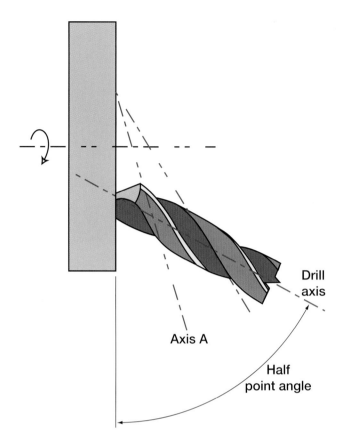

Figure 8.11 The geometry of twist-drill sharpening. To achieve the ideal tip geometry, the drill is swung around axis **A** as if it were in contact with the surface of an imaginary cone. The angle between axis **A** and the vertical face of the grinding wheel is a quarter of the point angle minus half the helix angle. At the same time the drill is fed forwards without rotation along its own axis, and held so that its axis is maintained at an angle of half the point angle to the face of the grinding wheel.[8] This ideal sharpening is done in special machines.

The sharpening process described above is even harder to replicate by hand than it is to visualize. Leonard Lee rightly calls the regrinding of twist drills by hand "a direct road to Hell."[9] If your resharpening is not symmetrical, the drilled hole will be oversize and the run-out greater. If the cutting-edge clearance (or relief) is too large, the drill will feed more quickly and require greater power and torque than normal. If the cutting-edge clearance is too small, the drill feed will be slowed.

There are at least three different methods for regrinding twist drills by hand which approximate to the ideal process: all are unlikely to yield a well-resharpened tip without practice.[10] But use any of the three jigs described in figures 8.12 to 8.16 and success should result.

Figure 8.12 A twist-drill grinding jig which is used on the circular face of a bench-grinder grinding wheel. This jig produces a tip geometry which approximates the ideal described in the previous figure. There are many similar jigs, all should be accompanied by detailed instructions.

The wheel guard shown has been rotated from the normal position because a felt wheel is normally mounted on this end of this grinder's spindle. The grinding wheel is rotating clockwise, and therefore moving correctly downwards past the drill tip.

Figure 8.13 Jig-assisted hand grinding. The fence clamped onto the grinding-jig tilting platform sets the point angle; the tilt of the tilting platform jigs the lip clearance. If the drill is short, you may need to clamp a narrow piece of wood on top of the tilting platform to be able to manipulate the drill readily.

Present the drill with a cutting edge horizontal, and push the drill's left-hand bevel gently into contact with the grinding wheel as shown in the upper photograph. Then without dwelling at the initial contact, steadily push the bevel up the surface of the wheel, at the same time rotating the drill slowly clockwise. Compare the two photographs to clarify the action. Do not rush the grinding movement and you will quickly get the knack. Repeat with the other bevel. When both cutting edges are sharp, compare their lengths, and if not equal, grind further until they are.

Figure 8.14 Twist drill sharpening with a homemade jig of my design. Two pieces of plywood, here 100 x 40 x 17 mm, are screwed together. Their inside faces are longitudinally and symmetrically grooved to locate the drill. When you mount a drill into the jig, have the drill's cutting edges parallel to the faces of the plywood. Jig the lip clearance angle with the tilting platform of a platform sharpening jig, and the point angle with a fence which you fit to the tilting platform. You have to measure or check by eye to ensure that the drill's cutting edges are equal in length. While it does not give the ultimate tip geometry, using this jig beats sharpening freehand. Its use is shown in the next two figures

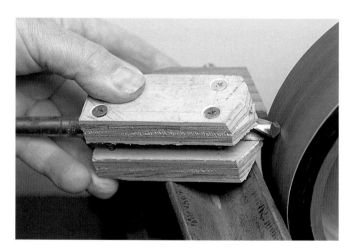

Figure 8.15 The plywood sharpening jig in use.

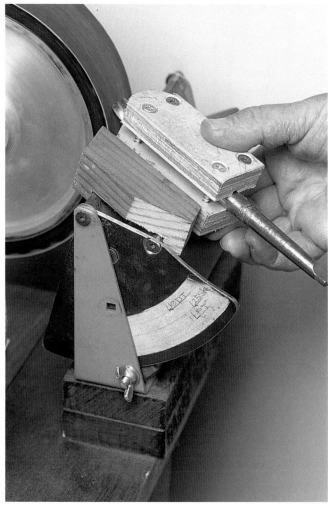

Figure 8.16 **The fence which jigs the point angle** is fitted to the nearside of the tilting platform which is tilted to jig the lip clearance angle.

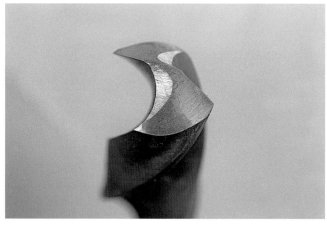

Figure 8.17 **Twist-drill web thinning.**

As you shorten a twist drill its web thickness (figure 8.8) increases. Large-diameter twist drills have inherently thick webs. You can restore or improve a twist drill's performance by thinning its web. Use a small grinding wheel, a rotating mounted conical or cylindrical stone, or an edge of your bench grinder's grinding wheel as shown in the next figure.

Figure 8.18 **Thinning a twist-drill web** on a bench grinder.

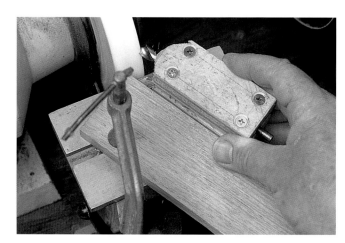

Figure 8.19 Brad-point twist-drill sharpening with my homemade jig.
You can refresh the cutting edges by honing the bevels and the insides of the spurs with a slipstone or a suitably-profiled diamond file. You can regrind on the edge of a grinding wheel. Keep the lip clearance angle at 15° to 20°.

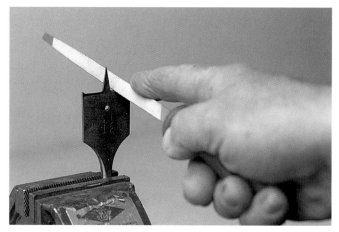

Figure 8.21 Sharpening a spade drill. If through your honing or filing the cutting edges and bevels cease to be identical to one another, the spade drill will at best cut an oval hole.

The sharpening in this and the following four figures is sourced from Leonard Lee's *The Complete Guide to Sharpening*. Lee's book gives greater detail and shows several jigs which you can make to increase your drill-sharpening accuracy.

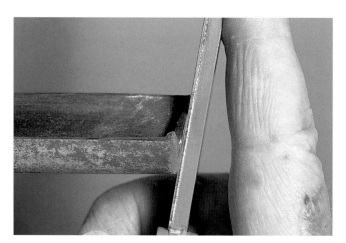

Figure 8.20 Sharpening a shell drill. Shell drills can be resharpened only a limited number of times. Use a fine file or hone. You should not file or hone the front bevel so much that you make it weak—shift to honing the top bevel of the cutting edge. Do not sharpen the long edge along the shell—it should not cut, if it did it would enlarge the hole and the drill would wander off line.

A gun drill can only be correctly resharpened by its manufacturer or by a specialist engineer in the field.

Figure 8.22 **Levelling the teeth of a sawtooth drill** by rotating the drill at the drilling machine's slowest speed. The center point of the drill is clear of the grinding surface, here a surplus grinding wheel supported on the drilling machine's table. You could use a bench stone instead of the grinding wheel.

Figure 8.23 **Sharpening the teeth of a sawtooth drill.** You need only file the front edge of each tooth. Have the vertical face of the file radial from the drill's center point.

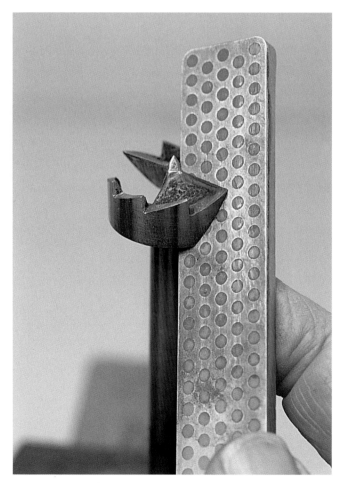

Figure 8.24 **Honing the radial cutting edges** of a sawtooth drill.

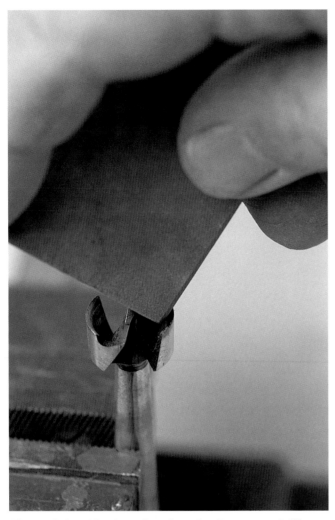

Figure 8.25 Honing the rim of a Forstner drill.
The drill's radial cutting edges are sharpened as shown in the previous figure.

A Forstner drill can cleanly enter a workpiece surface at other than 90° because the sharp rim projects a touch ahead of the two radial cutting edges. The rim is therefore vulnerable to overheating. Use Forstner drills only when you have to, do not run them too fast or cease to feed them, and keep them clean and dry-lubricated.

8.4 DRILL ACCESSORIES

Many drills have straight shanks which have to be held in the lathe in a suitable chuck (figure 8.26). Large-diameter twist drills usually have shanks which taper slowly, and therefore grip in a socket with the same internal taper. John Jacob Holtzapffel showed a round-hole drill chuck which uses this principle in 1881.[11] Within a few years, American Steven Morse had standardized the tapers which bear his name (figures 8.27 and 8.28, and table 8.2). Where a drill shank or chuck arbor do not have the same Morse taper as your lathe's headstock or tailstock swallow, you need to use an adapter (figure 8.28). The special accessories for drilling and long-hole boring are detailed in sections 8.5 and 8.6.

Figure 8.26 Drill chucks. *Left*, a four-jaw scroll chuck marketed by Axminster Power Tool Centre, Devon, England; *center*, a Jacobs chuck on a No. 2 Morse-taper arbor; *right*, a keyless or quick-release chuck.

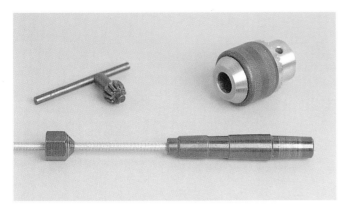

Figure 8.27 A Jacobs chuck with arbor and drawbar from Peter Child, England.

A chuck on a Morse-taper arbor held in a rotating headstock-spindle swallow will tend to creep to the right and rattle out unless continuously pushed in, or unless pulled into the swallow with a drawbar. The drawbar passes through the headstock spindle and the nut is screwed onto the bar's projecting left-hand end.

Some Morse-taper arbors are designed to screw into a chuck; some arbors have a short Jarno- or Jacobs-taper spigot which grips in a socket with the same taper in the chuck body.

Figure 8.28 Adapting Morse tapers. *Top left*, a 3 to 2 MT extension socket; *top center*, a 1 to 3 MT sleeve; *bottom center*, a twist drill with a No. 1 MT shank in a 1 to 2 MT sleeve; *top right*, a 3 to 4 MT sleeve with a drift; *bottom right*, a 2 to 3 MT sleeve.

Morse-tapered arbors, sleeves, and drill shanks can be housed in bigger tapered sockets by using sleeves, and in smaller sockets by using extension sockets. The narrow steel wedge which is driven through the slot in a sleeve to expel the item with the smaller taper is called a drift.

Table 8.2
Morse Taper Dimensions

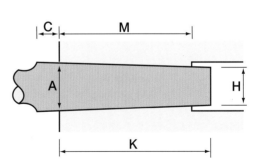

Number of Morse Taper	Diametrical Taper, in./ft.	Diameter at Gauge Line A, in.	Exposed Length C, in.	Contact Length M, in.	Diameter at Small End H, in.	Length of Arbor from Gauge Line K, in.
1	0.59858	0.475	$1/8$	$2\ 1/16$	$11/32$	$2\ 3/16$
2	0.59941	0.700	$3/16$	$2\ 1/2$	$17/32$	$2\ 21/32$
3	0.60235	0.938	$3/16$	$3\ 1/16$	$23/32$	$3\ 5/15$
4	0.62326	1.231	$1/4$	$3\ 7/8$	$31/32$	$4\ 3/16$
$4\ 1/2$	0.62400	1.500	$1/4$	$4\ 5/16$	$1\ 13/64$	$4\ 5/8$
5	0.63151	1.748	$1/4$	$4\ 15/16$	$1\ 13/32$	$5\ 5/16$

The Morse taper is about 1 in 20, or $5/8$ in./ft., and is a self-gripping taper.
Multiply by 25.4 to convert inches to millimeters

8.5 DRILLING METHODS AND EQUIPMENT

Your lathe's headstock-spindle axis and tailstock-ram axis must align well for drilling and axial boring to be successful. Misalignment will cause oversize holes, chatter, and run-out. Wear in the bed and tailstock will increase misalignment. Figures 8.29 to 8.37 show eight ways to drill in a lathe. Some of the operations could be done in a drilling machine or horizontal borer.

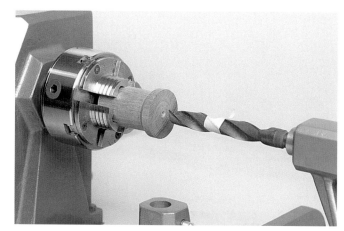

Figure 8.30 Drilling a short or shallow workpiece. The twist drill has a No. 2 Morse-taper shank which fits into the tailstock ram's No. 2 Morse-taper swallow.

Short workpieces can be mounted on a faceplate or held in a chuck. Here the body of a spring chuck is being held in the Shark jaws of a Vicmarc VM120 chuck. Screwchucks are rarely suitable because their center screw prevents drilling through the workpiece.

Figure 8.29 Homemade drill pads. *Left,* flat for general use; *right,* with a conical recess for boring small spheres.

A drill pad is a plate on a Morse-tapered shank. A drill pad acts like the horizontal table of a drilling machine. Manufactured steel drill pads were common, but wooden versions are adequate for light drilling. For heavier drilling, drill and tap a rectangular or circular steel plate and screw it onto a chuck arbor of the appropriate Morse taper. To drill into the sides of spindles use a drill pad with a transverse vee groove.

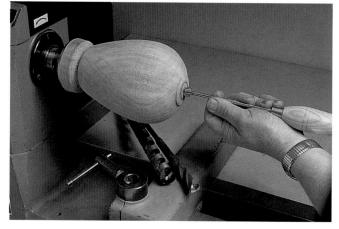

Figure 8.31 Boring with a hand-held drill to the bottom of a hollow turning. In hollow turning and sometimes in bowl turning, you bore a hole to the hollow's bottom before hollowing with gouges or scrapers. You have to hand-hold the drill if the workpiece is mounted outboard, or you may prefer to even when the workpiece is mounted inboard. (Note that for normally-sharpened drills used outboard, the lathe has to be run in reverse).

A long-series twist drill, a shell drill, and a spear-point drill are commonly used for hand boring. The drill needs to be mounted in a handle. If there is no locating, conical recess to start the drill on center, cut one with a detail gouge.

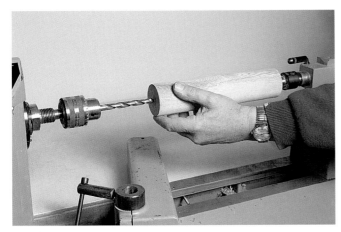

Figure 8.32 Hand locating the left-hand end of a workpiece is only advisable for small-diameter holes. If you start the drill into the larger recess left by a cone-type tail center after any preliminary roughing, the hole is more likely to be true.

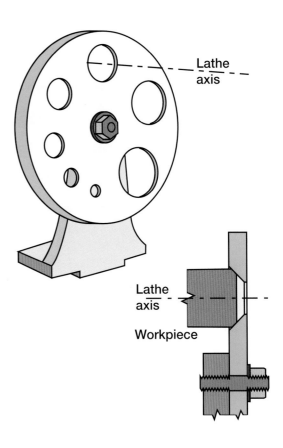

Figure 8.34 A boring collar was the earliest device for locating the right-hand ends of long workpieces during boring. Moxon showed an almost identical version over three centuries ago.[12] The circular metal plate contains several holes of different diameters whose centers are equidistant from the center of the circular plate. The circular plate is rotated to bring the appropriately-sized hole into coaxiality with the lathe axis, and the plate is then locked in position. The holes through the circular plate are conical with an included angle of about 90°. During a long-hole-boring operation, you may need to reposition the boring collar a little to the left to remove excessive play caused by the right-hand end of a workpiece compressing as it rotates within the conical hole.

Boring collars are related to steadies (pages 67 to 69). Some boring collars can be used as steadies and vice versa as shown in the next figure.

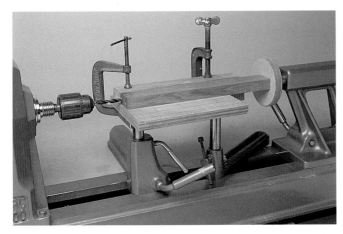

Figure 8.33 A horizontal drilling table supported by two banjos. If your lathe bed is level, you can precisely level the drilling table at the required height using a ruler and spirit level. The workpiece can be pushed to the left along the fence by hand or with the tailstock ram.

For larger workpieces you can make a cradle which fixes to the bed and along which you or the tailstock ram push the workpiece. Alternatively you can fix the workpiece to a cradle which slides along the bed. A vee cradle is best for boring a workpiece of circular cross section.

Long turned workpieces are more commonly bored using a boring collar.

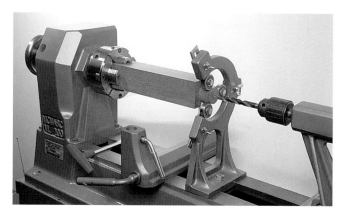

Figure 8.35 Boring into a long workpiece. The right-hand ends of long workpieces should be securely and axially located during boring. Here I have preturned a temporary pin on the workpiece's right-hand end. I can then accurately bore into the square cross-section by locating the pin in a three-wheel planetary steady acting as a boring collar.

Figure 8.37 Radial drilling with a simple shopmade jig. The shoulders on the vertical wooden posts are positioned so that drilling is automatically centered at lathe-axis height. Each drill diameter requires its own jig.

Figure 8.36 Radial drilling using a manufactured jig, the Robert Sorby Precision Boring System. This and similar systems enable you to accurately drill horizontal holes in any direction. The drill bush is usually centered at lathe-axis height. Bushes of different diameters can be housed in the post which fits into your banjo. If you need to drill a ring of holes in a workpiece, the ideal device to ensure equal hole spacing is a lathe's indexing facility.

You can make a similar system from hard wood as the next figure shows.

8.6 LONG-HOLE BORING

The legend of figure 8.2 explains that no drill or auger is self-centering. Therefore, to minimize the run-out when long-hole boring you need to adopt certain procedures:

1. If you feed a non-rotating workpiece against a rotating drill, the drill's tip will be more likely to follow non-axial grain or a zone of softer wood than if you feed a non-rotating drill into a rotating workpiece. The ideal is to contra-rotate both workpiece and drill, but this is neither feasible nor necessary in woodturning.

2. Because long-hole-boring drills steer by being held in alignment within the hole they have just bored, you must start the drill truly axially. You can achieve this by housing a bush in the tailstock-ram swallow or the equivalent, or by boring an axial pilot hole. The bush should preferably not rotate—if it does it can damage the drill. You should also try to keep the shank and the handle end of the drill in axial alignment during the boring (figure 8.42 shows a simple guide which can be useful for both).

3. You need to keep the diameter of the hole as tight as possible. If you do not withdraw a drill sufficiently often, the chips compact and enlarge the hole. The drill tip can then wander off line. You should therefore withdraw a shell drill at about 1/2-in. (13-mm) intervals to clear the chips.

4. If boring through the full length of a workpiece in one operation, take care that the drill tip will not smash into chuck jaws or similar as it emerges through the end of the workpiece. A safer method is to drill from each end, but this is unwise if any misalignment at the holes' meeting would, say, prevent a neat-fitting tube or rod being pushed through. While you should feel when a drill is considerably off line, you will not know by how much until the tip breaks through the side or end of the workpiece.

Figures 8.38 to 8.45 illustrate long-hole boring equipment, procedures, and precautions.

Figure 8.38 Dead, hollow tail centers. These No. 2 Morse-taper centers are manufactured with through-hole diameters corresponding to the commonly-available diameters of shell drill. Here a 5/16 in. long-hole-boring auger is projecting from the hollow tail center held in the tailstock ram.

Boring a workpiece through a dead hollow tail center held in the tailstock ram has two disadvantages: first, the length of the drill is effectively shortened by the length of the tailstock ram; and second, there is high friction between the workpiece and the dead center. The first disadvantage can be overcome by using a banjo-mounted hollow tail center (next figure), or by drilling a pilot hole (figure 8.41); the second by using a live hollow tail center or a modern boring collar (figures 8.40 to 8.45).

Figure 8.39 Aligning a banjo-mounted hollow center with a twist drill (or rod) mounted in a Jacobs chuck mounted in the tailstock-ram swallow. The diameter of the drill or rod and the internal diameter of the hollow center should be the same. After aligning the hollow center, screw it to the left to locate the workpiece's right-hand end.

Figure 8.40 Live hollow tail centers by Craft Supplies and Nova. These live centers have the advantage that the the workpiece is not charred and rotates more easily, but the disadvantage that the bush rotates and is more likely to damage the drill tip.

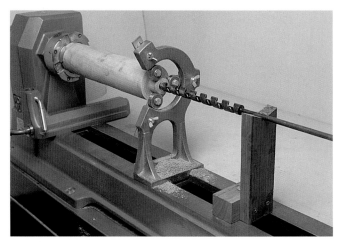

Figure 8.42 Boring through a predrilled pilot hole. The auger is hand-held. The wooden guide helps keep the auger in alignment with the lathe axis, thus minimizing run-out. Ideally the right-hand end of the drill should be held coaxial with the lathe axis by being mounted in or against the tailstock ram if the lathe bed is long enough. When the bed is too short, it would be worth making a wooden bed extension if boring many workpieces.

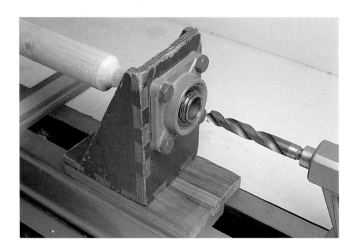

Figure 8.41 Boring an axial pilot hole with a twist drill held in the tailstock-ram swallow. Instead of the tapered-shank drill shown, you could use a straight-shank drill held in a Jacobs chuck. The right-hand end of the workpiece has been turned with a steep taper which locates into a boring collar made from a bearing bolted onto a plywood structure. The long hole is then bored using the pilot hole as a bush.

    This boring collar was shown being used as a steady in figure 3.18.

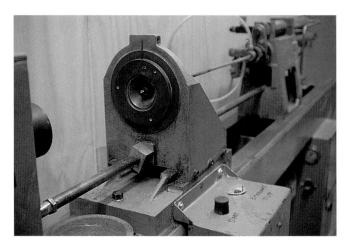

Figure 8.43 The fixed bush, live taper chuck arrangement of a Genini automatic pneumatic and hydraulic hole-boring lathe. The boring collar slides along a carriage which is positioned on the bed according to the length of the workpiece. The boring collar is moved to the left and right by the pneumatically-operated rod. The boring collar has a fixed bush surrounded by a taper chuck mounted in a bearing. The next figure shows a cruder equivalent.

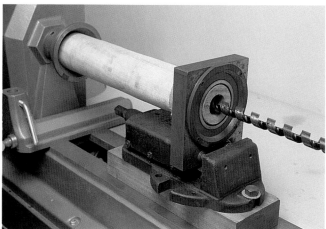

Figure 8.44 Boring a workpiece held between two taper chucks. A taper chuck is mounted on the headstock spindle. The workpiece's right-hand end is located in a hard-wood taper chuck held tightly within the inner race of a bearing which is housed in a plate screwed to the moveable jaw of a machine vice. By operating the machine vice the hard-wood taper chuck can be moved to the left and right to clamp and unclamp the workpiece. For large-volume drilling you might replace the screw operation by a pneumatic system.

The drill is the auger shown in figure 8.3, and its right-hand end is held in a Jacobs chuck mounted in the tailstock ram. A pilot hole has been drilled earlier with a twist drill mounted in the tailstock ram.

Figure 8.45 Boring a long hole in a large workpiece. The principles are the same irrespective of the workpiece size. The drill being fed by apprentices Nick Johnson (left) and Stephen Waite is similar to that shown in figure 8.3, and is welded to an extension rod. The boring collar is a larger, steel-bodied version of that shown in figure 8.41.

8.7 FINISH-TURNING AFTER BORING

You should bore spindles such as lamp stems which are to have full-length through holes before you finish-turn them. You then center the workpiece by the ends of the bored hole for finish-turning. Then even if the through hole was not bored truly, it will pass centrally through the finished turning. Figures 8.46 to 8.50 show common mounting methods.

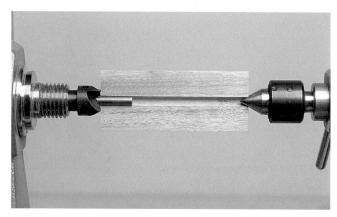

Figure 8.46 A drive centre and a cone tail center used to mount a bored workpiece for finish-turning. The drive center has interchangeable center pins of $1/4$, $5/16$, and $3/8$-in. diameters.

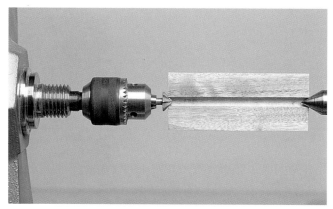

Figure 8.47 A rose countersink can be used to drive and center workpieces with small-diameter through holes.

Figure 8.48 **Using plugs to mount a bored workpiece.** Screws have been screwed through the drive plug to leave their points projecting sufficiently to positively drive the workpiece. The plug drive center need not be turned with a Morse-taper shank and held in the headstock spindle swallow as here—it could be mounted in a chuck, or on a screwcuck or faceplate.

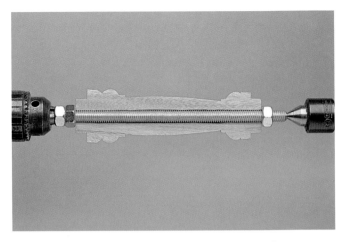

Figure 8.50 **A bored workpiece mounted on a screwed mandrel** made from a length of threaded rod. More sophisticated screwed mandrels with Morse-tapered left-hand ends may still be available.

Figure 8.49 **Using a live tail center** to locate the right-hand end of a bored workpiece. Like an engineers' pipe live tail center, the whole outside of this Nova live tail center rotates.

8.8 BORED, STEPPED, REAMED, TAPERED, AND COUNTERBORED HOLES

Figures 8.51 to 8.57 illustrate the equipment and methods used when more than one operation is needed to produce a hole.

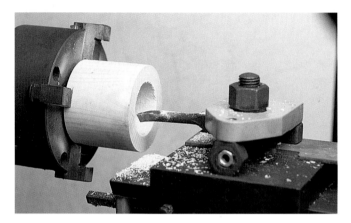

Figure 8.51 Enlarging a drilled hole with a carriage-mounted boring bar. This boring bar was forged with a square cross section at its right-hand end, and a cranked scraping tip at its left-hand end. Boring bars which mount in tailstock-ram swallows are also manufactured.

Figure 8.52 Drilling a stepped hole. Start with the largest-diameter drill and work down through the diameters. Take care to locate the tip of the next-largest drill in the center of the hole left by the previous drill. Alternatively, you could first drill to the full depth of the stepped hole with the smallest drill, and then drill progressively shallower holes as you step up in drill diameter. The later, larger-diameter drills are less likely to drill concentrically with this second method.

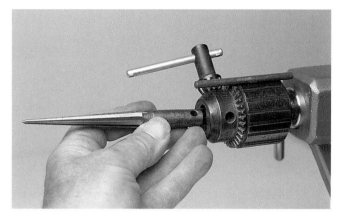

Figure 8.53 A tapered reamer which can be used by hand or mounted in a chuck.

You may want to drill a tapered hole. Tapered twist drills are manufactured, but in a limited range of sizes and tapers. The alternative is to drill a single-diameter or stepped hole which you then ream with a reamer or trim with a gouge or scraper.

In metalworking, drilled holes are smoothed, trued to size, enlarged, or profiled by reaming. In woodturning profiling is the main use.

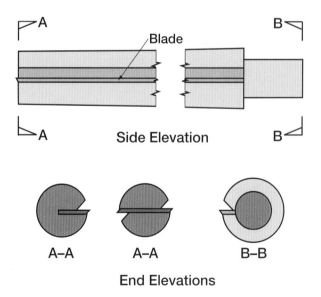

Figure 8.54 Single- and double-bladed reamers based on one shown in Hamelin-Bergeron, plate XXX. The bodies can be hard wood or metal. Two-bladed versions can be made by sandwiching a single, two-edged blade between two semicircular sections of hard wood.

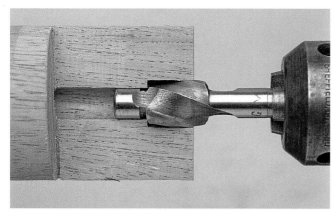

Figure 8.55 **Counterboring** is related to gun drilling in that the cutting edge(s) are steered by a non-cutting part of the drill which rotates snugly within a previously drilled pilot hole. In counterboring, however, the steering part of the drill tip precedes rather than follows the cutting part of the drill, and the steering hole is bored in a previous and separate operation.

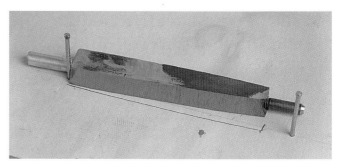

Figure 8.57 **Checking the grinding of the counterboring reamer shown in the previous figure.** By locating the reamer's projecting pins against the nails, I can draw the profile of the side and front cutting edges on one side, and then axially rotate the tool 180° to check how well the profiles of other edges agree.

8.9 ENDNOTES

Figure 8.56 **Deep counterboring** can be used to enlarge and to profile holes. The cylindrical centre pin at the front of this counterboring reamer is guided by the axial hole bored previously with a shell drill.

This tool was made from a piece of carbon tool steel. The tool steel was held in a four-jaw scroll chuck mounted on this wood lathe for the boring and tapping to receive the 5/16 in. and 3/8 in. bolt sections which form the pins at each end.

1 G.P. Wall, *Heat Treatment of Steel* (Sheffield: Magneto Works, no date).
2 L.T.C. Rolt, *Tools for the Job*, pp. 170–171. Also: Joseph Wickham Roe, *English & American Tool Builders* (Yale University Press, reprinted Lindsay Publications Inc., Bradley, Illinois, 1987), pp. 196.
3 Ernie Conover, "Drilling with a Lathe," *Woodturning* No 9, pp. 67–71.
4 Gun drill catalogue of Botek GmbH, Germany.
5 Frank Pain, *The Practical Wood Turner*, p. 137.
6 Illustration scanned from C.A. Martin, *Der Drechsler*, p. 145, fig. 318.
7 John L. Feirer, *Machine Tool Metalworking* (New York: McGraw-Hill, 1973), p. 219.
8 *Machinery's Handbook* (New York: Industrial Press Inc., 20th ed., 1976), pp. 1820–1821.
9 Leonard Lee, *The Complete Guide to Sharpening* (Newtown, Connecticut: The Taunton Press, 1995), p. 192.
10 Different methods are described in: Edward K. Hammond, *Modern Drilling Practice* (New York: The Industrial Press, 1919), pp. 129–133; J. Smith, editor, *Complete Engineer* (London: George Newnes, no date, vol 1), pp. 164–167; and John L. Feirer, *Machine Tool Metalwork*, p. 221.
11 J.J. Holtzapffel, *Hand or Simple Turning*, p. 206.
12 Joseph Moxon, *Mechanick Exercises or the Doctrine of Handy-Works*, plate 13 of the turning section.

Chapter Nine

WHERE NEXT?

Edmond Capon, director of the Art Gallery of New South Wales, has defined his job as "to keep switching lights on just over the horizon." But I have been impressed through researching this book by how many turners push forwards towards distant lights which they have themselves switched on. This is just as prevalent in the ranks of beginners and hobbyists as it is among high-profile professionals. For all, the horizon, like the end of the rainbow, keeps tantalizingly in view but is always ahead. And this is how it should be, for it is the journey which fulfills.

I wrote *Woodturning Methods* to help you on your turning journey. Some of its content will immediately appeal, may excite you to explore further; some content may appeal in the future; and some may never achieve any particular relevance. But even this last content is not without benefit.

In twenty years of professional jobbing turning I have never needed to use some of the methods detailed in this book. Some of the methods I was never attracted to. But I am glad that I have had to explore them for this book. I cannot say why or point to any discernible result, but greater knowledge brings with it subtle benefits, especially an increase in confidence.

Confidence is the vital factor for progress. Through *The Fundamentals of Woodturning* you will have gained confidence in your basic tool skills. *Woodturning Methods* will help you to increase your repertoire and widen your turning horizons by adding methods which build on those basic skills.

So grab hold of the methods you are attracted to. But don't reject those which seem irrelevant because just knowing of them will enrich your turning and may help you to overcome unexpected problems in the future.

The concluding pictures in the book are of a humble invention for the pediculous rather than a significant art piece for collectors. To turn it needed the hand steadying described in chapter 3. But it is not the only salve if this book has left you itching to get to your workshop.

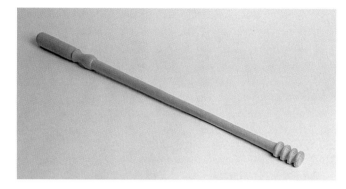

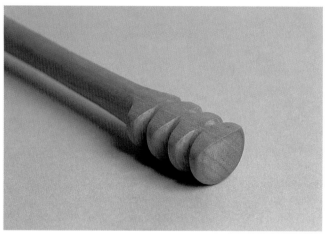

Figure 9.1 A backscratcher. The flattened end makes it easy to use when you're dressed.

Appendix

BIBLIOGRAPHIES

This appendix is provided for the growing proportion of turners who seek to expand their knowledge. There are four bibliographies:

1. Books in English on and relevant to hand woodturning. This bibliography concentrates on titles which are in print or have recently been. It also included titles on treen because many of the items described in them are turned.
2. Books on ornamental-turning.
3. Books on hand- and/or ornamental-turning in languages other than English.
4. Magazines which usually include woodturning content.

The bibliographies are not exhaustive. I have gleaned some of the titles from the bibliography published in the *American Association of Woodturners Annual Resource Directory*. I have not included the details of every edition of a particular book. Some books are published in different countries and at different times by different publishers; and sometimes with different titles. Where a facsimile of a book long out of print has been published, I have tended to list the details of the facsimile edition because it is easier to access. I have included books which detail both hand turning and ornamental-turning in both bibliographies.

The Internet is such a rapidly-growing and changing source of woodturning information that I have not attempted to list any of its woodturning sites.

I would be grateful for the details of new magazines and books, and of past books which I have failed to include: I will add them to the bibliographies in future editions.

BIBLIOGRAPHY OF HAND-WOODTURNING BOOKS IN ENGLISH

Abbott, Mike. *Green Woodwork*. Lewes, East Sussex: Guild of Master Craftsman Publications, 1989.

American Association of Woodturners Project Book. Minneapolis: American Association of Woodturners, 1993.

American Woodturner's Techniques & Projects. Minneapolis: American Association of Woodturners, 1996.

Art of Woodturning. New York: American Crafts Museum, 1983.

A Sampling of papers from the 1993 World Turning Conference. Philadelphia: Wood Turning Center, 1997.

Ashby, Peter, and Ashby, Tim. *Woodturner's Wooden Clock Cases*. Fresno, California: Linden Publishing, 1992.

Association of Woodturners of Great Britain. *Wonders in Wood*. 1998.

Audsley, George Ashdown, and Audsley, Berthold. *The Art of Polychromatic & Decorative Turning*. London: George Allen, 1911.

Barker, Harold. *Pictorial History of the American Wood Lathe (1800-1960)*. Ada, Ohio: Harold Barker, 1986.

Bell, R.C. *Fun on the Lathe*. Lewes, East Sussex: Guild of Master Craftsman Publications, 1997.

Bidou, Gerard, and Guilloux, Daniel. *Woodturning in France*. Dourdan, France: Editions H. Vial, 1998. There is also an edition in French.

Blandford, Percy. 24 *Woodturning Projects*. Blue Ridge Summit, Pennsylvania: TAB Books, 1990.

Blandford, Percy. *The Woodturner's Bible*. Blue Ridge Summit, Pennsylvania: TAB Books, 1975.

Blandford, Percy. *Wood Turning*. London: W. & G. Foyle, 1976.

Boase, Tony. *Woodturning Masterclass*. Lewes, East Sussex: Guild of Master Craftsman Publications, 1995.

Boase, Tony. *Bowl Turning Techniques Masterclass*, Lewes, East Sussex: Guild of Master Craftsman Publications, 1999.

Borre, William R. *The Art of Freehand Turning in Miniature*. Windsor, Ontario: B.J. Miniatures, 1982.

Boulter, Bruce. *Woodturning in Pictures*. London: Bell & Hyman, 1983.

Boulter, Bruce. *Woodturning Projects and Techniques*. Hemel Hempstead, Hertfordshire: Argus Books, 1986.

Bowen, Hilary. *Woodturning Jewellery*. Lewes, East Sussex: Guild of Master Craftsman Publications, 1995.

Bowen, Hilary. *Decorative Techniques for Woodturners*. Lewes, East Sussex: Guild of Master Craftsman Publications, 1996.

Bridgewater, Alan, and Bridgewater, Gill. *Winning Designs for Woodturning*. London: Unwin Hyman, 1987.

Bridgewater, Alan, and Bridgewater, Gill. *Woodturning Traditional Folk Toys*. New York: Sterling Publishing, 1994.

Brown, Emmett E., and Brown, Cyril. *Polychromatic Assembly for Woodturning*. Fresno, California: Linden Publishing, 1982.

Browne, Sam, editor. *Getting the Most out of your Wood Lathe.* Hinckley, Leicestershire: TEE Publishing, 1993. (Facsimile of 1935 first edition).

Cain, Tubal. *Workholding in the Lathe.* Hemel Hempstead, Hertfordshire: Argus Books, 1987.

Child, Peter. *The Craftsman Woodturner.* London: G. Bell & Sons, 1971.

Cole, R.W. *Woodturning.*

Conover, Ernie. *The Lathe Book.* Newtown, Connecticut: The Taunton Press, 1993.

Conover, Ernie. *Turning for Furniture.* Newtown, Connecticut: The Taunton Press, 1996.

Cox, Jack. *Beyond Basic Turning:* Hertford, Hertfordshire: Stobart Davies, 1993.

Crafts Alliance Gallery. *Works off the Lathe: Old and New Faces.* Saint Louis, Missouri: Crafts Alliance Gallery, 1987.

Crafts Study Centre. *David Pye: Wood Carver and Turner.* London: Crafts Council, 1986.

Cramlet, Ross C. *Woodturning Visualized.* Milwaukee: Bruce Publishing, 1966.

Crawshaw, Fred D. *Problems in Wood-Turning.* Peoria, Illinois: The Manual Arts Press, 1933.

Cripps, Mike. *Turning Goblets.* Atglen, Pennsylvania: Schiffer Publishing, 1997.

Cripps, Mike. *Turning Pens and Other Desk Accessories.* Atglen, Pennsylvania: Schiffer Publishing, 1997.

Cripps, Mike. *Wood Turning for the Garden.* Atglen, Pennsylvania: Schiffer Publishing, 1997.

Darlow, Mike. *The Fundamentals of Woodturning.* Exeter, NSW: The Melaleuca Press, 1998.

Darlow, Mike. *The Practice of Woodturning.* Exeter, NSW: The Melaleuca Press, 1985 and 1996.

Darlow, Mike. *Woodturning Methods.* Exeter, NSW: The Melaleuca Press, 1999.

David Pye: Wood Carver and Turner. London: Crafts Council, 1986.

Dinmore, Ernest Augustus. *Wood Turning.* London: Evans Brothers, 1947.

Dinmore, Ernest Augustus. *Wood Turning Designs.* London: Evans Brothers, circa 1951.

Ditmer, Judy. *Basic Bowl Turning with Judy Ditmer.* Atglen, Pennsylvania: Schiffer Publishing, 1994.

Ditmer, Judy. *Turning Wooden Jewelry.* Atglen, Pennsylvania: Schiffer Publishing, 1994.

Dixon, Philip H. *The Reading Lathe: A Link with the Anglo-Saxon Migration.* Newport, Isle of Wight: Cross Publishing, 1994.

Dunbar, Michael. *Woodturning for Cabinetmakers.* New York: Sterling Publishing, 1990.

Duncan, S. Blackwell. *Basic Wood Turning: A Layman's Introduction and Guide.* Englewood Cliffs, New Jersey: Prentice-Hall, 1986.

Easinger, Earl W. *Problems in Artistic Woodturning.* Woodcraft Supply Corp, 1954.

Enter the World of Lathe-Turned Objects. York, Pennsylvania: York Graphic Services, 1997.

Evan-Thomas, Owen. *Domestic Utensils of Wood.* Wakefield, Yorkshire: EP Publishing, 1973. (First published in 1932 by Owen Evans-Thomas, London).

Evans, Harry Thomas. *The Craft of Wood-Turning.* London: The Technical Press, 1957.

Expressions in Wood: Masterworks from the Wornick Collection. Oakland, California: Oakland Museum of California, 1996.

Faceplate Turning: Features, Projects, Practice. Lewes, East Sussex: Guild of Master Craftsman Publications, 1996.

Fairham, W. *Wood-Turning.* London: Evans Brothers, no date.

Fine Arts Museum of the South. *Out of the Woods: Turned Wood by American Craftsmen.* Mobile, Alabama: Fine Arts Museum of the South, 1992.

Fine Woodworking on Faceplate Turning. Newtown, Connecticut: The Taunton Press, 1987.

Fine Woodworking on Spindle Turning. Newtown, Connecticut: The Taunton Press, 1987.

Golden, Michael Joseph. *A Laboratory Course in Wood-Turning.* New York: American Book Company, 1897.

Gustavsson, Ragnar, and Olsen, Olle. *Creating in Wood with the Lathe.* New York: Van Nostrand Reinhold, 1968.

Haines, Ray E., editor. *The Wood-Turning Lathe.* New York: D. Van Nostrand, 1952.

Hasluck, Paul Nooncree. *The Wood Turner's Handybook.* London: Crosby Lockwood, 1887.

Hasluck, Paul Nooncree. *Lathe Work.* London: Crosby Lockwood, 1910.

Hetherington, A.L. *British Empire Hardwoods from the Point of View of Turnery.* London: H.M. Stationery Office, 1931.

Hodges, Lewis. *The Woodturning Handbook with Projects.* Blue Ridge Summit, Pennsylvania: TAB Books, 1984.

Hogbin, Stephen. *Wood Turning: The Purpose of the Object.* Sydney, NSW: John Ferguson, 1980.

Holtzapffel, Charles. *Materials; etc.* Vol. I of Turning and Mechanical Manipulation. Radford Semele, Warwickshire: TEE Publishing, 1993. (Facsimile of 1846 first edition).

Holtzapffel, Charles. *The Principles etc. of Cutting Tools etc.* Vol. II of Turning and Mechanical Manipulation. Radford Semele, Warwickshire: TEE Publishing, 1993. (Facsimile of 1875 first edition).

Holtzapffel, Charles, and Holtzapffel,.John Jacob. *Abrasive and Miscellaneous Processes, etc.* Vol. III of Turning and Mechanical Manipulation. Radford Semele, Warwickshire: TEE Publishing, 1993. (Facsimile of 1894 first edition).

Holtzapffel, John Jacob. *The Principles and Practice of Hand or Simple Turning.* Vol. IV of Turning and Mechanical Manipulation. New York: Dover Publications, 1976. (Facsimile of 1881 first edition).

Holtzapffel, John Jacob. *The Principles and Practice of Ornamental or Complex Turning.* Vol. V of Turning and Mechanical Manipulation. New York: Dover Publications, 1973. (Facsimile of 1881 first edition).

Hopper, Ray. *Multi-Centre Woodturning.* Lewes, East Sussex, England: Guild of Master Craftsman Publications, 1992.

Hunnex, John. *Illustrated Woodturning Techniques.* Lewes, East Sussex: Guild of Master Craftsman Publications, 1996.

Hunnex, John. *Woodturning: A Source Book of Shapes.* Lewes, East Sussex: Guild of Master Craftsman Publications, 1993.

Hutchinson, Thomas C. *The Pen Turning Manual.* Sturgeon, Missouri: Hut Products for Wood, 1995.

ICS *Reference Library Volume 10A.* London, International Correspondence Schools, 1903.

Iles, Ashley. *Memories of a Sheffield Tool Maker.* Mendham, New Jersey: The Astragal Press, 1993.

Intermediate Woodturning Projects. Lewes, East Sussex: Guild of Master Craftsman Publications, 1997.

Jacobson, Edward. *The Art of Turned Wooden Bowls.* New York: E.P. Dutton, 1985.

Jacobson, James. *Small & Exciting Woodturning Projects.* New York: Sterling Publishing, 1994.

Jacobson, James. *Small and Unusual Woodturning Projects.* New York: Sterling Publishing, 1987.

Jacobson, James. *Woodturning Music Boxes.* New York: Sterling Publishing, 1983.

James, Gerald T. *Woodturning: Design and Practice.* London: John Murray (Publishers), 1958.

Jones, Phil, and Mercer, Charles. *Woodturner's Project Book.* New York: Sterling Publishing, 1987.

Key, Ray. *The Woodturner's Workbook.* London: B.T. Batsford, 1992.

Key, Ray. *Woodturning and Design.* London: B.T. Batsford, 1985.

Key, Ray. *Woodturning with Ray Key.* London: B.T. Batsford, 1997.

Klenke, William W. *The Art of Wood Turning.* Radford Semele, Warwickshire: TEE Publishing, 1993. (Facsimile of 1954 first edition).

Krochmal, C. and Snipes, K. *Art of Woodturning.* Drake Publications.

Lathe-Turned Objects. Philadelphia, Pennsylvania: Wood Turning Center, 1988.

Lawrence, Terry. *Turning Wooden Toys.* Lewes, East Sussex: Guild of Master Craftsman Publications, 1994.

LeCoff, Albert, editor. *Challenge IV: International Lathe-Turned Objects.* Philadelphia, Pennsylvania: Wood Turning Center, 1991.

LeCoff, Albert, editor. *Challenge V: International Lathe-Turned Objects.* Philadelphia, Pennsylvania: Wood Turning Center, 1993.

LeCoff, Albert, curator. *Lathe-Turned Objects: An International Exhibition.* Philadelphia, Pennsylvania: Wood Turning Center, 1988.

Levi, Jonathon, with Young, Robert. *Treen for the Table.* Woodbridge, Suffolk: Antique Collectors Club, 1998.

Lindquist, Mark. *Sculpting Wood.* Worcester, Massachusetts: Davis Publications, 1986.

Lukin, James. *The Lathe and its Uses.* London: Trubner & Co, 1868.

Lukin, James. *Turning for Beginners.* London: Guilbert Pitman, 1906.

Lukin, James, editor. *Turning Lathes: A Guide to Turning, Screw Cutting, Metal Spinning & Ornamental Turning.* Mendham, New Jersey: Astragal Press, 1994. (Facsimile of 1894 fourth edition and 1896 Britannia Company Catalogue).

Lukin, James, editor. *Turning Lathes: A Manual for Technical Schools and Apprentices,* fifth edition. Colchester, England: 1899.

Macbeth, Alan. *Wood Turning for the Beginner.* London: Percival Marshall, 1949.

Marsh, Bert. *Bert Marsh Woodturner.* Lewes, East Sussex: Guild of Master Craftsman Publications, 1995.

Martin, Terry. *Wood Dreaming.* Sydney, Australia: Angus & Robertson, 1996.

Meilach, Dona Z. *Creating Small Wood Objects as Functional Sculpture.* New York: Crown Publishers, 1976 and 1987.

Meilach, Dona Z. *Woodworking: The New Wave.* New York: Crown Publishers, 1981.

Milton, Archie S., and Wohlers, Otto K. *A Course in Wood Turning.* Milwaukee: The Bruce Publishing Company, 1919.

Mortimer, Stuart. *Techniques of Spiral Work.* Hertfod, Hertfordshire: Stobart Davies, 1996.

Moxon, Joseph. *Mechanick Exercises; or the Doctrine of Handy Works.* New York: Praeger Publishers, 1970. (Facsimile of 1703 third edition).

Nish, Dale. *Artistic Woodturning.* Provo, Utah: Brigham Young University Press, 1980.

Nish, Dale. *Creative Woodturning.* Provo, Utah: Brigham Young University Press, 1975.

Nish, Dale. *Master Woodturners*. Provo, Utah: Artisan Press, 1985.

Northcott, W. Henry. *A Treatise on Lathes and Turning*. Fresno, California: Linden Publishing, 1987. (Facsimile of 1868 first edition).

O'Donnell, Michael. *Woodturning*. Hemel Hempstead, Hertfordshire: Argus Books, 1988.

O'Neill, Hugh. *The Complete Spindle Turner*. Marlborough, Wiltshire: The Crowood Press, 1998.

O'Neill, Hugh. *Woodturning: A Guide to Advanced Techniques*. Marlborough, Wiltshire: The Crowood Press, 1994.

O'Neill, Hugh. *Woodturning: A Manual of Techniques*. Marlborough, Wiltshire: The Crowood Press, 1989.

Pain, F. *The Practical Wood Turner*. London: Evans Brothers, 1965.

Peters, Geoff. *Woodturning*. Arco Books, 1961.

Phillips, Ann, and Phillips, Bob. *Make Money from Woodturning*. Lewes, East Sussex: Guild of Master Craftsman Publications, 1995.

Phillips, Ann, and Phillips, Bob. *Understanding Woodturning*. Lewes, East Sussex: Guild of Master Craftsman Publications, 1997.

Pinto, Edward H. *Treen and Other Wooden Bygones*. London: G. Bell & Sons, 1969.

Pracht, Klaus. *Woodturning*. London: Dryad Press, 1988.

Practical Tips for Turners & Carvers. Lewes, East Sussex: Guild of Master Craftsman Publications, 1995.

Practical Tips for Woodturners. Lewes, East Sussex: Guild of Master Craftsman Publications, 1995.

Pye, Chris. *Carving on Turning*. Lewes, East Sussex: Guild of Master Craftsman Publications, 1995.

Pye, David. *The Nature and Aesthetics of Design*. New York: Van Nostrand Reinhold, 1982.

Pye, David. *The Nature and Art of Workmanship*. Cambridge: Cambridge University Press, 1968.

Raffan, Richard. *Turned-Bowl Design*. Newtown, Connecticut: Taunton Press, 1987.

Raffan, Richard. *Turning Boxes with Richard Raffan*. Newtown, Connecticut: Taunton Press, 1998.

Raffan, Richard. *Turning Projects*. Newtown, Connecticut: Taunton Press, 1991.

Raffan, Richard. *Turning Wood with Richard Raffan*. Newtown, Connecticut: The Taunton Press, 1985.

Rebhorn, Eldon, and McKnight. *Woodturning*.

Regester, David. *Great Little Things to Make on a Small Lathe*. London: B.T. Batsford, 1996.

Regester, David. *Turning Bowls Step-by-Step*. London: B.T. Batsford, 1994.

Regester, David. *Turning Boxes and Spindles Step-By-Step*. London: B.T. Batsford, 1994.

Regester, David. *Woodturning Step-by-Step*. London: B.T. Batsford, 1993.

Resides, George H., and Diemer, Hugo. *Wood-Turning*. New York: McGraw-Hill, 1911.

Robertson, Peter. *Creating a Scottish Highland Bagpipe*. Glasgow: Leobyte Publishing, 1994.

Roszkiewicz, Ron. *The Woodturner's Companion*. New York: Sterling Publishing, 1984.

Rowley, Keith. *Woodturning: A Foundation Course*. Lewes, East Sussex: Guild of Master Crafsman Publications, 1990.

Rowley, Keith. *Keith Rowley's Woodturning Projects*. Lewes, East Sussex: Guild of Master Craftsman Publications, 1996.

Sainsbury, John. *Craft of Woodturning*. New York: Sterling Publishing, 1984.

Sainsbury, John. *John Sainsbury's Guide to Woodturning Tools and Equipment*. Newton Abbot, Devon: David & Charles Publishers, 1989.

Sainsbury, John. *Sainsbury's Woodturning Projects for Dining*. New York: Sterling Publishing, 1981.

Sainsbury, John. *Turning Miniatures in Wood*. Lewes, East Sussex: Guild of Master Craftsman Publications, 1991.

Sanders, Jan. *Colouring Techniques for Woodturners*. Lewes, East Sussex: Guild of Master Craftsman Publications, 1996.

Seale, Roland. *Practical Designs for Wood Turning*. London: Evans Brothers, 1957.

Sherwin, Reg. *Pleasure and Profit from Woodturning*. Lewes, East Sussex: Guild of Master Craftsman Publications, 1988.

Sing, Dick. *Pens from the Wood Lathe*. Derbyshire: Craft Supplies, 1997.

Sing, Dick. *Useful Beauty: Turning Practical Items on a Wood Lathe*. Atglen, Pennsylvania: Schiffer Publishing, 1995.

Sing, Dick. *Wood Lathe Projects for Fun and Profit*. Atglen, Pennsylvania: Schiffer Publishing, 1994.

Slater, David. *Wood-Turning Made Easy*. London: Cassell, 1931, revised 1953.

Small, Tunstall, and Woodbridge, Christopher. *Mouldings & Turned Woodwork of the 16th, 17th and 18th Centuries*. Hertford, Hertfordshire: Stobart Davies, 1987.

Spielman, Patrick. *The Art of the Lathe*. New York: Sterling Publishing, 1996.

Spindle Turning. Lewes, East Sussex: Guild of Master Craftsman Publications, 1996.

Springett, David. *Adventures in Woodturning*. Lewes, East Sussex: Guild of Master Craftsman Publications, 1994.

Springett, David. *Turning Lace Bobbins*. Rugby, Warwickshire: C & D Springett, 1995.

Springett, David. *Woodturning Wizardry*. Lewes, East Sussex: Guild of Master Craftsman Publications, 1993.

Springett, Christine, and Springett, David. *Success to the Lace Pillow*. Rugby, Warwickshire: C & D Springett, 1997.

Stokes, Gordon. *Beginner's Guide to Woodturning*. London: Pelham Books, 1974.

Stokes, Gordon. *Modern Woodturning*. London: Evans Brothers, 1973.

Stokes, Gordon. *Woodturning for Pleasure*. Englewoodcliffs, New Jersey: Prentice-Hall, 1980.

Stephenson, Eric. *The Auto-Lathe*. Sheffield, Yorkshire: Eric Stephenson Woodworking Techniques, 1978.

Stephenson, William L. *Victorian Woodturnings and Woodworks*. Loveland, Ohio: Chestnut Publications, 1995.

Stults, Tom. *Pen Making Made Simple*. Yukon, Oklahoma: CWT, 1996.

The Best of Fine Woodworking: Lathes and Turning Techniques. Newtown, Connecticut: Taunton Press, 1991.

The Woodworker Book of Turning, Hemel Hempstead, Hertfordshire: Argus Books, 1990.

Thorlin, Anders. *Ideas for Woodturning*. London: Evans Brothers, 1977.

Toller, Jane. *Treen and Other Turned Woodware for Collectors*. Newton Abbot, Devon: David & Charles, 1975.

Useful Techniques for Woodturners. Lewes, East Sussex: Guild of Master Craftsman Publications, 1998.

Useful Woodturning Projects. Lewes, East Sussex: Guild of Master Craftsman Publications, 1995.

Watson, Egbert P. *Manual of the Hand Lathe*. Philadelphia: Henry Carey Baird, 1869.

Weldon, David. *Shapes for Woodturners*. London: B.T. Batsford, 1992.

Wilk, Christopher. *The Art of Wood Turning*. New York: American Craft Council, 1983.

Wilkie, Ian. *Woodturning for Repair and Restoration*. Marlborough, Wiltshire: The Crowood Press, 1998.

Woodbury, R.S. *Studies in the History of Machine Tools*. Cambridge, Massachusetts: Massachusetts Institute of Technology Press, 1972.

Woodturning Techniques. Lewes, East Sussex: Guild of Master Craftsman Publications, 1995.

Woodturning: Tools & Equipment Test Reports. Lewes, East Sussex: Guild of Master Craftsman Publications, 1998.

Wooldridge. W.J. *Woodturning Techniques*. New York: Sterling Publishing, 1982.

BIBLIOGRAPHY OF ORNAMENTAL-TURNING BOOKS

Abell, S.G., Leggat, J., and Ogden, W.G. Jr. *A Bibliography of the Art of Turning and Lathe and Machine Tool History*. North Andover, Massachusetts: The Museum of Ornamental Turning Ltd, 1987. The starting point for researching references on ornamental-turning.

Bergeron, Louis-Eloy. *Manuel du Tourneur*. Paris: Vol. 1 1792, Vol. 2 1796. Second edition revised by Pierre Hamelin-Bergeron with supplements published 1816 to 1843. Second edition facsimile printed 1980 in two volumes plus loose plates by Jacques Laget, Nogent-le Roi, France.

C.H.C. *Ornamental Lathework for Amateurs*. London: Percival Marshall, no date.

Edwards, Ross. *Microcomputer Art*. Sydney, Australia: Prentice Hall of Australia.

Evans, J. H. *Ornamental Turning*. Mendham, New Jersey: Astragal Press, 1993. (Facsimile of first edition published in England in 1886 by the author).

Grace, G.A. *The Art and Craft of Ornamental Turning*. London: Society of Ornamental Turners, 1960. (The Society of Ornamental Turners also publishes booklets on specialist areas of the craft).

Hetherington, A.L. *British Empire Hardwoods from the Point of View of Turnery*. London: H.M. Stationery Office, 1931.

Holtzapffel, John Jacob. *The Principles and Practice of Ornamental or Complex Turning*. Vol. V of Turning and Mechanical Manipulation. New York: Dover Publications, 1973. (Facsimile of 1894 first edition). See the previous bibliography for the other four books in the Holtzapffel series.

Hulot. *L'art du Tourneur Mechanicien* (part of 25-volume series *Description des Arts et Metiers*). Geneva, Switzerland: Slatkin Reprints.

Jones, Bill. *Bill Jones' Notes from the Turning Shop*. Lewes, East Sussex: Guild of Master Craftsman Publications, 1996.

Jones, Bill. *Bill Jones' Further Notes from the Turning Shop*. Lewes, East Sussex: Guild of Master Craftsman Publications, 1997.

Knox, Frank M. *Ornamental Turnery: A Practical & Historical Approach to a Centuries-Old Craft*. Englewood Cliffs, New Jersey: Prentice-Hall, 1986.

Lukin, James. *Simple Decorative Lathe Work*. London: Guilbert Pitman, 1905.

Lukin, James. *The Lathe and its Uses*. London: Trubner & Co, 1868.

Lukin, James, editor. *Turning Lathes: A Manual for Technical Schools and Apprentices*, Fifth ed. Colchester, England: Britannia Company, 1899.

Lynn, Bob. *Woodworking: My First Seventy Years*. Ashburton, New Zealand: Lynn Historical Woodworking Trust, 1992.

Mathews, Martin. *Engine Turning 1680-1980*. Sevenoaks, Kent: Martin Mathews, circa 1983.

Maurice, Klaus. *Sovereigns as Turners*. Zurich, Switzerland: Verlag Ineichen, 1985. The text is in both German and English.

Moxon, Joseph. *Mechanick Exercises; or the Doctrine of Handy Works*. New York: Praeger Publishers, 1970. (Facsimile of 1703 third edition). There is also a more recent facsimile by Astragal Press of Mendham, New Jersey.

Northcott, W. Henry. *A Treatise on Lathes and Turning*. Fresno, California: Linden Publishing 1987. (Facsimile of 1868 first edition).

Ogden, Warren G. *The Pedigree of Holtzapffel Lathes*. North Andover, Massachusetts: The Museum of Ornamental Turning, 1987.

Plumier, Charles. *L'Art de Tourner*. Lyon, 1701. Other editions and translations 1706, 1749, 1776, 1975 (see next entry) and 1976 (Nogent-le Roi: Jacques Laget).

Plumier, Charles. *The Art of Turning*. Translation of the 1749 edition by Paul L. Ferraglio. Brooklyn, New York: Paul Ferraglio, 1975.

Walshaw, T.D. *Ornamental Turning*. Hemel Hempstead, Hertfordshire: Argus Books, 1990.

BIBLIOGRAPHY OF TURNING BOOKS IN LANGUAGES OTHER THAN ENGLISH

This list contains only those books I have seen. Even if, like me, you are linguistically challenged, the illustrations can be valuable to the knowledgeable turner. I apologize if some of the bibliographic details are incorrect.

Bidou, Gerard. *50 Modeles d'Objets a Tourner*. France: Editions Bricodif, 1991.

Bidou, Gerard. *Le Tournage sur Bois*. France: Editions Fleurus, 1995.

Bidou, Gerard. *Technologie du Tournage sur Bois*. Paris, France: Editions Eyrolles, 1987.

Bidou, Gerard. *Tournage sur Bois, Techniques et Creation*. Paris, France: Editions Eyrolles, 1990.

Bockelmann, Gottfried. *Handbook Drechseln*. Ravensburg, Germany: Ravensburger Buchverlag, 1997.

Darlow, Mike. *The Fundamentals of Woodturning*. A German edition will be published by Dornier Medienholding of Berlin in 2000.

Graef, A., and Graef, M. *Musterblatter Moderner Drechslerarbeiten*. Hannover, Gerrmany: Verlag Th. Schafer, 1982.

Knoppe, Hugo. *Handbuch der Drechslerei*. Hannover: Verlag Th. Schafer, circa 1989. (Facsimile of 1938 edition).

Knoppe, Hugo. *Handbuch der Ovaldreherei*. Hannover: Verlag Th. Schafer, circa 1986. (Facsimile of 1920 edition).

Knoppe, Hugo. *Meistertechniken der Drechslerkunst*. Hannover: Verlag Th. Schafer, 1986. (Facsimile of 1926 edition).

Martensson, Hans. *Drechseln nach alten Vorlagen*. Hannover: Verlag Th. Schafer, 1990.

Martin, C.A., and Spitbarth, Carl. *Die Kunst des Drechslers*. Weimar: Bernhard Freidrich Boigt, 1879.

Martin, von C.A. *Der Drechsler*. Hannover: Verlag Th. Schafer, 1990. (Facsimile of 1905 edition).

Schopper, Hartman. *Panoplia Omnium*. Frankfort-on-the-Main: 1568.

Spannagel, Fritz. *Das Drechslerwerk*. Hannover: Verlag Th. Schafer, 1981. (Facsimile of 1948 edition).

Spannagel, Fritz. *Gedrechselte Gerate*. Hannover: Verlag Th. Schafer, 1987. (Facsimile of 1941 edition).

Steinert, Rolf. *Drechseln in Holz*. Leipzig: Fachbuchverlag, circa 1993.

Sundqvist, Wille, and Gustafsson, Bengt. *Die Schaltechnik in der Drechslerei*. Hannover: Verlag Th. Schafer, circa 1991.

Valicourt, E. de. *Nouveau Manuel Complet du Tourneur*. Paris: Librarie Encyclopedique de Roret, 1872.

MAGAZINES AND JOURNALS

This list includes most of the commercially-published magazines in English which include or are likely to include material relevant to woodturning. The list also includes some of the major journals published by national woodturners' associations. (Appendix 1 of *The Fundamentals of Woodturning* lists national woodturning associations and their journals).

American Woodturner. Journal of The American Association of Woodturners, 3200 Lexington Avenue, Shoreview, MN 55126, USA. Published quarterly.

American Woodworker. RD Publications, USA. Published seven times a year.

Australian Handyman. Ceased publication in 1997.

Australian Wood Review. 430 West Mt Cotton Road, Mt Cotton, Qld 4165, Australia: Interwood Holdings Pty Ltd. Published quarterly.

Bulletin of The Society of Ornamental Turners. Contact: N.S. Edwards Hon. Secretary, 188 Bromham Road, Bedford, Bedfordshire MK40 4BP, England.

Contemporary Woodworker. Two issues only were published in USA in 1981.

Faceplate. Journal of the National Association of Woodturners New Zealand (Inc), published quarterly.

Fine Woodworking. The Taunton Press Inc., 52 Church Hill Road, PO Box 355, Newtown, CT 06470, USA. Published two-monthly.

Good Woodworking. Future Publishing Ltd, 30 Monmouth Street, Bath BA1 2BW, England. Published monthly.

More Woodturning. 950 S. Falcon Road, Camano Island, WA 98292, USA. A newspaper published monthly.

Popular Woodworking. Published two-monthly in America.

Practical Wood Working. Nexus Special Interests Ltd, Nexus House, Boundary Way, Hemel Hempstead HP2 7ST, England. Published monthly.

Revolutions. Journal of The Association of Woodturners of Great Britain. Published quarterly.

The Australian Woodworker. Skills Publishing Pty Ltd, 40-44 Red Lion Sreet, Rozelle, NSW 2039, Australia. Published two-monthly.

The New Zealand Woodworker. An excellent magazine published between 1988 and 1991.

The Woodturner. Nexus Special Interests Ltd, Nexus House, Boundary Way, Hemel Hempstead HP2 7ST, England. Published quarterly.

The Woodturner. This magazine ran to eight issues which were published occasionally and irregularly during the 1980s by Craft Supplies Ltd, The Mill, Millers Dale, Derbyshire SK17 8SN.

The Woodworker. Nexus Special Interests Ltd, Nexus House, Boundary Way, Hemel Hempstead HP2 7ST, England. Founded 1901, published monthly.

Touch Wood. Published in New Zealand between 1983 and 1988. It then became *The New Zealand Woodworker*.
Turning Points. Wood Turning Center, 42 W. Coulter Street, Philadelphia, PA 19144, USA. Published quarterly.

Wood. Meredith Publishing Group, 1912 Grand Avenue, Des Moines, IA 50309-3379, USA. Published nine times a year.

Woodturning. GMC Publications, 166 High Street, Lewes, East Sussex BN7 1XU, England. Published monthly.
Woodwork. Ross Periodicals Inc., 42 Digital Drive #5, Novata, CA 94949, USA. Published two-monthly.

Woodworking Crafts became *Woodworking International* became *Woodworking* became *Woodworking Today* which is no more. Guild of Master Craftsman Publications now publishes magazines which service specialist areas within woodwork, see *Woodturning* above.

INDEX